Literary Sociology
and
Practical Criticism

Literary Sociology and Practical Criticism
An Inquiry

JEFFREY L. SAMMONS

INDIANA UNIVERSITY PRESS
Bloomington and London

Published in Canada by Fitzhenry & Whiteside Limited, Don Mills, Ontario

Manufactured in the United States of America

Library of Congress Cataloging in Publication Data
Sammons, Jeffrey L.
Literary sociology and practical criticism.
Bibliography: p.
Includes index.
1. Criticism—Germany, West.   2. Literature and
society.   I. Title.
PN98.S6S3   801'.95'0943   77-74445
ISBN 0-253-33564-7   1 2 3 4 5 81 80 79 78 77

For Peter Demetz

Contents

PREFACE

The following essays have arisen out of a set of difficulties that confront me as a student and teacher of a foreign literature. The duality of vision that has emerged in my arguments certainly has something to do with the double optic that the native-born mediator of a foreign culture must strive to keep focused. Some critics, to be sure, keep the foreign culture at arm's length by the steady application of the common sense of their own; others become completely naturalized in the country of their interest and run the risk of losing track of its alienness. My own concern has been to avoid these extremes, though with what success it is difficult for me to say. The challenge, however, has become sharpened in recent years, especially for a Germanist. While Anglo-American and German literary criticism developed a mutually supportive relationship after World War II, what we call literary criticism and what the Germans call *Literaturwissenschaft* have again bifurcated, and, for a number of reasons having at least partly to do with the structure of German studies in the United States, the lines of communication function less well than they once did. A chief component in this development is the emergence in West Germany of a broad range of problems and attitudes that have become subsumed under the general heading of *Literatursoziologie,* a fundamental shift of interest and method that has had relatively little impact on literary criticism in this country, but that appears to me of sufficient importance to require our attention. These essays are the result of an inquiry into this development and are intended at least to exhibit the difficulties encountered by the American-trained practical critic in endeavoring to assimilate and judge a prominent aspect of contemporary literary study in Germany and in Western Europe generally. As I read criticism and theory, I sense the foreignness of my field as a disability in comparison to those whose center of experience is in the English and American tradition, regardless of their degree of international comparative commitment. But it may also be, if not an advantage, at least an alienation effect that reinforces the awareness of how strange and different a literary object can be. Added to this are certain elements of personal origin and background. It would be tedious and impertinent to speak of these at any length. Suffice it to say that they are of a nature to make me acutely aware that most of what we in universities consider literary experience, and all theory and criticism, are completely inaccessible to the majority of those with whom we share, not only the planet, but our immediate environment in our cities and towns and daily contacts.

By practical criticism I mean that scholarly activity that mediates between the corpus of literature, past and present, and the teaching of literature. The echo of I. A. Richards in the phrase is intentional. The problem he exhibited so dramatically in 1929, that literary texts easily elude the understanding of educated and literate people, is still with us. In much current German literary study in particular, there is a tendency to move directly from a paraphrastic, synoptic, or selective apprehension of the text to a comprehensive philosophical and social universe. The assumption generally is that the superficial meaning of a literary text is immediately accessible to the understanding, but all practical critics will be wryly aware of its unreliability.

As for "literary sociology," the term as used here does not designate any bounded and definable discipline. That it cannot be restricted to a technical branch of sociology will be made clear, although there is such a branch that is directly pertinent to my subject. What may appear to be the diffuseness of the term here is a consequence of my effort to follow and speak to the development of an appellative, didactic, and, in much of its own understanding, revolutionary process in literary study. My title could as easily have been *The Social Ethics of Literary Criticism* if it were not that my own views on this have less weight in what follows than the criticism of the assumptions, models, and results now before us.

My subject is an international one, and I hope I have done some justice to that aspect of it. If I show a particular tendency to advert to German materials, it is partly because they are the most accessible and familiar to me. But it is also because I think that developments in German *Literaturwissenschaft* are due for some attentive discussion in this country. American scholars in my field have not yet done as much as they might to transmit and criticize the new turn of events. One of the two important books about it, *Marxism and Form*, was written by a Romanist, Fredric Jameson, and the other, *The Dialectical Imagination*, by a historian, Martin Jay. Much of what Americans have done in these matters has been marked less by critical analysis than by faithful conversion to German academic radicalism. On a higher level, this is on the whole true of Jameson also, whose eloquent and felicitous account is limited, in my view, by a tendency to harmonize the difficulties and contradictions in the thinkers he treats and to regard the whole complex as a gospel that enables us not only to jettison the Old Testament of criticism but to consign our whole nation and civilization to perdition. Jay is more analytical and even-handed (although he is at least Jameson's equal in his feats of organization and explication of desperately difficult matters), but his history of the Frankfurt School, while indispensable as well as engrossing, ceases with the Institute's repatriation in Germany in 1950 and therefore has little to say about the current situation that has come in its wake. My own concern here is not to offer detailed explications of major documents of literary sociology and Marxist literary theory or to give examples of a practical criticism in touch with them, and certainly not to present a new social theory of literature. My study is a record of an encounter and its purpose is to animate a lagging and needful discussion on these matters.

I believe I ought to say, though at the risk of appearing to slight a subtle strain of contemporary theory, that I do not regard the text as "empty," a congeries of flexible signifiers more or less unfixed to particular significances. Rather I regard it as "full" of life and reality and concern, despite its indeterminacies that we as readers must further fill, and furthermore as relatively firm, an object whose fundamental constancy is founded in its genesis and intentionality, its time and place. I cannot see why this should deaden the text, why to keep it alive it must be stretched forward to meet us; rather, the greater benefit to us as readers would seem to me to stretch back to meet *it*, enriching ourselves, not speciously enriching the text. I regard as fallacious the argument that we cannot recover the universe of discourse in which the text of the past emerged and met its first audience. We shall generally find our efforts to do this difficult and imperfect, but difficulty and imperfection are not the same as impossibility.

As a literary critic, what strikes me in the current atmosphere is the fictionalization of everything, the transformation of all reality into a literary text. Rhetoric and emplotment are mobilized as the paradigms of history; myth becomes a central category of psychology; the formal reciprocities of poetic structure are employed for anthropological description; archetypes are promoted out of the latent storehouse of the imagination to universal epistemological patterns; language is regarded as controlling of the apprehension of the world rather than being ever and in any sense instrumental or referential. My disposition in these matters will be evident in what follows. But we should all be clear that one of the consequences of this trend is the disappearance of literature. If everything is literature, there is no literature. If there is no tension between imagination and reality, there is no category of the imagination; there is only a blooming and buzzing epistemological anarchy, conventionally or opportunistically ordered. Just as archetypal criticism disperses literary history and evaluative interaction with the variety of literary experience, so the fictionalization of everything evaporates fiction itself, for there no longer can be any concept of *poiesis* as a special form of alternative organization of and imposition upon reality.

The study of the relations of literature and society, as part of the intellectual climate of our times, is deeply infected with the trend toward the absorption of reality by synthesizing intellect. But at its core it contains an invulnerable resistance, which is doubtless one of the reasons it has been unpopular in the mainstream of criticism. It may seem strange to some, but it is perfectly logical, that literary sociology, far from dissolving literature into something extraneous to it, actually defends the integrity of literature. For it becomes quickly apparent that the relationship of literature and society, of imagination and reality, is reciprocal, or, as it is now common to say, dialectical; by treating literature in its real, local context of human relations and social construction of consciousness, by bringing literature and society together, it keeps them apart; by resisting the fictionalization of the world, it resists the disappearance of fiction in the world. My thesis, therefore, is that by regarding the genesis, substance, form, and affectiveness of literature from as realistic and non-mythical, non-fictional a vantage point as we can find, we protect the realm of art and the imagination.

I have a number of debts to discharge. It is in the nature of this book that I must make the customary disclaimer concerning the responsibility of others for its failings with more than the usual emphasis. I want particularly to stress that the dedication to Peter Demetz is an acknowledgment of his collegial generosity and the inspiration of his scholarly companionship, and is not meant to saddle so capacious a cosmopolitan in the disciplines of criticism with responsibility for the often pointed opinions that inform these essays. Professor David Miles of the University of Virginia has accompanied me in this project practically from its inception; our fruitful conversations and extensive correspondence, his erudition and critical acumen, and his steadfast encouragement have been of inestimable benefit. Professor Priscilla Clark of the University of Illinois at Chicago Circle has made valuable criticisms and on one occasion provided what Goethe in a well-known essay called "significant furtherance through a single brilliant word," which I hope I have taken to heart advantageously.

I am grateful to the John Simon Guggenheim Foundation for the fellowship that enabled me to do the bulk of the work in a concentrated way, and to the administration of Yale for permitting me to take a leave out of turn in order to accept it. The pleasure and usefulness of my stay in Vienna were greatly enhanced by the ready kindness of Dr. Wolfgang Kraus and Dr. Reinhard Urbach of the Austrian Society for Literature and Professor Werner Welzig of the University of Vienna.

An early version of part of Chapter III was published as "Truth and Time: A Literary-Sociological Inquiry" in *Colloquia Germanica* (1974; appeared Winter 1975/76):222–239; Professor Paul Stapf graciously gave permission to include an extensively revised version here. A passage in Chapter V originally appeared in my article, "The Threat of Literary Sociology and What to Do About It," *Yearbook of Comparative Criticism* 5 (1973):33–34; my appreciation goes to Professor Joseph Strelka for permission to reuse it.

Versions of several of these essays have been given as public lectures; as these occasions have been most valuable to me for discussion and criticism, I want to thank my hosts: Professors Theodore Ziolkowski of Princeton; Seymour Flaxman of the Graduate Center, City University of New York; William C. Crossgrove of Brown; Herbert Lederer of the University of Connecticut; and Herbert Arnold of Wesleyan.

So much friendliness and prompt good will are drawn upon even for a simple scholarly product. The experience of it reinforces me in my conviction that human relations in bourgeois society are not exhausted by non-communication, reification, and anomie.

New Haven, Connecticut
Summer, 1976; Winter, 1977

Literary Sociology
and
Practical Criticism

I

Introduction

IT MAY BE helpful to say at the outset that the very term "literary sociology" is likely to have a different ring in American ears than in contemporary Continental discussion. It will tend to denote to us a technical branch of the discipline of sociology dealing with the behavior of groups in what is sometimes called the "literary system": authors, producers (commissioning Maecenases and publishers), mediators and inhibitors (critics, scholars, educators, libraries, censors) and receivers or what, in more naive days, was called the reading public. It has long been an article of faith in our indigenous criticism that this branch of inquiry has little or no bearing on practical or theoretical criticism, which has its own areas of competence in the examination of specific texts or of a different kind of literary system, the historical continuum of form, tradition, and aesthetic meditation in which every literary event in Western culture subsists. Practitioners of this branch of sociology, who will here be called empiricists,* rarely if ever have challenged this division of labor. Whether indigenous[1] or Continental,[2] they regularly defer to the authority of literary criticism in regard to the interpretation of specific works and seem ready to acquiesce in the distinction humanists are concerned to enforce between science, the study of regularities, recurrences, and causalities, and their own realm of uniquely focused energies and inimitable achievements. Whether this territoriality has been wise or

*By their opponents they are usually called "positivists." However, this term has become a tendentious catch-all in current discussion and I shall normally avoid it. For the same reason I shall try to refrain from referring pejoratively to critics interested in the complex interior of texts as "formalists."

healthy is much discussed these days, but the dispute is not one of my main concerns here. A study of the subject makes it apparent that empirical sociology can contribute more to a realistic practical criticism than is generally recognized.[3]

Beyond the boundaries of this subdiscipline of sociology there is a broad and, one must say, ancient meeting ground of literary criticism and social involvement. Both Plato and Aristotle treat literature as matters of explicit social relevance, and most literary discussion through the nineteenth century has accepted as more or less self-evident Horace's yoked canons of usefulness and delight. In fact it is the modernist episode, with its reflex in the New Criticism and its belated German cousin once or twice removed, *werkimmanente Interpretation*, that appears as an aberration in the history of criticism in the purity of its concentration upon the verbal icon and the internal relations of a text. That mode of criticism is now under heavy assault and we are probably beginning to have learned as much from it as we usefully can. There is no profit in casting overboard the experience of the last fifty years; it was undoubtedly one of the great ages of criticism, and what we have learned about the subtlety, the layeredness, and the paradoxes of the literary work of art is too valuable and rational to be abandoned. At the same time, it is becoming clearer in retrospect that modern criticism, despite its effort to isolate its object and treat it in terms derived from itself alone, has not been without its own ideological complicities. It is arguable that modern criticism, like modernist literature itself, exhibits, if not universally, then with recurrent regularity, conservative and even reactionary allegiances. Associated with this—and worth mentioning, because the issue will recur in our own subject—has been a salvationist employment of literary art, attempting to place it in a void alleged to have been left by the weakening of religious and traditional authority at the center of modern advanced societies. The tendency that developed in New Criticism toward a Neo-Romantic irrationality and poetic religiosity can get on the nerves of even such an admirer of the movement as Richard Foster, who has warned of "the threat of criticism 'for its own sake'—or criticism-as-poetry—where criticism seems to absorb, even *become*, the object which created it and for which it exists as a dependent"; the critical approach becomes a "supplicative ritual" toward a talismanic object.[4] It is a process against which T. S. Eliot vigorously warned at an early stage in the history of modern criticism.[5] Indeed, it is possible, as Alvin Kernan has wryly suggested, that this priestly function serves as a justification for the hugeness and unlimited proliferation of academic literary criticism as exegesis of and service to a sacral scripture: "there can never be too many prayers, even if some of them are mumbled." [6]

Now it is a fact, though one not usually acknowledged by Continental observers, that radically formalist criticism has never held exclusive dominion over literary study in our society. Its enormous influence—buttressed, it is only fair to say, by enormous achievements—is incontestable. But naturally philology, literary history, literary biography, and integrated cultural study have gone on uninterruptedly, and it is doubtful whether practical education has ever been able to manage without transmitting the historical context and extrinsic referents of literary texts. Within criticism itself there have always been those who have sensed the futility of ignoring the social and political context of both literature and criticism. The appeal for a systematically sociological examination of literature was mounted in Germany in the 1920s and 1930s by established representatives of academic literary study.[7] In 1935 the comparatist Albert Guérard wrote plainly, and without benefit of Marxism or of any other system to speak of, that "there is no literature . . . that is not, in some measure, the joint production of author and public" and that "literature is a social product," assertions of the sort today presented as revolutionary novelties, though Guérard himself remarked that they were "hoary with age."[8] In 1948 Stanley Edgar Hyman argued that "the bodies of knowledge of most usefulness to criticism are the social sciences,"[9] and one need only look at the English Institute Essays of 1957, a date close to the confident peak of the New Criticism, to find cogent critiques of the principle of disinterested contemplation and of the possibility of an ideologically neutral criticism.[10]

In Europe, however, and especially in Germany, *Literatursoziologie* has become much more than a methodological alternative, an option to be probed and rediscovered. The definition of literature as a social product with a social function has developed into a fundamental issue of the ethics of intellectual work. This commitment has figured prominently in the convulsive politicization of German universities of the last decade or so, especially in the humanities; and, since instruction in the humanities in German universities is carried on primarily with the purpose of training schoolteachers, the struggle is quite explicitly one for the minds of the young. The effect has been pervasive; such a quantity of virtue has accrued to the concept of "society" that in West Germany today hardly a monograph on any literary topic can be published without some form of the word *Gesellschaft* in the title or jacket copy.

The history of how this came about has yet to be written. Among the factors to be considered would be, along with the haunted, intractable character of the German past, a certain persistent disproportion between democratic political institutions and retained authoritarian social structures in post-war Germany, the major irritant of the preserved hierarchical structure of the university, and the impression made by the conduct of the Western nations from Suez and Algeria to Vietnam. The Vietnam war greatly accelerated the decline of the once high prestige of the United States among younger Germans of the educated class, and a prominent symptom of that decline is the vociferous rejection of the individualistic, "bourgeois" education sponsored by American criticism. But I expect that when such a history is properly written, it will have to deal as well with certain continuities in the German tradition. For one thing, I think it will emerge that, despite the standing of poets like Rilke, Stefan George, and Gottfried Benn, the modernist mode, along with the intrinsic criticism it generated, never became deeply rooted in Germany. There was not, as far as I can see, a complete renunciation of the apprehension of literature as a vehicle of deeper extrinsic truth and higher cognition, of moral guidance and historical revelation. The tendency of the German version of the New Criticism, *werkimmanente Interpretation*, to become associated with existentialism and Heidegger's ontology indicates this; the vast industry of the study of trivial and commercially generated literature also does so, for its intensity is impelled by a more or less articulate sense of sacrilege. Even the reversals, like the notorious (and futile) proclamations of the "end of literature," reflect a betrayed faith. Furthermore, such an investigation would encounter a deeper continuity: the fear of the centrifugal tendencies of modern secular society, a longing for organic coherence, for supportive community, for the overcoming of alienation.

Here is located the evident link to the extraordinary revival of Marxism in German scholarship, which I consider one of the most significant developments in contemporary intellectual life, not least because of its demonstrable exportability. It also brings us to something of a paradox in our subject. For Marxist critics, or "materialist literary scientists," as they often prefer to designate themselves, frequently deny that they are literary sociologists at all,[11] owing to their objection to "bourgeois" or "positivist" sociology, the descriptive empiricism which, it is claimed, lacks a dynamic theoretical context—by which Marxists normally mean a philosophy of history—and therefore works to conserve social structures rather than to change them. More fundamentally, the denial derives from the Marxist ambition to a total comprehension of reality, including nature, history, and consciousness. Thus we read in a contemporary West German handbook of Marxist literary theory meant for beginning students of literature: "only the idea of the whole legitimates the study of the particular."[12] For the Marxist, everything we talk about is inextricably involved with everything else we talk about owing to the ideological filiation of consciousness. A steady concentration on a particular aspect of reality such as literature, not to mention upon a particular literary work, is not only difficult; it is actively discouraged.

Thus the empirical sociologist's complaint that Marxism does not allow social matters to stand alone for specialized study[13] is nugatory insofar as this is precisely what Marxism is concerned to prevent. Observers of the history of Marxist literary theory sometimes present it as though it were under an embarrassment due to its apparently weak foundation in the patristic texts. While Marx and Engels had a cultivated and attentive, if somewhat dissimilar, interest in literary matters, their specific criticism and observations on literature are really a peripheral segment of their writings and provide a narrow, somewhat shallow, and not wholly solid base for an elaborated theory. Nevertheless, Lukács' reiterated insistence that Marx and Engels provide an adequate foundation for a theory of literature is not unjustified. For Marxism is in a fundamental sense a theory of consciousness involved with a theory of history, and, if such a theory is sound, it should yield a foundation for our understanding of the products of the imagination and their relationship to our life in the world. There can be no question that the Marxist promise of a comprehensive understanding of reality, consciousness, and experience is its main attractive feature for people who otherwise have no obvious reason for holding to such a doctrine. Marxism militates against any isolation of literature from the total realm of experience and thus stands at the opposite pole from a critical tradition that insists upon seeing "literature as literature." The non-Marxist who puts no faith in this tautology but still would not like to lose sight of literature as a bounded subject is in a position of some awkwardness.

The liberal scholar will look upon literary sociology as the pursuit of a large number of open questions about the relationship of literature and society. He will hope for some illumination of literature in its relation to social environment on the one hand, and some understanding of society and history on the other, or at least he will be concerned to ask what the nature, value, and limitations of such an understanding might be. The Marxist is in a different position. He knows the dynamics of society and the meaning of history. The literary work will either reflect this reality, unveiling its potential development, or it will obscure the reality, seducing attention away from it. In a sense, despite the dialectical relationship of being and consciousness and the admitted productive energy of the creating subject, there is little that a Marxist literary inquiry can learn, apart from illustrative detail, for the truth is one, and it is known. "The Marxist doctrine," said Lenin, "is omnipotent because it is true. It is complete and harmonious, and provides men with an integral world conception."[14] Being true, Marxist doctrine cannot be in conflict with anything else that is true; it is therefore under a heavy obligation to assert coherences. It has been remarked justly that Marxism employs scholarship as a "*Praxis*-securing scholasticism."[15] The results are familiar to anyone who reads much Marxist literary study. In the West the rhetorical mode is polemical and is meant to serve what bourgeois university students imagine to be the class struggle; with regard to literary texts themselves, there is a predictable monotony of conclusions. In the East, where the Trotskyist program of salvaging the great tradition for the people has silently become the ruling practice, there is a steady concentration on the emancipatory aspects of the classics.[16] In neither case can there be much imaginative expansion of critical experience, concepts, or results. It is not clear to me that even the most recent linkages with semiotics relieve this difficulty, for the order of the world to which the aesthetic sign system is related continues to be rather abstract and fixed. Indeed, the long-term problem in Marxist criticism may not be its imprecise apprehension of texts, but its reductive view of life and the world at large and especially its relatively rigid historiography, "dialectic" or not. The orderly purposiveness of the Marxist approach, which appears as one of its strengths, inhibits the excitement of discovery and that expansion of the literary experience that has long been the aim of criticism.

All of this is well known and leads to an impatience with Marxist literary criticism. Yet the fact is that Marxism has done more than anything else to give the questions concerning literature and society and our critical practices an urgent impulsion. More than thirty years ago an especially acute observer remarked that liberal, pluralistic criticism is "an anti-Marxist text in a Marxist context,"[17] and this is certainly much more true today. The insistence upon the interrelatedness of social environment, history, consciousness, and creativity that Marxists have brought to bear has had a purgative effect on contemporary critical practice that is evident perhaps most clearly in recent utterances of established non-Marxist scholars. But the greater debt to Marxism is owed to the questions it has pointed at the critic's consciousness itself. This is the true and, I think, indestructible achievement of what Peter Demetz has called the Fifth International of Western Marxists and others have called para-Marxists.[18] No more will the responsible literary scholar be able to understand his proper activity as the confrontation of a personal sensibility with a literary work. The neo-Marxist assault on individualism is overwrought and dangerous, and perhaps not even genuinely Marxian, but within limits it has the virtue of reminding us of how large a part of our apprehending consciousness is subject to unexamined ideological presuppositions and group-specific rationalizations or defense mechanisms. Up to now it was customary to see this only as critical practices receded into a historical distance. Marxism has created an awareness of the present historicity of our minds, of our responses and opinions and standards of evaluation as located in a changing and alterable flux of historical time. We need not, as some radicals imply, abandon our allegiances once we begin to understand how largely they relate to social conformation and social intent, but the resulting self-directed skepticism ought to put an end to that most dubious of Neo-Romantic revivals, the *criticus vates*.

Despite the Marxist resistance to the academic discipline of sociology, the convergence of Marxism with literary sociology in the broad European sense cannot be ignored. It has had, however, two consequences that make our subject complicated to handle and even to define. One is the continuing skirmishing over the boundary between the discipline of sociology and dialectical cultural philosophy, which has led on both sides to a whole catalogue of dualistic distinctions between "literary sociology" and "sociology of literature."[19] In the foreground of these distinctions there are two common concerns. One is a desire for communicable precision and verifiability in scholarly results. On the empiricist side of literary sociology there is a more or less articulate impatience with what is perceived as uncontrolled speculation in cultural philosophy. The empiricists would like to prove something about literature to be true. Therefore they avoid the deep waters of interpretation and evaluation, concentrating on demonstrable facts of behavior. It would be wrong to say that they are therefore in shallow waters. Empirical sociology of literature has many sobering things to tell us and provides ballast for a criticism that invests its activity with aesthetic enthusiasm. When empiricism is rejected in favor of prior theorizing, the tendency is to move in the direction of general cultural philosophy. American exemplars of this mode of criticism are rather uncommon; the best are, I suppose, Kenneth Burke and his shrewd disciple, Hugh Dalziel Duncan. Illuminating and even realistic as their aguments may be, their force of conviction is at least in part rhetorical, and they are not easily subject to refutation either by accumulated facts or different perceptions of the dynamics of society. The empiricists are more concerned with grasping certain concrete, real problems about literature that criticism may have failed to bring into view. A second concern among some empiricists is a degree of anti-Marxism, which naturally arouses irritation in some quarters.

In the background, however, is a problem of more general consequence. Marxists and others dissatisfied with the empirical approach object that it severs the literary work itself from the sociological inquiry. There is a separation from the work itself of a pre-work phase—the determinants of content, creation, and form, up to and including the individual consciousness and intention of the author—and a post-work phase—its distribution, reception, and endurance. "A sociology 'of' the novel," remarks Michel Zéraffa, "is distinct from a sociology 'via' the novel."[20] Contrary to the claim often made by unsympathetic critics that literary sociology seeks to abolish the autonomy of the work of art, the empiricists often assert their respect for autonomy. But autonomy is a question-begging concept itself, and it does often appear that the inner sanctum of the imaginative product is tabu territory for the empiricists. They are sensitive to the charge of "sociologism" and do not want to appear to be operating within the work with tools that are inadequate to it. While evading this charge, they open themselves up to the contrary one of giving objective support to the claims and practices of "bourgeois" criticism—though it might be remarked that "bourgeois" critics evince little gratitude for this alleged support. Nevertheless, it is troubling that the empiricist equation contains a permanently mysterious unknown. It seems odd that a thing may be said to have certain determinants and certain effects, while nothing specific may be predicated to that thing in direct relation to those determinants and effects.

Here one can see more clearly the benefits that accrue to Marxism. Its belief in the dialectical unity of consciousness and reality makes these problems ever so much simpler. There is little stewing about the autonomy of the work of art, though contemporary Marxists will sometimes defend the concept in their own terms; dialectics enables one to refine the problem of causality or perhaps even abolish it; the accumulation of facts and statistics is subordinate to larger perspectives that do not oblige one to separate out the work of art from the real process surrounding it. Thus it is not surprising that in an introductory manual of methods of criticism, which is supposed to be informational, students are told that only Marxism can be the "necessary foundation" of literary sociology, which deals with the total phenomenon of literature, "not . . . because literature can be seen in this way among others, but because literature is essentially the expression of a socially living individual."[21] How many difficulties are buried in these assertions the student is left to find out for himself; and since under present conditions only the most exceptionally self-motivated and innately curious German students are likely to find out much for themselves, this state of affairs in German literary study is a cause for some concern.

The second complication is that the bulk of literary-sociological discussion that is not primarily empiricist is concerned with theoretical disputation and employs literary phenomena illustratively; furthermore, it is a philosophical discipline whose disputes are carried out on the ground of epistemology. It is no doubt these features of the Continental discussion that have caused the time lag of its reception in English-speaking countries. Europeans, and Germans in particular, do not like to undertake literary studies without first securing a theoretical framework. The resulting density of exposition often goes against the grain of our tradition, in which clarity, communicability, and even elegance of expression in literary criticism are held in high regard. American students of the German tradition are sometimes surprised to discover that an extremely high level of abstraction in literary-critical expositions is regarded as an admirable feature, insofar as it superordinates totality to particularity, whereas "abstract" is often a pejorative epithet in our scheme of values. It is not always clearly seen that the issue here is not purely a matter of stylistic felicity and lucidity of mind. In the first place, the abstract, technical language is part of the campaign against individual response in literary studies, an effort to relieve "literary science" from dependence on the giftedness or sensibility of the practitioner by putting it on a general theoretical basis.[22] But this does not account for the profound abstruseness of much of the discussion, which has rather to do with the reflection of mind upon itself, a questioning of initial and conditioned responses as to their sources and reliability, a philosophical effort to reach beyond one's own given horizon of intellectual perception. "The unique texture of an Adorno or Benjamin essay," comments Martin Jay, "and the studied intricacy of their prose styles defy translation, not to mention reduction to their fundamentals. Their mode of reasoning was rarely inductive or deductive, a reflection of their insistence that every sentence must be mediated through the totality of the essay in order to be understood fully. . . . The principle that Adorno attributed to the symbolists also informed their work: 'Defiance of society includes defiance of its language.'"[23] A serious problem of communication thus emerges, which derives from the philosophical assumptions common to the discussion.

For example, Lucien Goldmann says: "I set out from the fundamental principle of dialectical materialism, that the knowledge of empirical facts remains abstract and superficial so long as it is not made concrete by its integration into a whole."[24] Ernst Bloch disposed of those who pride themselves on pragmatism and working toward conclusions from given literary texts or empirical observations in an exceptionally biting phrase as "asses of induction."[25] And the argument has reached our shores at last: Fredric Jameson asserts that it is "imperative to pass beyond the individual, empirical phenomenon to its meaning: abstract terminology clings to its object as *sign* of the latter's incompleteness in itself, of its need to be replaced in the context of the totality,"[26] and he praises that type of severely convoluted and obscure style exemplified by Adorno. On the one hand, philosophical or dialectical abstraction is said to yield the higher wisdom of a holistic, comprehensive view—a claim that will cause us much difficulty before we are through; on the other, the stubborn assertion of non-comprehension on the part of opponents is identified as a defense mechanism against the results of thought. The extremely dense and difficult Jürgen Habermas has complained bitterly of the "don't get it" (*Kannitverstan*) strategy of the "positivists," claiming that this is an effort to force the "critical theorists" to accept their opponents' own, ideologically distorted language.[27] Roland Barthes makes the same point more archly:

> You can of course judge philosophy according to common sense; the trouble is that while "common sense" and "feeling" understand nothing about philosophy, philosophy, on the other hand understands them perfectly. You don't explain philosophers, but *they* explain you. You don't want to understand the play by Lefebvre the Marxist, but you can be sure that Lefebvre the Marxist understands your incomprehension perfectly well, and above all (for I believe you to be more wily than lacking in culture) the delightfully "harmless" confession you make of it.[28]

Well, that makes me feel bad, as it was intended to do. But it does not altogether meet the problem. Not long ago a German scholar, while arguing that there is a generally felt need for a "scientification" (*Verwissenschaftlichung*) of literary studies, was obliged to observe that this process at the same time inhibits its purpose of making communication between disciplines and ultimately with the "uninitiated reader" easier, because the codes of communication become harder and harder to crack.[29] The Continental scholars, however, tend to repudiate clarity as a deceptive form of obfuscation. This is not only true of Marxists; the phenomenologist Erwin Leibfried warns cheerfully that "for many a literary historian·and interpreter there may be some passages that are tough to read; that was not to be avoided";[30] he certainly kept his promise. Goldmann also intimidates us with a cheerful and sovereign gesture: "Too much clarity darkens, wrote Pascal, and I have preferred genuine clarity to any purely formal and apparent clarity."[31] Jameson, as usual, faithfully transmits the argument; clarity, he says, "seeks to hurry the reader past his own received ideas." Dialectical thinking, however, is "thought to the second power"; it reminds us "that the simple is in reality only a simplification, and that the self-evident draws its force from hosts of buried presuppositions."[32]

There is something compelling about these assertions. As Marx said, "all science would be superfluous if the form of appearance and the essence of things directly coincided."[33] But perhaps they, too, need to be seen as an expression of ideological interest. George Lichtheim has observed that, to Continental Europeans, the Anglo-American world has long appeared a "de-centered totality," "a philistine culture with a void at the center," lacking in a comprehensive philosophy of life or society. "What is currently known as empiricism commonly goes with liberalism in politics and subjectivism in morals,"[34] which at least suggests that the attack on empiricism may go with illiberalism in politics and a morality bound to a potential communal standard. However that may be, and with all due respect for the massive intellectual energy concentrated on the theoretical disputation, there may be a somewhat worrisome trend for the subject to fold back over itself and thus fail in the long run to supply the openings and linkages for which, presumably, it is devised.

Therefore it has seemed to me best not to attempt to construct this inquiry around the traditional nodes of dispute with the sociological approach to literature—the autonomy of the work of art, the theories of mimesis or reflection, and the question of causal determination—since their relevance has receded in the current discussion. Instead I have retreated to a more elementary critique of some pervasive contemporary themes. For it is apparent that the topic is in need of efforts to locate fresh angles of vision. The problem is no longer one of a peripheral methodological alternative, but rather one of the meagreness of firm results in

proportion to an immense intellectual investment. Where firm results
can be delivered—most by empiricists—they not always but frequently
appear as a codification of the self-evident and somewhat remote from
the concerns of the critic; the answers that would truly be helpful are
obtained with such severe difficulty that progress has been slow and even
hard to identify.

But the situation is changing rapidly. The areas of inquiry are becoming better demarcated, the argumentation more exact and methodical,
and the awareness of pitfalls and antinomies sharper. Most remarkable is
the increasing subtlety and precision of Marxist theory. Even in East
Germany, where the practice of criticism, in my experience, tends to be
as complacent and tone-deaf as ever, theoretical developments of remarkable flexibility and catholicity are emerging from the Academy of
Sciences. International communication has much improved in recent
years and there is a tendency among Marxists, most remarkably in
Yugoslavia but also among Czechoslovaks and Poles, to moderate the flat
repudiation of "bourgeois" literary theory in favor of a dialogue with
major critical traditions. Unfortunately the dialogue is not well established in this country. The failure of American criticism, increasingly
fascinated by the current French fireworks, to come to terms with modern Marxist theory is the greatest single hindrance I have encountered in
this project; I have only partly been able to make up for it by my own
efforts. What is needed is for some of the great intellectual resources in
our departments of literature to be brought to bear on the maturing
Marxist development. In the absence of a genuinely critical and informed confrontation, Marxist discussion in the United States proceeds
in sectarian innocence, unobliged to deal with serious opposition or to
relieve its inherited ignorance of a world outside its own disputes,* while
at the same time American academic practice is, in this regard, falling
behind significant advances in literary study. The same is true of literary
sociology as a whole, despite the fact that American scholars have made
significant contributions to it. The whole complex of questions is cur-

* This too may be changing. Particularly deserving of mention is Stefan Morawski's
Inquiries into the Fundamentals of Aesthetics (Cambridge, Mass.: MIT Press, 1974), a finely
crafted example of the Eastern European intersection of Marxism with a mature mastery of
modern criticism. I cannot point to a recent example of an American non-Marxist critic
taking up the Marxist challenge at the same level of knowledge and understanding. The last
serious effort to do this is my colleague Peter Demetz's *Marx, Engels, and the Poets* (Chicago:
University of Chicago Press, 1967). But the core of this book is more than twenty years old
and no one, to my knowledge, has continued the critique in a similar spirit in English.

rently in productive disarray, and the inquiry will show that it continues to carry some curious doctrines that may require increased scrutiny before greater headway can be made. One of the deepest rooted of these will be the concern of the following chapter.

II

Analogy, Homology, Equivocation

> Had we but an Act of Parliament to abridge
> Preachers the use of fulsom and luscious Meta-
> phors, it might perhaps be an effectual cure of all
> our present Distempers.—SAMUEL PARKER, 1670,
> quoted by M. H. Abrams.

A GOOD MANY years ago, Arnold Hauser issued a warning that ought to have been better heeded than it has been:

> There is scarcely any greater danger for the sociological interpretation of cultural structures than . . . equivocations and none to which it is easier to fall victim. For there is nothing easier than to construct striking connections between the various styles in art and the social patterns predominating at any particular time, which are based on nothing but metaphor, and there is nothing more tempting than to make a show of such daring analogies. But they are just as fateful traps for truth as the illusions enumerated by Bacon and they might well be put on his list of warnings as *idola aequivocationis.*[1] *

The chief weakness of literary-sociological discussion is not sins against the alleged autonomy of art or naiveté on the head of determinism, but

---

* The ubiquity of the problem is perhaps best exemplified by noting that Hauser did not always take his own advice. Cf. the equivocations César Graña points to in his critique of Hauser's treatment of Impressionism, in *Fact and Symbol: Essays in the Sociology of Art and Literature* (New York: Oxford University Press, 1971), pp.72–79. ·

its tendency to undisciplined equivocation. At its worst it turns into a matching game of frivolous tendentiousness; it has some affinities to poker, including the element of bluff. But it is a danger that accompanies literary sociology at every level; no enterprise that seeks to put one area of experience into relation with another can avoid some postulation of analogical relationships, for no matter how radically the interpenetration of literature and society may be seen, it is logically impossible to assert that they are congruent and coextensive.*

Equivocation in the special sense employed here is illegitimate excess of analogy, and without analogy we can hardly discuss the external relations of literature at all. M. H. Abrams has said that "critical thinking, like that in all areas of human interest, has been in considerable part thinking in parallels, and critical argument has to that extent been an argument from analogy." Analogy, simile, or metaphor are fundamental to language usage; "metaphor . . . , whether alive or moribund, is an inseparable element of all discourse." When our discourse is reflexive in the sense that it is discourse about consciousness and expression, then analogy may be the only language resource we have. "Mental events must be talked about metaphorically, in an object-language which was developed to deal literally with the physical world." Some analogues, Abrams observes, are constitutive of theory and in turn select the facts to which the theory attends; he points to Coleridge's dictum that facts are not conclusions, but parts of premises, a position that anticipates the Marxist view concerning the priority of theory over observation. But Coleridge also pointed out that "no simile runs on all four legs," and Abrams observes that "the endemic disease of analogical thinking is hardening of the categories." [2] This is not its only consequence. Analogy carried to the extreme of equivocation severely undermines shared discourse. The partner in communication is put into a position somewhat like that of a person expected to appreciate a joke; if he refuses to make the required jump between vehicle and tenor of the analogic or metaphorical connection, the argument it is meant to carry goes dead.**

* From a certain point of view, the problem is not resolvable, insofar as the effort to get behind metaphor leads to an infinite regress, as I take what I understand of Jacques Derrida's thinking to mean ("White Mythology: Metaphor in the Text of Philosophy," *New Literary History* 6 [1974/75]:5–74). But I think that for practical purposes we must be careful about philosophical investigations of essences that end up with a paralysis of discourse, for the communication and intersubjective understanding that obviously occur in the world are thereby lost sight of and no account of them can be given.
** Perhaps I can illustrate the point I am trying to make by mentioning a similar problem that emerges in the genre of satire. An apposite example is Barbara Garson's cabaret skit

This, as I shall try to demonstrate, recurrently damages the persuasiveness of this branch of literary discussion for practical criticism.

Robert Musil, who possessed an annihilating instinct for intellectual absurdity, offered, apropos of Spengler, a good satire on what equivocation looks like at its worst: "There are lemon-yellow butterflies, there are lemon-yellow Chinese; in a certain sense, therefore, one may say: butterfly is the Central European winged dwarf Chinese. . . . That the butterfly has wings and the Chinese none is only a superficial phenomenon." It is as if, observes Musil, "a zoologist were to include among the quadrupeds dogs, tables, chairs, and equations of the fourth degree."[3] The elementary nature of illicit equivocation comes clear from these examples: like or similar abstract predicates of two phenomena are adduced in order to drag them into a relation of equivalency, however disparate their nature might otherwise be. It is what Empson in *Some Versions of Pastoral* called "pantification," the equating of everything with everything via symbolic reasoning. Metaphors can only be understood situationally, so that we readily recognize which predicates are being set into a relation of congruence and which are left out ("this man is a lion" does not mean that he has a tufted tail). Therefore our apprehension of a highly metaphorical discourse must be alert to the possibility of the smuggling of coherences that are not justified by the range of the initially

---

Macbird, which is an extended analogy insofar as it puts Lyndon Johnson into an equation with Shakespeare's Macbeth. No doubt it was my general lack of regard for Johnson that enabled me to find this satire funny, though I should think it would take a solemn admirer to refuse altogether the comedy of Johnson's ham-fisted language of power in the framework of Shakespearean rhetoric and the resulting contrast between purgative, tragic culture and the sight and sound of real politics in our time and place. But the link between Johnson and Macbeth that motivates the analogous connection is a postulate that Johnson bore a responsibility for President Kennedy's assassination similar to Macbeth's for the murder of Duncan. If such an accusation were made in earnest, it would not yield comedy; if false, it would be an intolerable libel; if true, it would be a political atrocity that would stifle laughter. I conclude that the analogy was not made in earnest; rather, it was a fictional exploitation of a feeling about the character of Johnson that derived not from domestic politics at all but from abhorrence of his prosecution of the war in Vietnam. Now there are three possibilities. First, one is so infuriated at Johnson and the system he represents that the analogy is not taken realistically, but only as a relatively diffuse expression of this feeling; the response is internally supportive in the community of the like-minded, but walled against the majority of others. Second, one takes the fiction in earnest and rejects it as the expression of an intolerable libel. Third, one takes it as a fiction, a symptom of a larger dismay with inhuman politics, while remaining uneasy at an implied accusation that threatens to spread over the boundary of the tentativeness of fictionality. My fear is that the first of these responses is more like the way equivocation works in literary sociology, whereas the third, by keeping in the forefront of one's mind an awareness of the pitfalls of tendentious equivocation, seems to me more in keeping with the exigencies of intellectual responsibility.

posited relation. One might call the equivocation the misapplication of synecdoche as congruent analogy.* What begins as an illustration, an act of mental suppleness, can end by being reified as a real correlation; its tentativeness, its necessary temporariness in the reasoning process are forgotten. The elementary violation of the independent structure of each of the phenomena and the lack of skepticism about linguistic prediction are obvious enough, one would think. The persistence of dubious equivocation in literary sociology therefore arouses some curiosity.

The problem is not confined to literary discussion, and a couple of examples from areas less strenuous will help to illustrate the practice. Among the currently thriving sociologies is the sociology of sport. It pursues such questions as the relative decline of the importance of baseball in American life and its displacement by football. Baseball, although a team sport, is largely a game of individual effort, as its obsession with personal statistics shows. As sports go, it is a game of gentlemanly practices. One might also add that it is a game of extraordinary physical grace; few sports yield such a quantity and variety of beautiful photographs as professional baseball. Clearly it is an expression of a dying bourgeois culture, in its individualism, its relative mannerliness, its aesthetic appeal, and its deliberate pace, which reflects the unhurried tempo of nineteenth-century society and is widely held to be a cause of its decline in relative popularity. Football, on the other hand, though not without individual heroics, is a game of collective effort, a whole team moving at once in a complex pattern of planned cooperation. Little do Gerald Ford and the rest of its not notably revolutionary audience guess (false consciousness!) that it is thus expressive of the coming of socialism. The dynamic, pulsating tempo of football reflects the same qualities in modern industrial civilization, and its stress on a constant application of physical force and power, displacing the episodic ballet of baseball, points to the brawn of the proletariat, which is its main audience. On the other hand, football contains, as a dialectical contradic-

---

*Hayden White, following Kenneth Burke, observes in a discussion of the tropes of historical explanation: "Synecdoche . . . would sanction a movement . . . toward integration of all apparently particular phenomena into a whole, the quality of which was such as to justify belief in the possibility of understanding the particular as a microcosm of a macrocosmic totality, which is precisely the aim of all organicist systems of explanation" ("Interpretation in History," *New Literary History* 4 [1972/73]:311). If this is right, and I am correct that the analogizing of Marxism and speculative sociology leads toward synecdoche, it would illustrate the rootedness of these doctrines in German organicism and thus, in a wide but perhaps important sense, in Romanticism generally.

tion, the violence and aggressiveness of late capitalist society and thus reflects the attitude of a large part of its audience toward the war in Vietnam.

I am extemporizing somewhat, and I do not wish to appear scornful of serious undertakings. It was, after all, an analogy drawn between the practices and manners of poker with those of capitalism that supplied the foundation for modern game-theory analysis of political, economic, and military situations. But one can sense, I think, the temptation in this mode of argument to elegant equivocation, which, because of the obvious analogies (*ego quoque*) between sport and art, are similar to those that emerge in our subject. Sport is only one topic among many that hold this promise. Among my collected curiosa clipped from German newspapers is an interesting example of philatelic sociology. It concerns a series of Greek postage stamps depicting the deeds of Hercules. After a moment's reflection, we will admit that Hercules is an allegory of George Papadopoulos, liberating Greece from vermin and fighting for law and order; the various defeated beasts are the enemies of the regime. Hercules defeats the Hydra, who represents the many-headed intelligentsia. He downs the Stymphalides, birds who according to legend could shoot with their feathers—journalists, obviously. He defeats Antaios by separating him from the source of his strength in mother Earth; thus the enemies of the regime are separated from their base in the people. And so on. If there is an element of parody in this disquisition, it is extremely straight-faced. Now, the political and symbolic function of postage stamps needs no elaboration, and, doubtless like all symbols whose import may be in some sense displaced or veiled, they are subject to a semiotic interpretation that reveals their full communicative range. But a complete insouciance about intentionality can cause speculation to get out of control.

To take a literary problem of the more comprehensive sort, let us consider the tension established in high medieval literature in the courtship of a totally unattainable lady—because she is married to a lord—by a supplicant knight. Such a relationship can occur, of course, any time and any place, but when it is persistently elaborated by the best European poets of an age, it seems eccentric and unnatural and thus appeals for an explanation. The social situation of the knights in question was changing; they were near the beginning of the long process that would turn knights into soldiers. If one thinks of love as oriented on a form of possession, an equation suggests itself; since the knights had lost their power base in landed property (making of the knight-poets a kind of anticipatory version of free-floating intellectuals), "the renunciation of possession in love corresponds very logically to the renunciation of property imposed by historical reality."[4] "The very logical correspondence" seems to me a queer one indeed, for if I were a dispossessed knight, I could think of several more logical responses than eloquently to require my dispossession in love as well. Why not, indeed, write poems about how it feels to be a landless and homeless knight? Walther von der Vogelweide did. The explanation appears to foreshorten the medieval tension of function between knight and poet and perhaps excessively to personalize a poetry that draws its delight from its extremely formal connections. In any case, I prefer as more realistic, if more pedestrian, the account given by David Daiches of the function of marriage at the medieval court and its effect in forcing love and sentiment to seek other channels.[5] *

Almost anything can be amalgamated by the analogical method. Just as Ernst Bloch assures us that the calculus could not have been understood until the dynamics of capitalism had appeared,[6] so Edoardo Sanguinetti asserts that the museum and the market are "essentially" the same thing: "The museum and the market are absolutely contiguous and in communication; better, they are two façades of the same social edifice. Price and value are equivalent words, for they designate in the work of art its aesthetic quality just as well as what it costs."[7] This is a good example of the way in which an issue can simply be dissolved in a flood of assertion, here employing, from phrase to phrase, an escalating rhetoric of increasing identification, for of course anyone associated with museums has a clear sense of the difference between price and value and is concerned about it. It is at least marginally worth remarking here that in early capitalist America, the very courts ruled in one case that "a picture was not like any other chattel, the property of the purchaser when ordered" but "belonged to the creative mind which had originated it and could never be wholly transferred," and in another that an artistic achievement could not be considered a "fixture" of a commercial enterprise.[8] The fascination of Christopher Caudwell lies largely in his gift for

---

* I am, of course, not fully equipped to judge these matters. For a professional critique of Köhler's stand, see Ursula Peters, "Niederes Rittertum oder hoher Adel?" *Euphorion* 67 (1973):244–260. It has recently been doubted that the object of love in the Provençal lyric was commonly either married or of higher rank than the poet. See William D. Paden, Jr., "The Troubadour's Lady: Her Marital Status and Social Rank," *Studies in Philology* 72 (1975):28–50. After all, some of this poetry was written by *princes*, like the Duke of Aquitaine and Emperor Henry VI. Köhler elsewhere has reflected on the limitations of sociological criticism and on the inertia of literary form. See Hans Norbert Fügen, "Literary Criticism and Sociology in Germany: Emphases—Attitudes—Tendencies," *Yearbook of Comparative Criticism* 5 (1973):257–258.

maintaining a chain of equivocating assertions with glib velocity. Since England was the most advanced of capitalist countries, he argues, it led the world in poetry for three centuries, as modern poetry (that is, post-Elizabethan poetry) is "capitalist poetry," a kind of redoubled equivocation that commands respect. Elsewhere Caudwell comes closer to Plekhanov and his forerunner Bücher in deriving poetic meter from the collective rhythm of work, the breakdown of which, if it is a good thing, must be ominous and deplorable: "it is obvious that the final movement towards 'free verse' reflects the final anarchic bourgeois attempt to abandon all social relations in a blind negation of them, because man has completely lost control of his social relationships."[9] It would be interesting to observe an application of this principle to Heine's *North Sea* poems or the poetry of Mayakovski. A similarly acrobatic feat would be the application to Kafka or Solzhenitsyn the assertion of Roland Barthes that the grammatical use of the narrative past indicates conscious or unconscious acceptance of the ruling social order.*

Some difficulties in these correlations have been caused by the awareness that major writers, in modern times at the very least, have been out of step with or in opposition to their societies. But this difficulty can be solved dialectically, for opposition can be negatively correlated, a line of argument that also goes back at least to Plekhanov. Thus Ernst Fischer is typical in seeing all art and literature since Rousseau as a protest against utilitarianism and reification;[10] even the Romantic-conservative rejection of the French Revolution can be seen in this light, as a protest against alienation and toward a recovered wholeness. This last is beyond doubt, though an observer with less enthusiasm for the obsession with wholeness may look upon this aspect of Romanticism in a more ambivalent light. Fischer's argument leads to a set of difficulties that oblige him to distinguish between artists who create false myths of totality (Racine, Wagner, Anouilh) and those who create true myths (Mozart, Goethe, Blake, Hölderlin, Melville, Kafka, Brecht, Faulkner, Beckett, Genet), a problem we shall encounter again. But to anticipate for a moment, I want to stress that the critique being developed here does not apply exclusively to Marxism. That it involves a broader issue can be perhaps

---

*Writing Degree Zero (Boston: Beacon Press, 1970), pp.30–34. Cf. Günther Schiwy, *Der französische Strukturalismus: Mode, Methode, Ideologie* (Reinbek: Rowohlt, 1969), p.60. But this, of course, refers to the French narrative past, which no longer exists in the spoken language. The argument is therefore embedded in particular socio-historical problems of French style; the fact that the observation is not transferrable to all Western literary languages weakens its force.

shown by a quick juxtaposition of two positions. Roland Barthes, in his
Essais critiques of 1964, demanded a "rapport between the *whole* author
and the *whole* work, a *rapport of rapports*, a homological and not analogical
correspondence."[11] In Northrop Frye we read: "almost any kind of
analogy may be significant."[12] What these views have in common will, I
hope, emerge at length.

One of the truly inspired analogizers of our time is Theodor W.
Adorno. His influence today is somewhat weaker than it was a few years
ago, partly because in his last years he would not agree with his followers
that the logical consequence of his views was to destroy the university or
turn it into a base camp for direct revolutionary action. But his methods
continue to echo in West German cultural studies, and, if the eloquent
defense by Fredric Jameson is any sign, their importation here is as-
sured.[13] Among the several peculiarities of Adorno's style is an infinitely
resourceful equivocation; the reader may stumble over an assertion that
strikes him as outlandish, but he is carried forward by the élan of
Adorno's confidence and ingenuity, which gives the impression of illuminating the subject from unexpected angles without, perhaps, always
doing so at all. "At times its methods," remarks Martin Jay of Adorno's
argumentation, "seemed to emphasize analogy more than cause and
effect in the traditional sense. . . . Characteristic of much of the [Frank-
furt] Institut's writing, and Adorno's in particular, was a sometimes
dazzling, sometimes bewildering juxtaposition of highly abstract statements with seemingly trivial observations."* Jay accounts for this by the
Hegelian need to link the complexly mediated concrete with the abstract.
But, lifted out of their seductive context and translated into something
like normal language, these equivocations sometimes develop bad limps.
As Adorno has a considerable reputation as a socio-philosopher of
music, we may take as an example his claim, cited by Jameson, that the
saxophone merely simulates the life that the traditional instruments
expressed directly.[14] I submit that this sort of statement is without
intelligible meaning; it is a rhetorical flourish in an assertive flow that
cannot have any instructive or illuminating force for the reader who
does not have an a priori commitment to Adorno's cultural criticism. The

---

*Martin Jay, *The Dialectical Imagination: The Frankfurt School and the Institute of Social
Research, 1923–1950* (Boston: Little, Brown, 1973), p.82. Some other remarkable examples
of Adornian equivocations are given by Jay on pp.67–70 and 261. For some similarly
extraordinary examples in Benjamin, see René Wellek, "Walter Benjamin's Literary Criticism in his Marxist Phase," *Yearbook of Comparative Criticism* 6 (1973):172–173. Related
examples in the sociology of music are noted by Vladimír Karbusicky, "The Interaction
Between 'Reality—Work of Art—Society,'" *International Social Science Journal* 20 (1968):653.

chaining together of such assertions lies outside the fundamental mode of intellectual discourse, which is *argument*. To account for this particular example, one needs to look, not at the context of Adorno's views, but to the generalized deafness of Central European intellectuals of an older generation, whatever camp they were in, to American jazz. Ernst Bloch, whose "principle of hope" is theoretically so open to the newness of things, spoke of jazz as "American filth" that was flooding the world: "Nothing so raw, vulgar, and stupid as the jazz dances since 1930 was ever seen before . . . —idiocy got completely out of hand."[15] This sheltered insensibility has no relation at all to a progressive cultural criticism, but is completely of a piece with the similar response of a decidedly unprogressive observer like Hermann Hesse and has even more unappetizing relatives.* The point here is not so much that the ideologues of modern Marxism are as much in need of ideological criticism as our own literary critics, but that equivocations purporting to illustrate massive sociological correlations can be founded on such provincialisms.

A more detailed example may help to show how Adorno's practice can contribute confusion to practical criticism. It concerns Heinrich Heine's *Buch der Lieder*, which is the foundation of the poet's international reputation but has a low standing among contemporary critics who are concerned to stress Heine's allegedly revolutionary middle period and his critique of what he called "poesy" as irrelevant to the political demands of modern times. Adorno tells us that Heine's early poetry is the application to literature of the industrial technique of mass production and that his theme of unrequited love is not what it seems at all but rather a simile for his rootlessness in society, which in turn has become the rootlessness of us all under capitalism.[16] The analogy between *Buch der Lieder* and mass production calls forth several objections. The volume contains about 240 poems, most of them very short, and it evolved over a period of some ten years. An average of two short poems a month, while not inconsiderable (and of course they were written in spurts of activity), is hardly a mass-

---

*Adorno wrote on jazz before experiencing it at first hand in the U.S., which, in what I hope is a wry comment by Martin Jay (*The Dialectical Imagination*, p.186), "allowed his dialectical imagination full sway," though he did not modify his opinion after coming to the U.S. Like Hermann Hesse, Adorno failed to distinguish authentic jazz from big band music; cf. my comments on this aspect of Hesse's cultural criticism in "Hermann Hesse and the Over-Thirty Germanist," *Hesse: A Collection of Critical Essays*, ed. Theodore Ziolkowski (Englewood Cliffs, New Jersey: Prentice-Hall, Inc., 1973), pp.125–126. Unlike Hesse, Adorno ultimately admitted that high-fidelity had made his criticism of radio's lack of space and presence obsolete (Jay, p.193). Adorno shares with Hesse, however, what Jay courteously points to as "a provincial streak in his make-up" (p.187).

production rate. Anyone familiar with Heine's way of working knows that his poems were not easily pieced together out of ready-made parts, but meticulously crafted with many revisions, which are almost always improvements and show a refined concern with nuances of sound and rhythm. If an analogy must be drawn, therefore, it would be with preindustrial artisanship and not with mass production. It is true that there are ready-made parts—the phrases and epithets of late Romantic verse—but, far from making Heine's creative process easier, they made it harder; his poems are full of skepticism about their truth-value and worry about what still can be done with them, if anything. Heine initially employed a conventional and familiar diction out of an inherited attitude of Romantic populism, seeking an unalienated naturalness in the common idiom, and did not seem to recognize, at least at first, that his model in this endeavor, the *Lieder* of Wilhelm Müller, itself exhibited an artistic consciousness broken by irony and self-awareness.[17] Furthermore, the bulk of the poems were written in the early and mid-1820s, long before there was anything in Heine's environment like industrial mass production; the analogy therefore intends (dialectically?) not only to denigrate the poetry, but also to predicate to it a "protention" (to borrow a term from phenomenology) with a very long reach and therefore has an abstract and almost mystical quality of prophecy.

As for the equation of Heine's theme of unrequited love with capitalist alienation, it is hard to know how to refute it, as it is an unverifiable aperçu. Heine was not rootless, though he certainly was dislocated in several ways, psychologically, socially, and politically. It is true that, toward the end of this early period, he began to defend the special dignity of being a poet, despite his dissonances, by connecting it with the disharmonious state of the world at large; the poet's heart, he said, is the center of the world and the rip in his heart the great rip in the world.[18] Doubtless it is true that the collapse of the bulwark against alienation that the Romantics tried to carpenter out of poesy, to which Heine's poetic struggle bears thoroughgoing witness, is a symptom of a modern condition and there would be much of interest to say about it. But to say that the major emotional experience of his protracted adolescence was not what he felt it to be at all, but was "really" an analogue to an impersonal, historical situation is to disrespect the poet's conscious life and his rational self-awareness. By casting such a wide net, Adorno obscures Heine's specific treatment of the subjective catastrophe of unrequited love as a threat to the poet's dignity and as something that must be overcome via poetry if the artist is to survive.[19] Once we have become clear about this, we may *then* begin to speak carefully about alienation and its particular relevance to the artist's being, but not before. The confluence of radical anti-individualism with the concept of false consciousness and socio-historical equivocation results in a flat misrepresentation. The difficulty is a fundamental one of broad extrapolation from a critically fuzzy apprehension of the literary work.

I am aware that elsewhere in Adorno's criticism there are valuable and sensitive insights, and I am not trying to pick a nit with him here. Nor am I here primarily concerned with the misfortune that Adorno's view has been uncritically accepted into contemporary Heine scholarship and the commentary to editions, although, since Heine scholarship is prominently characteristic of what is now happening in German literary criticism, this is a point of more than local significance. What we want to know is why so superlative an intellect works so oddly and how so explicitly rational a doctrine as Marxism comes to be associated with assertions of unverifiable equivocation. We will remember Roland Barthes' demand that analogy be supplanted with homology. From our point of view, this appears as an effort to meet the arbitrariness of equivocation not by increased skepticism and caution—more analysis—but by more rigorous equations—greater synthesis. Homology is a stronger word than analogy; it promises congruities rather than similarities. If the equivocal nature of illicit analogy is due, as Musil suggested, to the arbitrary selection of predicates without respect to the total structure of the phenomena compared, homology proposes to set whole against whole and promises a congruent totality. It is a daring concept, and the question is whether it relieves the inadequacies of equivocation or leads us into deeper difficulties.

We associate the concept of homology primarily with the work of Lucien Goldmann. I shall leave by the way here Goldmann's specific applications to Pascal, Racine, and Jansenism, and the novels of Malraux; others are much better qualified to assess this work and there has been a substantial response to it.* It has, to be sure, sometimes been

---

*Goldmann's methods certainly do not always assure cogent critical argument. In applying to Goethe the Marxian paradigm of Balzac as a writer whose import deviated from his own ideological allegiances, Goldmann remarks apropos Goethe's relationship to the French Revolution that, while his three counter-revolutionary dramas are now forgotten, his works embodying a revolutionary spirit—*Faust* and *Pandora* [!]—are deathless masterpieces (*Recherches dialectiques* [Paris: Gallimard, 1959]: pp.49–50). This disproportionate yoking of a work of world literature with a fragment known only to a minority of specialists occurs in a passage in which Goldmann is arguing for the necessity of close reading. One wonders what he would have said of *The Campaign in France*, where Goethe's conservative

doubted that Goldmann's massive theoretical apparatus was wholly necessary to gain his specific insights, but he always claimed that, experientially, they made his scholarly task efficient and led straight to the desired results. Nor can this be the place for a critique of Goldmann's highly resourceful and impressive work. But he is always at pains to make his core assumptions explicit, and it is those that concern us here.

Goldmann, unlike many earlier literary sociologists and Marxists, is a text-oriented critic with a concomitant concern with literary form (though it has been pointed out that his "form" is what others may be inclined to call "content"[20]). For this reason he regularly argues against the citing of literary works as a documentation or a reflection of a collective consciousness; for him, the relationship between work and consciousness is much more intimate. There is, he says, a "rigorous homology" between the form of the novel and the quotidian content of life in a liberal market economy.[21] Goldmann's concept of the collective consciousness is directly drawn from structuralism in that he sees it as a dynamic pattern seeking equilibrium. The homology cannot be one between consciousness and content, for this would ignore imaginative deviation from reality; it must therefore be one between social structure and literary form. The social group or class develops a coherent though, of course, not fully articulated "vision of the world"; the exceptionally creative individual drives this coherence to its limit and gives it imaginative or conceptual expression.[22] This structural interrelatedness between consciousness and society Goldmann terms, with another strong word, "global": "The central idea of this book [*The Hidden God*] is that facts concerning man always form themselves into significant global structures, which are at one and the same time practical, theoretical and emotive, and that these structures can be studied in a scientific manner, that is to say they can be both explained and understood, only within a practical perspective based on the acceptance of a certain set of values."[23] An individual can never generate a coherent vision of the world on his own; such a global structure can only arise out of the daily life of the members of the group[24] —Marxist *Praxis*.

Many difficulties arise here. Much of Goldmann's argument is assertive, and it is not obvious that his strategies have abolished the problem of equivocation. His view that the modern novel reproduces the transfor-

instincts, his vision of a world of civil and pacific values, and a realistic appraisal of aristocratic and even royal preposterousness, republican virtue, and revolutionary competence are held in a finely nuanced suspension that firmly rebuts Goldmann's denial of complexity and multivalence in the great writers. (See below pp.49–50.)

mation of use value into exchange value, largely derived from Lukács, begs the question of whether the underlying Marxist principle is correct, or, even if it does have a heuristic validity in economic history, whether Marxist philosophy does not generalize it more than it will bear. The radical neo-Marxist will object against Goldmann that the homologous relationship does not leave room for the writer's anticipation of things of the future.[25] While this objection throws up another difficulty that will be discussed in the following essay, Goldmann is not wholly able to avoid the static quality for which structuralism is often criticized. The stress upon the state of equilibrium reached or sought for by the collective consciousness binds new things in literature inescapably to the displacement of one social group by another, and the denial that new coherences (or just newness as such) can be an individual achievement contradicts much literary experience. Perhaps it can be made to apply to Pascal and Racine, or to a weathervane novelist like Malraux, but I should imagine it would offer substantial difficulties in coping with Catullus, or Wolfram von Eschenbach, or Kafka, or Faulkner. All arguments that postulate complete conformity between literature and its audience ought at least to bear in mind that Aristotle succinctly classified as second-rate those works in which "the poet is guided in what he writes by the wishes of his audience" (*Poetics*, XIII, 7). Moreover, I am made quite uneasy by Goldmann's statement that the literary work is characterized by a universe that is "à peu près" coherent with the group vision of the world;[26] even though, in my experience of reading him, it is an isolated instance, it is an enormous qualification in the midst of an argument insisting upon global homologies. It reminds one of Friedrich Engels' late hedging about the direct relationship of basis and superstructure, and, in the same way, solves a pragmatic problem while introducing severe logical difficulties into the foundation of the argument. It could be that the space opened by this "à peu près" is just that region, perhaps a narrow one, that is exciting to the practical critic.

There is, however, a broader implication of Goldmann's method that leads beyond his own work to a problem of a fundamental nature. Concepts of "homology" and "globality" postulate or strive for holistic visions. Goldmann is quite clear about this. "The category of totality," he writes, " . . . is at the very center of dialectical thought." Indeed, he goes so far as to supplant the traditional dialectical triad with the hermeneutic circle: "The central image dominating any dialectical thought is that of the sphere or circle, and from this point of view we must not allow ourselves to be misled by the many dualistic or triadic expressions—two

infinites, thesis, antithesis and synthesis, etc.—that we find in the theoretical writings of dialectical thinkers." He also informs us whence this
insistence on totality comes. It is impelled by an unwillingness to tolerate
a world of contingency. "As men, we cannot try to achieve the absolute,
but, at the same time, we cannot as men remain satisfied with any
understanding that does not strive after it. . . . It is the illusion of sen-
sualists and sceptics [!] to maintain that we can find in the world of reality
values which, although only relative, are sufficiently valid to make life
bearable."[27] It is primarily for this reason that Goldmann's position is
"rigorously monist."[28]

The epistemological postulate of totality, what Lukács, following
Hegel and Lenin, calls "the direct unity of the general and the particular,"[29] and the corollary concern with the recovery of an allegedly lost
community of man is so pervasive, not only in Marxism and literary
sociology, but in much modern criticism generally, that it may appear
futile to raise objections against it. Indeed, it has been said that the basic
conception of sociology itself is totality.[30] But as a philosophical obsession
it requires a more than methodological explanation. The modern self-
awareness, the maturity of which Kant spoke, brought with it both a
promise and a threat of freedom. While promising the emancipation of
man from his material and political oppression and increasing the potential of the individual to gain control over the range and order of his own
life, liberating him from an existence preordained by time, place, and
custom, it also generated a constantly recurring fear of the dissolution of
binding ties and objectively governing principles of human life. Idealism
and Romanticism are associated with the drive to close the resulting gap
of individuation or alienation. In theory, Marxism perceives this condition in dialectical balance; both the uprooting emancipation and the
pressure toward a new harmony of life achieved in conscious self-
awareness are major categories of the historical dialectic. In practice,
however, Marxism has tended to break up the emancipatory achievements, in the political realm especially, by an overriding pressure toward
the achievement of totality and community, and the neo-Marxist stress
upon the issue of alienation serves even further to repress Marxism's
Enlightenment heritage. This shows up in contemporary Marxist literary criticism, and in that respect it may not be so different from the
critical position it opposes.

"Since the early part of this century," observes Geoffrey Hartman,
"and already since the Romantic period, we have turned to art in order to
sustain our diminishing sense of 'the common nature' of man."[31] The

clearest and firmest link between the practices of Right and Left in literary studies is the concept of community, involving a strong sense of alienation in modern life and usually an argument or conviction about the potential, though currently frustrated, community-forming capacity of art. If the concept of community is highly and prominently valued, there will be a tendency to see hopeful congruences between, on the one hand, both the Romantic tradition and modern conservative criticism, and, on the other, socialist views of various kinds; such is, for example, the case of Raymond Williams. The radical sociologist will argue that organicism is a healthy response provoked by liberalism and will cheerfully admit that Marxism shares a common ground with conservatism.[32] If, however, the concept of community seems to the observer trapridden and not infrequently found in the neighborhood of illiberal, irrationalist, or totalitarian arguments, its appearance will be for him a signal to begin reading with close attention; such is my case. It does no good to point out that the fear of freedom and the pressure toward totality and unity are the most effective impulses of totalitarianism, for there is good totality and bad totality. Kenneth Burke, in his celebrated analysis of Hitler's *Mein Kampf*, observed that "the yearning for unity is so great that people are always willing to meet you halfway if you will give it to them by fiat, by flat statement, regardless of the facts," and he described with acuity the Fascist trick of turning the great human dislike of division and dissension against those who call attention to the fact of disunity. But Burke is not about to suggest that the dislike of division and the pressure toward unity is therefore to be opposed; on the contrary, Hitler's doctrine, which "provided a 'world view' for people who had previously seen the world but piecemeal" was the "*bad* filling of a good need."[33]

Everywhere we turn on this territory we find variations of a Lost Paradise myth; its reverberations will concern us further in the following essay, but it emerges here in the recurrent conviction that somewhere in the past—in Classical antiquity, or in the Renaissance, or in the preindustrial age—man and society were whole, and, as a corollary to this, literature and society were homogeneous.* Goldmann's principle of ho-

---

*It is interesting that the erudite Marxist Classicist George Thomson argues in an opposite direction. Much too close to and learned in Classical antiquity to make any use of it as a Lost Paradise, he is instead concerned to detect a progress toward democracy in ancient Greece. Thus, in his account, the "aristocratic" thought of Anaximander tended "to divide, to keep things apart," while the popular religion of Orphism "implied the reunion of what had been sundered, the recovery of what had been lost"; the Orphic Empedokles opposes Strife with Love. "The tendency of popular thought was to unite" (*Aeschylus and Athens: A*

mology radicalizes this view across all history, but it reflects the same concern. For Q. D. Leavis, to take a conservative example of which there will be more to say later on, literature and its public were in harmony until the emergence of modern economic divisions; and she expands this opinion to a truly paradisiacal vision of premodern society: "The closer one looks the more fully one is persuaded that the life of the people at the end of the seventeenth century and of the shopkeeper class at the beginning of the eighteenth century was in general both finer in quality and more satisfying in substance than that of their descendants."[34]

This view is not so different from the strong conservative and classicistic thrust of much Marxist literary evaluation, of which Lukács is a notable but not isolated example. The reasons for this should emerge more clearly in the following chapter. But it is necessary to mention here that Lukács' insistence upon all acts of consciousness as mirrorings of the same, unitary reality leads him to a vigorous defense of analogy, with characteristic allusions to Hegel and Goethe, although, of course, he must appeal to Hegel's differentiation between "superficial" and "fundamental" analogy.[35] Marxist criticism, writes Jameson, "is thus essentially a *form* or a pretext for a new politicization of our thinking, which gives us to understand what kinds of future social renewal and regeneration are available to us by allowing us a glimpse of the healthier, socially functional art of the past." Our contemporary literature cannot serve this purpose, for in the United States today there is nothing left in art or society worth salvaging.[36] *Les extrèmes se touchent*, or, to put it another way, the intellectual cultural criticism of our century exhibits some important common strands.

Thus the "hunger for wholeness," which Peter Gay has described as a particular irritant of the Weimar period in Germany,[37] is a much wider phenomenon and goes far to explain the prevalence of analogy, homology, and equivocation in literary sociology, and to connect it with European patterns of cultural philosophy from Hegel through Burckhardt to Wölfflin and Dilthey.[38] On the one hand, art is the preserving vehicle of this yearning; Ernst Bloch tells us that art is full of "symbols of perfection"; the phenomena of the imagination are related not only to the "whole of their epoch" (Goldmann's homology) but point

---

Study in the Social Origins of Drama, 3rd ed. [London: Grosset & Dunlap, 1968], pp. 145–146). It is important to notice this movement, for Thomson is arguing on the base of a philosophy that has eschatological roots. Marxism frequently undergoes such mutations when it gets down to cases. But my point here is rather the incompatibility of Thomson's pattern with the family resemblance of Marxism and conservatism.

to the "utopian *totum*" that they potentially contain.[39] According to Ernst Fischer, the loss of magic, the distance from nature and from the tribe as a collective organism, destroy more and more the equilibrium of the individual with his environment; the division of society is an impoverishment: "Individuation was secretly sensed as a tragic *guilt*, the yearning for an original unity was inextinguishable, the dream of a 'golden age,' of an innocent 'paradise' transfigured a distant and dark past." Since, however, "the essential content of personality is and remains the social element," the communicative power of art is a return from the individual to the collective. Art repairs "the destroyed unity of man"; "in every genuine work of art, the split of human reality into individual beings and collective being, into the particular and the general, is sublated, but these remain as sublated elements in the restored unity."[40]

Are we not here moving toward religion, much as the New Criticism tended to depart from its original rational base for a Neo-Romantic view of literature as secularized religion and not infrequently wound up in religious orthodoxies? I think so. Bloch, of course, is profoundly respectful of religion as an elemental vehicle of the principle of hope, and Jameson extrapolates from this circumstance an affinity between Marxism and Christianity, which he appears to regard positively.[41] But it takes the straightforwardness of Goldmann to confront the issue head-on, or almost so. We must, he says, understand "social reality as a whole, in an organic unity which links together both values and actions. In my view, this attitude can best be described by using the word faith—provided, naturally, that we dissociate it from any exclusively religious connotation." But Goldmann does not so dissociate it, for elsewhere he says that Marxism "is, certainly, a religion, but a religion with no God, a religion of man and of humanity." Marx and Lukács knew, he says quite surprisingly, "that there is no empirical way of proving that progress existed in the past and that it will continue in the present," a statement that appears to me to erase Engels' reiterated analogy between natural and social evolution as a basic postulate of historical materialism. Pascal's idea of the wager turns out to be central here; we must assume that history has a meaning; indeed, we do not choose the wager, but have already made it one way or another.[42]

Such arguments have uncomfortable implications. But we need not puzzle them out for ourselves; we may rely still further on Goldmann's remarkable candidness. One small difficulty with the Marxist philosophy of history is that it has been a poor predictor of the future, just as the

Christian eschatological prophecy has had to be indefinitely postponed. But if one has true faith, it cannot be overthrown by the resistance of reality. The kind of hope held out by Marx, Engels, Lenin, and Lukács "cannot be destroyed by any external difficulty. These thinkers merely discover that values are realised slowly, and that"—here it is worth listening carefully—"compared to History or to Eternity, one single human life has scarcely any importance." Thus, in this Christianized Marxism, the Inquisition lurks in the wings. To the ethical question of how one ought to live, "the reply is already implicit: by situating one's life inside an eschatological or historical whole in which it inserts itself by faith. The essential truth of Augustinianism and of dialectical materialism is that we must believe in order to understand reality and to act in a humanly efficacious manner. and it is for this reason that there is no autonomous and independent Augustinian and Marxist ethic."[43] *

In one possible mood, the radicality of the "hunger for wholeness" and its insouciant susceptibility to totalitarian resolutions can be mitigated by regarding it as a rhetorical hyperbole that is understandable in the face of the distressed experience of atomization and alienation. Ernst Fischer writes: "Obviously man wants to be more than himself. He wants to be a *whole* man,"[44] a theme that runs constantly through Lukács' aesthetics as well and is legitimately grounded in Marx. But the jump from more to whole is by no means necessary and is, in fact, fallacious; surely there is a broad middle ground between separation and identity. The failure of many major intellectuals to locate this middle ground was one of the accompanying misfortunes of the Fascist era. Requiring a strong position against the bad totality of Fascism, yet convinced that "the negation of totality, of the objective interconnections between the individual complexes, is also dangerous, producing disorientation, the defence of fragmentation, the psychology of the meaninglessness of one's actions,

*Goldmann's use of the word "autonomous" here masks his meaning. If he means no immutable ethics given outside of history, then that is doubtless true of Marxism, though the link to Augustinianism becomes obscure. If he means an ethics distinct from the system as a whole, then the point is trivial. Marx does argue, for example, that in the obligations of commercial relations there can be no question of justice, they being mere forms determined by the relations of production. See *Das Kapital*, Section 5, Ch. 21 (Karl Marx, Friedrich Engels, *Werke*, ed. Institut für Marxismus-Leninismus beim ZK der SED, XXV [Berlin: Dietz Verlag, 1964],351–352). But if Goldmann means that in Marx's doctrine there is no anterior, fundamental ethics driving the argument with recognizable constancy, then this is surely mistaken. The question of Marxist ethics is a problematic one, but Marx's own thinking was actuated by principles of freedom and harmony, probably related to those of Hegel, as desiderata in human existence. See Eugene Kamenka, "The Primitive Ethic of Karl Marx," *Marxism*, ed. Michael Curtis (New York: Atherton Press, 1970), pp.118–127).

the cynical rejection of morally inspired activity, and the powerless acceptance of one's conditions, however inhuman they might be,"[45] they found themselves impelled to opt for Stalinism, the one approximate manifestation of the good totality. The pattern repeated itself often and is often defended today. What is postulated is an indissoluble link between liberalism, skepticism, relativism, and induction on the one hand and nihilism, disorientation, moral dissolution, and the absurd on the other. It is, in fact, a late chapter of the shock effect of the collapse of a religiously sanctioned order of society. I do not myself believe that this philosophical logic of the excluded middle is congruent with reality. The complexity of human affairs, like that of the relations of literature and society, is not reducible to formulas of the type: if A, then not-B.

The desire to perceive the world as a totality, or to advance a restoration of totality that is prefigured for us in art, is the explanation for the tendency toward uncontrolled analogy and equivocation. Metaphor itself, especially in Romantic doctrine, presses toward the reconciliation of disparities; the restoration or construction of a unity in diversity is crucial to any serious implication that metaphor and analogy yield truth rather than ornament or illustration. The parallel to the conservative canons of modern criticism is very striking. "What Frye, [Philip] Wheelwright, and others are saying" observes Gerald Graff, "is that the poet's use of metaphor inescapably commits him, provisionally at least, to a kind of transcendentalist monism." The consequence for critical apprehension is that "according to this theory a poet cannot possibly say in his poem that subject and object are *not* one, that matter is *not* spirit."[46] In a sense, the poem understood this way is itself an equivocation. The obsession with the wholeness of things and an unqualified yearning for the harmonious community of man shared by the radical, materialist doctrine is marked by the same tendency. Empson, in one of his arresting argumentative ellipses, remarked that "once you have said that everything is One it is obvious that literature is the same as propaganda."[47] The French sociologist of art Jean Duvignaud has said that the "aesthetic of the absolute community . . . implies above all the absence of what today we call art,"[48] and this accounts, no doubt, for the strikingly conservative taste and anti-modernism of many Marxist literary theorists. Bloch, who is on the whole an exception in this regard, connected Lukács' conservative canon with the vision of totality and traced it to the traditional idealism of German philosophy.[49] But Bloch differs from Lukács only in that he sets totality as a future-oriented desideratum rather than as an existing abstraction; the values are similar, as they must be in any system in which alienation is so important a concept.

The synchronic concept of epoch, which permits equivocation in the first place, is in itself problematic. It is well known that attempting to define stylistic homologies among concurrent arts often creates embarrassments.[50] For Lukács, the stylistic incongruities of, say, the Baroque arts could not be fundamental, for all the arts, in their differentiation through the various senses, are reflections of the same reality.* If Goldmann were to apply his structural concept of homology to a problem like this, he would have to argue that Baroque painting and music corresponded to the world-view of different social groups, a position I should think would be difficult to maintain, though Escarpit does suggest it.[51] Nor can one easily doubt that there are internal, formal pressures within the various arts that give them a measure of internal diachronic development. To be sure, it has been said of Lévi-Strauss's structuralism that "all the aspects of the same society do not evolve simultaneously, they are not all in accord; it follows that analogy on the one hand can go hand in hand with very great differences on the other"[52] —which is very likely derived from the Marxists' operational category of non-simultaneity but in my view brings us back to Musil's butterfly and Chinese.

R. S. Crane also mounts logical objections, which he, too, associates with visions of totality; he regards as illicit the "assumption that we can deduce particularized actuality from general possibility," an assumption drawn from a "quasi-Platonic" postulate of "the participation of the Many in the Being of the One." Like Musil, Crane sees Spengler as a particular offender in this regard, in whose assertion of "'deep uniformities' among the most disparate historical phenomena" there is a "lurking presumption of causal efficacy," but "no obligation to render this explicit or to argue its plausibility for the relationship in question. . . . Extreme devotees of *Geistesgeschichte*" constantly exhibit "irresponsible analogizing, uncontrolled by any dialectically rigorous criticism of terms and hence debased to the level of mere verbal equivocation."[53] It is important to bear this in mind, as well as the possibility that neo-Marxism may, in this respect, be closer to *Geistesgeschichte* than it would care to

---

*It is a very interesting assertion made by James S. Ackerman that there has been no Marxist architectural criticism because the patronage of the powerful on which architecture depends appears in no situation to be the progressive force in society ("Toward a New Social Theory of Art," *New Literary History* 4 [1972/73]:321).

admit. But it must also be said that Crane's logical requirements are of such a degree of rigor that they would inhibit just about any extrinsic discussion of literature; neither history nor sociology proper could function under such strict canons of causality as he proposes.[54] There are decisive necessities interrelated with fortuitous and contingent events that can be plausibly identified without belaboring causality as a logical relation. We can say, for example, that the European middle-style *comédie larmoyante* accompanies increasing middle-class self-awareness, which is thus a contextual determinant without which the genre would not have emerged or thriven. To deny that we can make such statements would be to align ourselves with those who refuse to make sense out of historical facts.

René Wellek makes the familiar counterargument when he asserts that the situation of the German artist at the turn of the nineteenth century cannot "account for" Novalis' *Heinrich von Ofterdingen*.[55] But it is inconceivable that *Heinrich von Ofterdingen* could have been written in 1600 or 1700, and just about as inconceivable that it could have been written fifteen or even more than two or three years earlier than it was. Equally unimaginable is that, in 1800, it should have been written in France, or in Poland, or in Massachusetts. If we are convinced of this, as I assume we all are, then there are reasons for this conviction that can be specified without requiring that they account for every aspect and nuance of a work which, while most imaginative, is nevertheless a response to and therefore in determinate dialogue with an environmental context. Whether, in order to codify this conviction, it is necessary to find analogies of content and homologies of structure is, of course, another question altogether. But that the passivity and stasis forced upon society by the backward German political order impelled the bourgeois intellectuals and the educated nobility in touch with them to seek an aesthetic solution to the emancipation of man at this time is now hardly doubted by any historian or literary scholar. Novalis, indeed, consciously sought to break out of this passivity, not only by poeticizing the world, but also by the practical conduct of his short life, at the end of which he had become a public official, a kind of ombudsman, in his community.

An uneasiness about equivocation is not uncommon among critics, including literary sociologists, although it is naturally always someone else who is guilty of it. Harry Levin bluntly calls Goldmann's homologies "naïve parallels."[56] Goldmann, in turn, warns that "organic analogies are very dangerous—and Marxist thinkers have always underlined this fact";[57] although whether his own concept of globality is so different from Classical-Romantic organicism is a question worth some study. Norbert Fügen, while being obliged to state that "all branches of current literary sociology are based at least on the assumption that the parts of a social system are dependent upon one another, that writers can be seen as parts of the system and that their utterances can be regarded as social behavior," complains that "under the influence of a scholarship with strong artistic ambitions there sneaks in a metaphoric manner, no longer subject to scientific criticism, that draws its legitimization from a more or less successful resemblance to literature."[58] Another observer complains of Fügen's methods "that they equate their object with analytic categories whose justification is derived primarily from the degree of their operability," while criticizing Adorno and Goldmann for a priori assertion and the neglect of empirical social aspects: "the more global and indefinite the social whole that emerges in the interpretation, the more arbitrary appears its connection with detail."[59]

So it goes in our subject; the problems will not come to rest, and every man's hand seems to be raised against every other. For it is not likely that literary sociology can be conducted without *some* form of analogy and *some* sense of coherence in the social and historical fabric. The problem, as Jameson rightly says, has its "origins in the Romantic era along with the invention of history itself, for it depends on some prior theorization about the unity of the cultural field." This theorization is the "will to link together in a single figure two incommensurable realities, two independent codes or systems of signs, two heterogeneous and assymetrical terms." But Jameson's claim that this manner of "metaphorical composition," such as we find in Adorno, yields "truth" seems to me mystical. If the realities and terms are incommensurable and heterogeneous, if setting them together is, as Jameson says, "contingency temporarily transmuted into necessity,"[60] then we must not lose our awareness of the experimental and tentative aspect of this thinking process. The sociologist George A. Huaco offers as a substitute for the rigid concept of homology the term "isomorphism," and suggests that its legitimate Marxist use is instrumental rather than existential; according to Marx, in Huaco's reading, "*sometimes* a social pattern produces its mirror image in some symbolic domain of culture," and "a group of literary works *might* exhibit shared mythical patterns without these or other patterns being isomorphic to anything going on in society."[61] Whether this is a correct reading of Marx or not I should hesitate to say, but it does offer a prospect of restraining the excesses of equivocation. Pierre Macherey, meanwhile, has argued for the concept of rapport, which keeps the difference between metaphorical or analogical terms in view and is concerned with distance as well as likeness.[62] But a far more fundamental consideration is that society, especially modern society, is likely to be far less coherent, less clearly patterned, and more centrifugal than any aesthetic representation it generates.[63]

I am convinced that we can make legitimate sociological statements about literature and that they can be pertinent to the meaning of literary works as such as well as their meaning for us. Where artistic social behavior is first correlated with larger social structures and formal conclusions are drawn on this base, as Alan Lomax has done with types of musical performance in various societies,[64] compelling results may emerge. But it is altogether clear that a strict concept of social and historical globality has the same consequence that some years ago was ascribed to the autonomous, self-sufficient view of poetry: that it "in some mysterious way puppetizes the poet and does the job for which, in its innocence, common sense has traditionally held him responsible."[65] When Goldmann's genetic structuralism combines with contemporary French anti-humanism, this effect becomes quite explicit; the Italian structuralist Fernando Ferrara asserts that "the author does nothing but gather and transmit" the values generated by the social group; "he is therefore negligible and, in fact, can be ignored in our model."[66] It appears to me, however, that a literary criticism without authors is not likely to have much educational or cultural fortune, and therefore a practical criticism firmly committed to a dehumanization of literature may turn out as bleak and indifferent as the uninspired exercise of immanent criticism. If we lose track of the probable inadequacy of our structural grasp of society and history, if we transform contingency *permanently* into necessity, and if we allow our dismay at alienation and atomization to lead us into fantasies about global totalities and a secularized *unio mystica*, we shall be led into equivocations that loosen the language of argument from the object of discourse and become purely operable out of a priori interest.

III

Truth and Time

Durch praktische Gesetze, nicht durch gekün-
stelte Geburten der theoretischen Vernunft soll
der Mensch bei seinem moralischen Handeln
geleitet werden.   —Friedrich Schiller,
Briefe über Don Carlos, xi

The discussion of equivocation and analogy took us to some larger
postulates or concerns that emerge behind these curious practices and
help to explain them. We find an urge to apprehend or recover a
coherent, total world of experience and a desire to seek in the work of art
a structure congruent with such totality, or, in other cases, anticipatory of
its recovery. This raises at once another large issue that has been separated from the preceding one only with some difficulty. All analogy and
homology imply that the work of art, in some fashion or other, via
content or form, gives information about the world around it or anterior
to it. This implication raises problems of cognition that confront us
everywhere in literary sociology.

There are actually two different problems of cognition involved. One
is the hermeneutic question of how we know a work of art and what the
nature of the object is that is thus known. This is, of course, an irrepressi-
bly contentious topic. The line of inquiry leads to the role of the reader in
constituting or reconstituting the reality of the literary work and is
therefore of direct literary-sociological interest. The French—Sartre and
Escarpit in particular—have been inclined to stress that a book or a poem
is not a literary work but only a physical object; the literary work is a
content of consciousness constituted by reading or hearing. This argument, incidentally, is quite similar to that propagated a generation ago in

American philosophy by John Dewey.[1] Its apparent plausibility and at least partial correctness nevertheless lead to some difficulties, especially if one believes that a work is substantially formed by a socially determined consciousness of historical transitoriness. If a work is ontologically that which is constituted in the reader's consciousness, what is apprehended by a later reader subject to different social determinants will be a different work. The work, by this argument, appears to lose the quality of a real existent with a fixed historical location, and in that regard there is no great difference from the New Critical process that, by denying intentionality and discrediting attention to concrete context, threatens to make of the literary work a freely manipulable object of interpretation. In recent years E. D. Hirsch has been mounting a persistent opposition to this view, and he has observed: "Only recently has historicism turned back upon itself to announce that we *are* imprisoned in our own culture willy-nilly, and we must therefore return to a quasi-medieval conception of interpretation, namely that the best meaning (or for that matter any meaning) must be anachronistic whether we like it or not."[2] Furthermore, the "reader-consciousness" theory sometimes seems disrespectful of the limitations that even a "quasi-medieval" hermeneutic would impose; Erwin Leibfried has pointed out that the Song of Songs may be interpreted as dealing with profane or with sacred love, but it may not be treated as a discourse on warfare or the manufacture of wine.[3] If such limits can be imposed on a text, then it seems to me that in all probability they can be drawn more tightly and we may be permitted to doubt that sacred love can be the meaning of the Song of Songs in any but an arbitrary, imposed sense. The seventh and fifty-third chapters of Isaiah and Vergil's fourth Eclogue cannot *mean* the future coming of Christ, no matter how many centuries of interpreters used the texts in this fashion. This is worth remembering as a paradigmatic limitation on the value of reception history as illuminating of the text.

Vexing as the problem is, it is not peculiar to literary sociology; it emerges in any type of fundamental literary theory. While we must acknowledge its presence and be alert to the difficulties it generates, it does not loom as large in our questioning of literary sociology as the other issue of cognition: what knowledge of the world, if any, does the literary work apprehend and communicate? When I was in elementary school, one of the things we were encouraged to note in our discussion of literature was something called "signs of the times." In retrospect, it appears to me that the teachers who devised this method must have been influenced by a pre-New Critical view of literature that, under the impact

of the Depression and the severe deterioration of the political atmosphere in the world, reached its peak in the 1930s—a form of practical
literary sociology. As a pedagogical device for ten-year-old readers, the
approach had clear virtues. It sharpened the awareness of the difference
between our own experiential consciousness and that embodied in the
story at hand; in this way it worked against a naive assimilation of the
literary work by present and provincial consciousness. I assume the
purpose was to increase the understanding and, hopefully, the positive
acknowledgment of cultural and historical differences as experiences of
enrichment—a democratizing purpose of high priority in the multi-
ethnic and biracial environment in which I lived. Behind such a method
lies a straightforward view of cognition: the literary work communicates
a picture of a world different from our own. Such a view also implies a
predilection for realism. As far as I can recollect, all the reading we were
given in school between the imaginative story-telling at the beginning
and the futile attempts to introduce us to high culture at the end was in
the realist mode.

Certain kinds of critics have always been concerned to deny that a
cognitive aspect can be predicated to a fictional phenomenon. Sometimes the purpose of this denial has been to defend the freedom of
literature from censorious overseers; Sir Philip Sidney's claim that fiction
cannot lie because it affirms nothing is an example of this strategy; and it
may appear that if literature cannot lie, it also cannot tell truth and thus
has no cognitive aspect. This has been the position of modern logicians,
and Tzvetan Todorov is not alone in extrapolating from it the view that
the literary reading of any text is one in which the question of truth does
not arise.[4] Yet even Richards' theory of "pseudo-statements" would seem
to suggest that fictional utterances are at least mimetic of real ones, even
if they ought not to be verified or falsified.[5] Sometimes a polemic is
mounted as though it were necessary to deny that literature communicates the same kind of knowledge in the same way as nonfictional
discourse; thus Ingarden asserts that literature is not intended "to permit a conceptual and judgmental form and a fixation to a scientific
perception, nor does it serve to communicate such results. . . . It is
therefore quite mistaken to query literary works and interpret them as
though they were disguised philosophical systems."[6] But as sociologists
have pointed out recently, there can be two meanings of "true": "in the
linguistic sense of not being falsifiable by other evidence, and also in the
ontological sense of being 'true to the world.'"[7] Perhaps we may agree
that literature cannot be true or false in the first sense, and much

egregious misreading, not to speak of censorship and oppression, derives from a simple failure to observe this. Still, certain kinds of literature
tend so far to the assertive that this kind of truth appears to be trying to
engage the reader; one might think, in German letters, of Stifter or
Gotthelf, or of modern documentary theater. The quarrel of the Soviet
dissidents with their persecutors is a more complicated case than either
the judges or the defendants are prepared to recognize. But so far as
"truth to the world" as reflective cognition is concerned, a statement like
Ingarden's does not dispose of the likelihood that literature can stand in
some important relation to perception or to philosophical systems and
that this relation may interest us. Of course, genuine extremists will
attempt such a denial. Northrop Frye writes:

> poetry knows nothing of progress, only of recurrence. Whatever science
> may say, the poet's world continues to be built out of a flat earth with a
> rising and setting sun, with four elements and an animate nature, the
> concrete world of emotions and sensations and fancies and transforming
> memories and dreams. . . . The four elements are still there in Dylan
> Thomas and the Eliot Quartets, and are likely to remain in poetry until that
> remote time in the future when chemistry, or whatever the appropriate
> science will then be, will have discovered that there are in fact four elements,
> and that their names are earth, air, fire, and water.[8]

This playing at atavistic know-nothingism cries out for protest. The
argument against science, which recalls Keats, suffers, as M. H. Abrams
has said, from "the fallacy . . . that when a perceptual phenomenon is
explained by correlating it with something more elementary than itself,
the explanation discredits and replaces the perception—that only the
explanation is real, and the perception illusory,"[9] an objection that,
parenthetically, also applies to some applications of the Marxist basis–
superstructure scheme. The response, however, cannot permissibly be
to deny the realm of truth either in natural science or in the economic
basis. As several examples in modern literature show, the insistence upon
rejecting the claims of this realm and seeking alternatives mires the
intellect in an occultism that has difficulty distinguishing between the
imaginative and the imaginary. Such constructed alternatives are ineffectual in the long run because they are arbitrarily private and cannot be
socially shared except by coteries often marked by bad faith insofar as
they are aware of the willfulness and waywardness of such constructions;
and when larger groups, like our contemporary youthful astrologers,
drug-cultists, black magicians, and Jesus people, fall victim to them, the
result is not the conquest of a new territory of the mind, as the cultists

insistently claim, but a vacuum left behind by their departure, which then fills up with more baleful elements of the reality they believe they have defeated. In the face of provocations of this kind, I have trouble following Geoffrey Hartman's judgment that "Frye is our most radical demystifier of criticism."[10] Obscurantism is certainly not the road to demystification.

However, insofar as Frye's statement is more than a joke, it asserts that it is the poets who are right and that science will ultimately be obliged to come around to the vision Frye imputes to them. It is indeed of interest for our purposes that the most irrational criticism often ascribes a truth value to literature and therefore a kind of transcendental cognition, as though we were still in the age of Hesiod, believing that the gods instruct men through inspired poetry. This imputation is especially prominent in the more idealistic kinds of hermeneutics. Thus Richard Palmer, discussing Gadamer, explicitly predicates cognition to art, which "is not sense perception but knowledge." It is not a new knowledge, however, but a reinforcement of what is already within our horizon; we assent to the work of art and "come home" in it; art "reveals being" and "the artist has said what *is*."[11] * Here there is certainly a fundamental quarrel with those who believe that the exploration of art and literature is a way of leaving home, and who would regard the proper activity of the intellect not as a revolving spiral directed inward, but as a stretching beyond the parochially given limits of awareness. But before we conclude that a "materialistic" literary theory grounded in social considerations will be a wholly unambiguous instrument for combatting this concept of cognition, we had better take a look.

The modern idealistic revival of the notion of the poet as a divinely inspired seer, of poetry as revelatory of eternal forms or of a unified transcendental truth, is well known. From a historical point of view, it has a tendency to be revived, with greater or lesser ingenuousness, when poets are convinced that they are at the forefront of a surging intellectual development, or when, as in our time, they face the threat of being pushed altogether to the farthest periphery of society. As we shall see when we come to speak of the problems of endurance and elitism, the empirical branch of literary sociology tends to call into question any universalistic and transcendental pretensions of this kind. But where

---

*This is not a peculiarity of religiously derived hermeneutics; Richard Foster has pointed out that several New Critics "share with Ransom the general conviction that poetry provides ontological knowledge" (*The New Romantics: A Reappraisal of the New Criticism* [Bloomington: Indiana University Press, 1962], p.145).

literary sociology is more speculative, and particularly where it is under the influence of Marxism, a countertrend becomes evident. Marxism has always had a gingerly relationship to cultural tradition. Heine's expectation, apparently influenced by what he knew of Babouvism, that Communism would be iconoclastic, that the liberated proletariat would destroy the accumulated treasures of art and blanket the world in a grey utilitarianism, planting potatoes in his laurel forests and using the pages of his volume of poems for grocery bags,[12] has proved to be poor prophecy. Despite the recurring efforts to stimulate an indigenous proletarian literature, and despite the official repudiation of Trotsky's cultural politics, which argued that the proletariat needed to acquire the level of bourgeois culture, Marxism has been highly attentive to and conserving of the art and literature of the past and has encouraged the use of the past as a model for the present. The initial iconoclasm of Bogdanov's *Proletkult* was soon scotched by Lenin. It may be that the large amount of cultural opportunity made available by the European Communist countries is in part a revival of the Metternichian policy of distracting the population with circuses in lieu of freedom. It has been argued recently that the Marxist preoccupation with past art is indeed a deviation from original Marxian principles and is a consequence, in the East, of the need to abandon revolutionary principles in favor of the existing order, and, in the West, of resignation before the refusal of the revolution to occur.[13] In any case, in the literary realm it involves principles of cognition that in their general pattern bear some resemblance to conservative and idealistic claims.

In the history of literary sociology, even the positivist Taine was convinced, according to René Wellek, "that the artist is necessarily the man of the deepest insight into truth, not only truth in a general or transferred sense, but also the truth of an age or a nation";[14] and Walter Abell, who has supplied us with a most interesting and sober psycho-social theory of art, rather surprises us at the end by stating that the experience of art should be a religious one and that the "voice of God" speaks from it.[15] But it is the Marxists who make especially large claims for the special insights of the artist. Ernst Fischer is still among the most cautious: the artist's subjectivity, he writes, "consists not in that his experience is fundamentally *different* from that of his fellow men and contemporaries (or class comrades), but that it is stronger, more awake, and more *essential*, that it reveals the newly arisen and newly arising human relationships, brings them to the consciousness of their contemporaries, calling out to it: *Hic tua res agitur*."[16] This is a well-formulated statement and it is reasonable on its own premises. If consciousness is socially determined, then the artist's consciousness cannot be radically different from that of his social group; the necessity of the artist, therefore, which is Fischer's concern in this place, must lie in the greater intensity, alertness, and accuracy of his insight. But there are at least three problems here. For one thing, it is not clear why this should be especially true of the artist; could it not be said also of the philosopher or of any kind of intellectual oustanding in his own time? Second, although the statement is couched in general terms, it contains an unspecified value judgment; for we all know that there are writers whose substance is not *tua res agitur*, who "betray" the cause of their social contemporaries. Are they artists, or what? Fischer himself, it is true, came to a broadly tolerant position with respect to the varieties of modern literature, but by that time he was hardly a Marxist at all any more. Third—a point connected with the preceding one—it can often happen that the quantitative difference in insight between the artist and his contemporaries becomes a qualitative difference that leads him away from or against the consciousness and self-awareness of his contemporaries. In that case we must make a decision; either the artist has engaged in a "betrayal" and has departed from his communal responsibility, or he takes on the role of the prophet disregarded in his own country, expressing on behalf of his social contemporaries a truth that properly belongs to them but that their false consciousness inhibits them from seeing. In Communist countries the Party usually makes the former decision; in assessing works of the past or "bourgeois" literature, Marxists will normally tend to the latter choice. Ernst Bloch characteristically argues that even if "the receptivity of an age is not itself at the height of that age . . . , the inspiration that comes to perception [*sich vernimmt*] in an individual of genius comes from the age's mission."[17] (Note the highly typical stylistic strategy of making an inanimate force the subject of an action for which the human being is a vehicle.)

The stress on genius is an unexpected peculiarity of Marxist literary discussion; Lukács approvingly quotes Hegel to the effect that "originality is . . . identical with true objectivity,"[18] an argument not insignificantly similar to one mounted by Coleridge.[19] The "born artist" for Lukács has the gift of finding with "infallible certainty" the form or the renewal of form that has an exact affinity to the "solid content" (*gediegener Gehalt*) of the reality with which he is confronted.[20] Lukács is, of course, constrained to avoid any notion of *individual* genius as the wellspring of creativity. For the preservation of particularity in the exceptional artistic consciousness, he therefore employs the Hegelian category of "special-ness" (*Besonderheit*), which mediates between individuality and univer-sality. As a mediating category between atomized empirical perception and generality, Lukács finds it in Goethe, as a fundamental confirmation, incidentally, that Goethe was a realist, for the creation of typical repre-sentation occurs in this category. "Specialness" gathers into human di-mensions the inhuman infinitude of the extensive world. By intensifying (and expanding) individuality, it makes man the measure; Lukács thus hopes to open the way to a humanistic, materialistic aesthetics. It seems clear, however, that since "specialness" is closely related to the subjectivity of the artist's perception, its reunion with universality is only possible by means of priestly and prophetic claims made of the artistic vision.[21] From others we hear not infrequently assertions such as that "the genius is . . . the sum of the possibilities of his time."[22] Both the imprecision and the Romanticism of such a claim are striking, and one may be surprised to find it recurring in the context of what regards itself as "scientific socialism."

It might be mentioned here parenthetically that the stress on genius is part of the quarrel with empiricism. Empirical sociology of literature has achieved some of its best results with non-canonical or trivial literature. It has been true, in modern times, at least, that what we regard as the best literature has tended to have a fairly narrow audience and often exhibits a substantial time lag in public acceptance. Researchers primarily in-terested in sociological results therefore have a natural tendency to turn to literature widely read in its time, in which the ideological accommoda-tion to the public is likely to be much closer. The results are also much less problematical; the method achieves observations to which the reader is likely to assent without too much difficulty, and thus, for both scholar and reader, the enterprise is in some ways more gratifying. But the study of trivial literature, which is especially amenable to empirical methods and has been flourishing in recent years, has, I think, run itself into a set of difficulties that are turning out to be awkward to resolve. Chief among them is that the concept itself preserves a value hierarchy that the students of the subject insist they are determined to set aside. That the *Kitsch* of one observer or one age is the charm of another is a familiar experience in quarrels about taste, and recently one German scholar has made the revolutionary suggestion that the whole concept of *Kitsch* is meaningless and useless.[23] It is not always clear what we are talking about when we speak of trivial literature. If it means, as it did at the outset, mass-produced ephemeral literature, the subject is clear but easily

exhausted; if it tends to spread into all literature short of the enduring
aesthetic canon, the concept becomes diffuse, discriminatory, and probably inoperable.

Industrialized subliterature, often written under contract and for the
most part by authors who are under no illusions that they are producing
something worthwhile, has shown a remarkable stability of form and
content for some two hundred years, despite the appearance of apparently new genres such as pornography and subliterary science fiction,
and it is so formulaic and so rigidly adapted to minimal reader expectations that the study of it tends monotonously to the same results and
observations. In my experience of studies of popular literature, I have
come to think that it would be more fruitful to distinguish subliterature
from the more or less serious, non-canonical literature of wide public
resonance, what one may for convenience call the best sellers. Here the
dynamic of significant and changing social values appears in its most
unmediated form, and the study of such literature yields not only purely
sociological results, but fleshes out a context that sharpens our awareness
of what is conventional, what is related to social expectations, and what is
unique and original in the finest literary achievements. An older but in
some ways still exemplary study of best sellers is E. K. Bramsted's *Aristocracy and the Middle-Classes in Nineteenth-Century Germany* (1964; originally
published in 1937), a perceptive study of novels that had a wide national
and, in some cases, international renown in their time but today are
hardly read except by a few specialists in nineteenth-century German
literature. The book is indispensable to students of the period and ought
to lead them, more than it perhaps has, to the novels themselves, which
are neither incompetent nor uninteresting and greatly modify official
German notions of the national importance of the Classical-Romantic
literary canon developed in Imperial Germany.*

There is much to be said for attention to popular literature. Sometimes it exhibits epigonal imitation of fine literature or what is popularly
regarded as such, and thus teaches us something about the way great
works are generally perceived. It tends almost without exception to be in
a realistic mode; and since its existence is generally dependent on the
common denominators of large audiences, such writing reflects with the
greatest fidelity the values, the vision of life, and a concept of the socially
probable held or believed to be held by its audience; and as long as one

---

*A more recent example of this approach, focused in detail on a single decade, is
Friedrich Winterscheidt, *Deutsche Unterhaltungsliteratur der Jahre 1850–1860* (Bonn:
Bouvier, 1970).

remembers that it is not an aesthetic "reflection of reality," but an attempt to reproduce the perception of reality common to its consumers, much can be learned from it. That the best results in a sociological study of literature are obtained in connection with inferior or mediocre literature is a view held by a good many literary critics, insofar as they have any interest in the subject at all—Sartre, indeed, founded a contemporary review on this principle[24] —and I myself used to think so, although I am no longer convinced that this is either a necessary or desirable restriction. For one thing, it obliges us to assume the canon, which is itself one of the objects of literary-sociological inquiry. For another, while certain rather strict conventions allow us to draw a plausible line between subliterature and literature, the levels of true literature are much harder to distinguish.* Furthermore, most great writers have produced failed or mediocre works, and it also sometimes happens that work of enduring quality will emerge from an otherwise indifferent oeuvre; this is especially the case with poets. Thirdly, an exclusive stress on popular literature is somewhat humiliating, for it suggests that the sociological enterprise is impertinent to what is specifically and outstandingly literary, just as literary critics have so often asserted. The Marxist, furthermore, cannot bear *any* exclusion from his purview, and the cultural-political need to link tradition with the cause of the "people" joins with universalist concerns to move the greatest of literature into the center of inquiry. If the greater writer continues to be regarded as "special," then his specialness must be made congruent with sociological interpretation and evaluation. It also seems plausible that the work with the stronger and profounder vision ought to yield stronger and profounder answers to sociological questions if they are correctly put.[25]

The critic with the largest and most unqualified claims in this regard is once again Lucien Goldmann. For him, the "representative great writers" are "those whose work comes nearest to be the complete expres-

---

*For an exceptionally well-reasoned argument on this point, see Helmut Kreuzer, "Trivialliteratur als Forschungsproblem. Zur Kritik des deutschen Trivialromans seit der Aufklärung," *Methodenfragen der deutschen Literaturwissenschaft*, ed. Reinhold Grimm and Jost Hermand (Darmstadt: Wissenschaftliche Buchgesellschaft, 1973), pp.463–486. Kreuzer would not grant my boundary even between commercial subliterature and popular literature, and argues for a vertical examination of stylistic phenomena through all synchronic aesthetic levels. Diachronically, he would define "trivial literature as the denomination of a literary complex aesthetically discriminated against by the dominant culture-bearers in a contemporaneous situation." (p.478) and thus moves close to Escarpit in making value a function of socio-cultural standing. Yet it is clear in Kreuzer's argument that familiar axiological discriminations are still intact in it, and thus it contains an unsolved problem.

sion of the way a particular class looked at the world." If a text or a writer
is lacking in this overall meaning, it "has no fundamental or philosophical interest."* It is clear that Goldmann does not distinguish in this
regard between literary artists and philosophers, for he says of both that
they are "exceptional individuals who either actually achieve or who
come very near to achieving a completely integrated and coherent view
of what they and the social class to which they belong are trying to do."
"Exceptional individuals," he continues, "can give a better and more
accurate expression to the collective consciousness than the other members of the group." Goldmann is far from believing that the commonplace or mediocre literary work is the most susceptible to literary-
sociological analysis. In a difficult passage, he argues that average or
inferior texts are hard to analyze "precisely because they are the expression of particularly complex average individuals who are, above all, not
very typical representatives of their group."[26] This distinction between
average and typical is no doubt crucial, although I find it somewhat hard
to unravel. Doubtless it is related to Lukács' category of "specialness."
But the typical is a category that Marxists have traditionally applied to
realistic characterization. A typical character unites in himself in, as it
were, ideal form, significant aspects of the representatives of a group; he
stands, therefore, as a concentration of the significant features that are
otherwise distributed in the variety of individual behavior and character.
I do not know of anyone before Goldmann who has applied the concept
to the writer rather than to the fictional character—although he again
exhibits here a dependence upon Lukács' canonical values. An interesting Classicism emerges, with a concomitant anti-Romantic bias against
what used to be called *original* genius. The great writer appears to be a
receptacle and focus of the most significant forces of his time; this seems
to be what is meant by typical. It is striking that the average individuals,
who are *not* the great writers, are "particularly complex." Indeed, in
another place, Goldmann puts great stress on the non-contradictory
character of the great work; while individuals may have anomalies, that
is, non-coherent views, "there can be no true philosophy and no truthful
art that is at the same time Christian and immanent, Classical and
Romantic, humanistic and racial." Genius, rather than original, appears
here to be natural, or naive, much in the spirit of Schiller's view of

---

* The similarity to Wilhelm Dilthey's conception of *Geistesgeschichte* is striking and causes
one to wonder how new and trailblazing this form of literary sociology really is. For a
concise critique of this aspect of Dilthey relevant to our problems, see Winterscheidt,
Deutsche Unterhaltungsliteratur der Jahre 1850–1860, pp.11–18.

Goethe: "a writer of genius needs only give expression to his intuitions and feelings in order simultaneously to say what is essential about his age and the transformations it is undergoing."[27] With these judgments, many of the evaluative criteria of modern criticism—complexity, intensity, irony, ambiguity, and so on—are dismissed. Clearly these latter are connected with notions of individual achievement, or original genius, if one likes, which in a bourgeois-Romantic tradition are the hallmarks of greatness. In this claim of Goldmann's, therefore, there is a crucial challenge to a whole conception of art.

But the concept of typicality does not quite emancipate us from original genius. For one would like to know how it comes about that one specific human being rather than another becomes this profoundly typical spokesman, just as the student of historical determinism may sometimes wonder how such comfortably born German bourgeois as Karl Marx and Friedrich Engels acquired the insight that transcended their class consciousness. Why Racine rather than La Fontaine? They were born into the same time, locality, and social stratum.[28] Or are their works homologies of the same form, and, if so, what links them? This question appears to me to be one of the most crucial junctures of Marxist criticism, and I have yet to encounter a treatment of it that convincingly resolves the difficulties. In Marx and Engels it seems that artistic creativity and perhaps intellectual creativity generally retain a degree of subjective spontaneity that has a priority over material production.[29] Such a view is perfectly comprehensible from the humanist sources of Marxism, and indeed it is difficult to understand how a humanistic dialectic could function any other way. But one does not have to be a radical individualist or anti-determinist to point out that *Paradise Lost* and *Capital* were not written by "man" or even classes of men, but by people named Milton and Marx, and this consideration will not stop nagging us. Jameson also touches on the point and appeals as a solution to "Sartre's recent descriptions of the way in which each individual *reinvents*, in his own unique style and fashion, that social class of which he is a member," pointing to the importance of childhood as "a *mediation* between individual existence and the structures of the social group."[30] This seems to me fairly feeble; in any case it is a solution that hardly obliges us to carry the load of Marxism.

In Goldmann it develops that, despite the reification caused by bourgeois society and its ineluctable tendency to turn all values into exchange values, there are nevertheless individuals who orient themselves on qualitative rather than quantitative values, who, because of their sensitivity to the degradation of qualitative values in bourgeois society, become problematic and thus creative human beings.[31] Now, I have here juxtaposed an argument from his sociology of the novel, where the subject is a bourgeois genre, with one from *The Hidden God*, where he is investigating a modern Classical literature, and perhaps to do so is unfair to the historical nuances of his arguments. Nevertheless, it seems that he leads us into some problems when we put to him the question of how it is that the great writer is preeminently a vehicle of truth about society. On the one hand, he is a typical representative of his time, his social group, and its world view; Goldmann frequently adverts to Lukács' concept of "possible consciousness" (*zugerechnetes Bewußtsein*), the consciousness that people would have if they were totally capable of grasping their situation and that the great artist somehow acquires with special lucidity. On the other, as Laurenson and Swingewood reproduce the argument without considering the difficulties, "great writers alone can withstand [the] pressures" of that process of class division that causes "the loss of totality and universality in literary works."[32] It is hard to see how one can be sociologically typical and sociologically resistant at the same time within the same global world view. Goldmann's rescue of the great writers for literary sociology seems therefore not wholly to have succeeded. Furthermore, in a late statement Goldmann suggests that the advent of the creative individual who gives the alternative expression to the world vision is purely fortuitous—i.e., he might have had an upbringing in different ideological surroundings or not have emerged at all, an admission that severely weakens the link between sociology and criticism.[33]

One will occasionally meet with objections to the extreme veridical claims made for the great writers.[34] Both Lukács and Goldmann have been taken to task for their restriction to the refined canon; Lukács is able to write an extensive work on the historical novel, it is pointed out, without once mentioning Alexandre Dumas.[35] The sociologist of art Jean Duvignaud objects to Lukács' fixation on Goethe as "the representative of everything his time contains, of all the possibilities of experience contained by his epoch."[36] What of other authors, Duvignaud asks, with non-Goethean perspectives: Lenz, Büchner, Kleist, Hölderlin? The question is well put. It is hard to see how a literary sociology can be persuasive that so drastically shrinks the canon or ignores the broad landscape of synchronic literature. It seems clear that the great variety of literary phenomena poses problems for large claims of veridical cognition, and perhaps also for a strict dialectical relationship of apprehension and production. The practical critic often finds that these systems can be transferred to cases other than those originally used for illustration only with great difficulty.

The ultimate incongruity of strict veridical claims with the fictionality of literature shows up as a contemporary problem. It is widely believed in some quarters that Brecht's great innovation was to involve the audience in a direct cognitive process, and writers who have come in his wake, like Peter Weiss, are praised by Marxist critics as suppliers of "information."[37] I frankly do not see how this claim can be maintained. Altogether too much is made of the assertion that Brecht's rationally distancing dramaturgy leads to a critical insight into what is depicted, for one is not, in most cases, encouraged to come to any *other* conclusion than that suggested by Brecht. His sarcastic but unironic authorial presence firmly endeavors to urge particular interpretations upon the audience. The assumption is that the false consciousness of the audience holds certain presuppositions and prejudices that are disillusioned by the alienation effect. I cannot see that anyone has ever provided any demonstration of this assertion, and Brecht's constant problems with audience response suggest that real audiences are not quite as simple as those projected by Brechtian dramaturgy. The tirelessly reiterated claim that the success of the *Three-Penny Opera* was due to the fact that the bourgeois audience, recognizing its own amorality and gangsterism, was so irretrievably degenerate as to be delighted by this portrait of itself, lacks credibility. Suppose one were to make such a claim of the audience of Molière; would that not be absurd? Is it not as likely that the audience responded to Brecht's art and originality and, as is common among audiences of social comedy, ruefully and even gratefully to what is perceived as exaggerated caricature of its own worst side? Perhaps Brecht simply could not avoid the harmonizing, purgative, and safety-valve function that Empson ascribed to its model, *The Beggar's Opera*, which appears to have absorbed rather than stimulated insurrection.[38] Peter Weiss shows the problem in a more elementary form. No matter how intimately we may agree with Weiss's opinions on Vietnam and Portugal, his theatrical pageants cannot supply information on these subjects by their very fictional nature, though they make use of information in a selected, organized manner. Weiss's documentary plays, especially the one on Auschwitz, may well invite reflection on the part of the audience, especially by confronting it with the abuse and denaturing of language that is a feature of political atrocities; they may sharpen the attention in a world where such a plethora of stimuli and disasters competes for it; but there is no reason why Weiss's fictionalized opinions should lead to belief; the information communicated in these works concerns the opinions of Peter Weiss and perhaps those of the social group that holds him in regard; it is not reliable cognitive information about the subjects of the plays themselves. The fiction-maker goes a step further than the supplier of information or even the expository defender of a thesis in occupying territory in the minds of readers and audiences. Not only are facts sorted, organized, and weighted, but the reader's work in evaluating them, following and testing an argument, is preempted in favor of a dramatization of the reader's appropriate response on his behalf. It may yield good drama, but it is not history or political science and the reader cannot properly use it that way.[39] Rather than continuing the critical opposition characteristic of "bourgeois" literature, Weiss's plays function, for their own audience, in the same way as the patriotic plays of Elizabethan England, "concerned to stabilize or invigorate a mode of feeling [in our case we might rather say 'opinion'] that is generally considered desirable amongst the group addressed."[40] Therefore the tendency of these works is to become mystery plays reinforcing the convictions already held by a major part of the audience, and from that point of view are not emancipatory, but affirmative in terms of the group to which the audience belongs. For this reason, some contemporary writers have abandoned fiction-making altogether and have gone to direct documentary and reportage; calling themselves *Schriftsteller* rather than *Dichter*, they regard their literary talent as no more than a skill in writing that is to be directly employed for social change. There is nothing to be objected to in this decision—for one thing, it reduces the quantity of minor literature somewhat; but it evades, it does not solve, the problem of truth in literature.

Of course, on occasion a literary work *can* open up a public and social process of cognition with great force, although this is not common. The great German example of our time we owe neither to Brecht nor to Weiss, but is Rolf Hochhuth's foursquare melodrama, *The Deputy*. Despite the vast amount of research that enters into and (in a quite formal sense) surrounds that play, the cognition is not contained in the work, nor in the audience's response to it; rather, the play was the impetus for a process of cognition, for historical, social, and moral questioning, and the answers to this questioning, insofar as we have them at all, are located in the factual and reflective debate that followed upon the play, though the play's own vigor, ingenuity, and, to be frank, modest aesthetic and intellectual achievement, not only precipitated the process of cognition but continuously intersected with it. If *The Deputy* released a cognition itself, it was a cognition of the larger public's ignorance, tabus, and moral obtuseness; a useful result, no doubt, but not to be confused with a veridical perception of things in the world. What may be communicated, under certain circumstances, is knowledge about perception from one social context to another. When art emerges from the self-awareness of a social group and communicates to those outside it, certainly knowledge of a form of consciousness, of experience, of self-understanding different from our own is transmitted. A pertinent example would be the impressive recent achievements of the Black theater in the United States, but almost any meeting across cultures or historical epochs through an artistic medium has this character. It is important, however, to be clear about what we are learning, what kind of truth is refracted in this way. It is a communication of subjectivities and appearances, not of analytic understanding, for which fiction can be no more than evidence.

If we were undertaking comprehensive literary theory, this would be the place to introduce a discussion of realism. It is doubtful, however, whether such a discussion would carry us very far in achieving an assessment of the possibilities of literary sociology. It would take a considerable optimist to claim that the realism debate of the last thirty or forty years had yielded very stable results. The difficulties of explaining how a product of the imagination with artistic materials (or any sign system, for that matter) can be an isomorphic reproduction of reality are great—they start with the modifications Aristotle was immediately obliged to make upon his principle of mimesis—and Lukács, in his two-front war against expressionism and naturalism, so bedeviled the issue that it became almost unmanageable; "man," he tells us, "wants to see his own clear, heightened mirror image, the mirror image of his social *Praxis*, in epic poesy."[41] The mirror image cannot be intellectually unmediated, for that would be naturalism; therefore it is "heightened" by an awareness of the truth behind the empirical surface of things—another Classicist element in Lukács' mimetic theory[42] —and this qualification naturally reopens all the initial questions about truth in literature. Aesthetic reflection can only be effective "if its central content [*Gehalt*] is the reproduction of the truth of life without the least concern whether this truth is verifiable as a mirror image of details. . . . Genuine art . . . as a reflection of the essential, human-oriented reality must lead beyond the level of any particularity, not only as a whole, but in all its details."[43] The distance from Lukács' early idealistic formulation that life is only raw material for the writer[44] is not all that great. The experiential world as it presents itself to us cannot be accepted, for that would be conservative affirmation of things as they are. Thus for a typical younger contemporary critic, truth in literature is not a function of a mirroring process, but the question "whether it presents a critical model opposed to the world of experience or whether it contributes to the veiling of the historical-social reality."[45] The traditional response of literary criticism to this sort of argument has been to question the status of external reality itself to literary imagination, concerning itself rather with the structure of reality, the intentional world given in the work.[46] Whether this latter is actually a concept of realism cannot be discussed here, although it seems to me not as incompatible with Lukács' reflection theory as one might think.[47] But the insistence that literature builds its own reality, though a useful heuristic principle for criticism, threatens to deny any mimetic aspect, which, even if mimetic only of semiotic systems by which we structure the world, is so familiar a part of our basic experience of literature that its denial must in consequence be dismissed as fallacious. Fictions would be wholly incomprehensible if they did not refer constantly to phenomena of external experience. Ways of talking about realism are themselves ideological, insofar as they are concerned with an apprehension of what is possible or probable, and historically realism theory has constantly sought recourse to the claims of truth over reality or to negative correlation,[48] so that introducing the question of realism here would tend to make the present argument circular.

Of course the problem can be made a great deal more difficult than this. One good way is to appeal to Hegel. The extreme complexity of Hegel's views on the subject-object relation make this branch of literary theory defeatingly difficult for the practical critic. A recent explicator has stressed that art is not illusion but "eidetic reality," a formulation that asserts an identity between the symbols formed in the socially constructed imagination and reality itself.* The idea is real, with man as its subject; the character of totality in art is the identity of subject and object. Art is not the mimesis of this totality, but the discovery of reason in reality, and in that sense is cognitive. "The kernel under the motley crust of facts, the *Praxis* of subject and object as a real historical dialectic, becomes, in the medium of sensual illusion, the meaning of art as well. Far from being a mere occasion of aesthetic contemplation or her-

---

*Stefan Morawski, more cautiously, applies "eidetically given symbolic meanings" to primitive art only, in contrast to the heightened individuality of advanced civilization (*Inquiries into the Fundamentals of Aesthetics* [Cambridge, Mass.: MIT Press, 1974], p.67).

meneutic intuition, art is a form of knowledge, the *theoretical* appropriation of reality."[49] It is hard to cope with this without moving irretrievably
into a philosophical realm; indeed, the last clause makes us wonder
whether there is in fact any difference between art and philosophy other
than a superficial "motley crust." The essentialist insistence upon a firm,
rational core of reality with which the apprehending subject is in immediate dialectical contact seems to require an act of philosophical faith
and makes the variety of literature and art difficult to comprehend. For it
always turns out that there are correct and incorrect, legitimate and
illegitimate apprehensions, and this reopens the argument about truth
once more.

In practice, however, the justification of the truth of art is generally less
strenuous than this, if not less problematical. Goldmann's concept of
globality is a spatial metaphor, and his structuralist-inspired position is,
in the eyes of some observers, somewhat static. In this respect Goldmann
is a little unusual, for speculative sociological arguments of the truth of
art are more commonly related to a concept of historical time. Indeed, it
is remarkable how much Marxist literary theory collapses if one denies
that history has an ascertainable, prospective meaning. Such a denial
would, of course, strike at the root of Marxist analysis, for the dialectical
vision perceives facts and events as elements in a totality of process;
history flows through the cultural phenomena, carrying into them aspects of tradition and out of them anticipations that found our contact
with them in the present. Art thus is a conduit of historical time, but
simultaneously a particularly concentrated eddy of human consciousness that both captures and releases dynamic, historical truth. This is an
exciting concept with many ramifications, and I doubt that any modern
literary criticism or history can remain totally unaffected by it. But it
turns problematical when an essentially philosophical doctrine not only
becomes confident that the specific shape of history is reliably ascertainable from the past into the future, but also that the artistic consciousness
has, or can have, a specially privileged character of insight into historical
process. The strictly sociological tradition has been skeptical of this view
of history. Durkheim argued emphatically that "a discipline that looks to
the future lacks a determinate subject matter and should therefore be
called not a science but an art."[50] I think it a misfortune that the dispute
on this point has come to be perceived as split along conservative/
progressive lines; the repudiation of futurism is associated with conservatives such as Durkheim or alleged conservatives like Popper, while
Marxism aggrandizes the progressive ground. But this is by no means

logically necessary for several reasons, one of which is the para-religious nature of transcendent historicism.

It is by this means that the ancient, prophetic dignity of the poet has been restored in a secular doctrine. Christopher Caudwell, whose work presents itself as a Marxist defense of poesy, argues that society "secretes poetry . . . by projecting man into a world of superior reality—a world of more important reality not yet realised, whose realisation demands the very poetry which phantastically anticipates it." Thus poetry transcends the immediate context to "a whole new world of truth."[51] For Bloch, a utopian presentiment of the future is the very explanation for the existence of illuminating and intellectual products, for how else could they emerge from false consciousness? "Without a utopian function, class ideologies could only have achieved transitory delusion, not models in art, science, philosophy."[52] Now this is an elegant way of resolving the antinomies inherent in the concept of false consciousness, and the orientation of the imagination on future possibilities is no doubt a useful element of a defense of poesy and helpful in explaining how art transcends immediate time and circumstance. However, if we wish to assign a reliable veridical quality to the utopian imagination, this can be done only by appeal to a myth of history, and here the rational difficulties begin to appear. "All previous great culture," asserts Bloch, "is the pre-illumination [Vor-Schein] of something better achieved."[53] * Is it?

The similarity of the Marxist historical dialectic to Christian and other eschatalogical doctrines has often been remarked upon; and indeed it is not surprising if one traces back the links from Marx to Hegel to Swabian Pietism, which in turn was much involved with eschatalogical utopias and millenarian expectations. Furthermore, we can locate Marx in the general Romantic pattern of fall and redemption without too much difficulty.[54] This imputation angers some Marxists; others, if they have been able, like Bloch, to amalgamate the utopian promise of religion with a Marxist view, accept it with equanimity. The historical dialectic not

---

*Lukács does not go so far here; his stubborn realism impels him to deny that a true aesthetic can be utopian, and he speaks more narrowly and less mysteriously of the "not yet existing, still subjective reality of the human race" that can come to expression in art (Ästhetik [Neuwied: Luchterhand, 1972], II, 122, 125). It would be a worthwhile historical exercise to query how this aspect of literary sociology relates to the persistent futurism of those oppositional authors in the time of Marx who felt themselves unpleasantly trapped in a profoundly unsatisfactory, transitional present; it is an important feature especially of nineteenth-century novel theory and practice, and is adumbrated as early as Schelling. See Gerhard Friesen, The German Panoramic Novel of the 19th Century (Bern: Lang, 1972), pp. 121–122, 155 n.230.

only points to a utopian future, but it also carries with it the familiar vestiges of a myth of the Lost Paradise. The very nature of Marxist concepts like alienation, the division of labor, the transformation of use value into exchange value, suggests a time in the past when these disruptions had not yet occurred. I have the impression that there is some vagueness about when this time might have been. In the immediate preindustrial age (cf. the enthusiasm for Goethe)? In Classical antiquity? In prehistory? Perhaps in a backward-oriented utopian imagination? For Lukács, following Engels, the division of labor begins practically with the origin of the race, with the functional differentiation of the senses of sight and touch;[55] in *The German Ideology* Marx develops an argument that appears to connect the division of society and consciousness with the first manifestations of the divison of labor, which in turn is related to the differentiated function of the sexes. Thus any conception of a primeval unity is located so deep in the mists of the past as to be virtually archetypal, and it draws alienation on such a large anthropological canvas that it loses much of its bite as cultural criticism. Marx himself instinctively took over the common German view of his time that Classical antiquity was the model age of wholeness, raising a problem that we shall meet in another place. I have long suspected that the real underlying experience is the shock of the advent of the rapidly ramifying nineteenth-century world upon what was retrospectively perceived as the stable and relatively uncatastrophic order of the eighteenth century, a retrospect to which Goethe gave thoughtful expression in his autobiography.[56] Thus the Golden Age can float back and forth over the cultural patrimony at the behest of received opinion or argumentative opportunity.

When Marxists look beyond their usual obsession with the nineteenth century, they normally have no difficulty detecting class divisions and divisive ideologies at any point in past history, and Marx's mature analysis of society was not restricted to a dualistic class opposition. But it is interesting that, as long ago as Seneca, the loss of paradise was ascribed to the introduction of private property,[57] and the retention of the Lost Paradise myth in Marxist literary criticism is striking. In this regard, Christopher Caudwell's snorting about "Golden Agers"[58] is appealingly uncharacteristic. Ernst Fischer is quite explicit: "That this dream [of utopian anticipation] has been dreamed ever again, above and beyond castes and classes, has its primary cause in the memory that there was once such a condition, a Golden Age, a Lost Paradise."[59] And a contemporary young Marxist activist argues that bourgeois society is historically eccentric, while ancient culture retains the lost sense of the totality of a society.[60] Here there is the danger of a kind of primitivism, which seems to be encouraged by structuralist anthropology; another Marxist has pointed to Lévi-Strauss, rightly, I expect, as a Lost Paradise thinker.[61]*

The responsible literary critic must endeavor to make some distinctions here, which sometimes get blurred in the metaphorical habits of, especially, German thinkers. Whether futurism is a specifically German view, impelled by the misery of political reality, is questionable, but its persistence, not only in the proto-realistic theories of the Young Germans around 1835, but even in the foundation of German realism itself, gives one pause.[62] Müller-Seidel has warned us against an excess of rationalism, and reminds us that "the recovery of paradise after its loss is a literary motif of high rank."[63] Of course it is, but when we are examining the cognitive claims made for literature, a distinction between real history and imaginative myth seems urgent. Wolfgang Binder has remarked that no post-medieval writer has believed literally in the myth of the Golden Age, that it is "not a creed, but a method."[64] I am not as confident about this as I should like to be, and, anyway, some cultural criticism tends to handle myth ambiguously, offering it as metaphor, but nevertheless acting upon it intellectually as though in some sense it were history. When a philosophy of history that contains obvious mythical elements becomes the framework for estimating the truth of literature, then our troubles multiply.

It perhaps ought to be said that there is a way of escaping the contentiousness of the quarrel about the religious structure of Marxism. For whatever may be the true interpretation of the Marxist reading of history, a shorter-range pattern of historical interpretation is emerging with increasing clarity as the body of Western Marxist cultural interpretation grows and becomes more coherent and subtle; it is now so firmly entrenched that it has become a commonplace of contemporary German literary study. It might be called the truncated eschatology of the bourgeoisie. In its nuances it differs from author to author; there is much vagueness about chronological perimeters and particularly about the actual congruence of the development of capitalism and especially industrialism with the bourgeois awakening. It also makes a considerable difference whether one is talking about England, France, or Germany, but the somewhat elusive pattern is nevertheless firm doctrine and in its

---

* Martin Jay, in *The Dialectical Imagination: A History of the Frankfurt School and the Institute of Social Research, 1923–1950* (Boston: Little, Brown, 1973), pp.271–273, mounts a rather difficult argument to distinguish the Frankfurt School from a potentially reactionary primitivism.

general outlines looks something like this: Once upon a time, the bourgeoisie was the progressive class. In its rebellion against feudalism, absolutism, and the imprisonment of mind and conscience by the Church, the bourgeois class applied the revolutionary claim of reason to existing conditions and generated in its imagination a utopian vision of liberty, equality, and fraternity, thus developing universal and humanistic categories of an emancipated mankind. This was the Golden Age of the bourgeoisie. It encompasses what Adorno liked to call the "great philosophy," that is, German philosophy from Leibniz and Kant to Hegel (whose ultimate harvesting was, of course, accomplished by Marx), and what with increasing frequency is now referred to as the Great French Revolution. This was the age in Germany that abandoned the relational thinking of the Enlightenment and its pragmatic analysis of present reality in favor of a search for a unified substance of spirit and matter that could, of course, nowhere be located in the present and thus linked Homeric antiquity with an essentially aesthetic vision of an organic utopia.

There occurred, however, the Fall. Its outward manifestations in Germany are Romanticism, especially its latter phase, and eventually the failure of the revolution of 1848; in France the halting of the Revolution, marked by the defeat of Robespierre. The Fall is caused by the pressure of the burgeoning proletariat, perceived as the "mob." The bourgeoisie resists the extension of liberty and emancipation to this class and, with that refusal, reason ceases to be its ally and its imagination is impoverished. Its consciousness becomes a false consciousness, reifying its universalistic categories, for, though they continue to be enunciated, they apply to the bourgeoisie alone. Thus matters have stood from that day to this, though continually worsening. The claims of the bourgeoisie to be the model of modern humanity become increasingly grotesque through capitalism, colonial imperialism, Fascism, anti-Communism, economic imperialism, and so forth. Society is riven, culture decays, and the public community, through which reason articulates itself and which is the basis of eighteenth-century constitutionalism, gradually disappears; along with it disappears a genuinely public community of the arts. Under the circumstances of "late capitalism" a fulfilled individual existence is no longer possible, while the disintegrating and mendacious society continues to judge itself incongruously by a Goethean ideal of the meaningfully integrated, self-realizing individual.

I call it a truncated eschatology because the vision of redemption in it is vague and explicitly utopian, with only the slenderest of concrete links to present reality. The "Fifth International" has become reticent about the supersession of a proletarian culture and civilization; this was already apparent in Lukács, and marks an impassable boundary between Western neo-Marxism and orthodox Communism. The reasons for this are not very obscure, having to do with the failure of the industrial working class to behave according to the Marxian view of what its true consciousness must be, and all of us are familiar with the various surrogate proletariats that have been suggested to us in recent years: perhaps the students; perhaps the students in alliance with non-white minorities; perhaps the real proletariat has been exported and is now constituted by the Third World. The points relative to our subject are these: the cultural present, and, indeed, the whole cultural tradition since the Fall, whenever that might have been, is regarded with a bitter aversion, except where continuing, relatively unfalsified traces of the original emancipatory purpose can be discovered. While the worm is constantly being discovered in the original apple, there is a continuing investment in the Golden Age—an example in German studies is a renewed allegiance to Schiller—and the similarity to conservative cultural criticism becomes clearly evident. The disappearance of the present may be a common feature of the intellectual interpretation of the modern condition, but it appears to me most profound in the German tradition, doubtless owing to the recurrently unsatisfactory nature of the German social and political environment. It is a Romantic inheritance, and that inheritance conditions the tendency to look for redemption in the artistic imagination. Nietzsche commented on this in *Beyond Good and Evil* in connection with Wagner.[65] One of Novalis' veiled, oblique aphorisms, ca. 1798, reads: "Nothing is more poetic than memory and presentiment or idea of the future. Our ideas of prehistory attract us to dying, to evanescence. Our ideas of the future drive us to invigoration, to abbreviation, to assimilating activity. Therefore all memory is melancholy, all presentiment joyful. . . . But there is a mental present that identifies both through dissolution, and this mixture is the element, the atmosphere, of the poet."[66] Perhaps the most telling word here is "abbreviation" (or "foreshortening," *Verkürzung*); by a mental or imaginative act the present is collapsed into the future and becomes less real than even the elegiacally regarded past.

The hatred of the present, however, can degenerate into reactionary primitivism and assaults on civilization. Fascism is an especially instructive example, as is its relation to the so-called "conservative revolution" and the wave of irrationalism that beset European intellectuals around and after the First World War. "Hatred of art," remarked Ortega y Gasset, "is unlikely to develop as an isolated phenomenon; it goes hand in hand with hatred of science, hatred of State, hatred, in sum, of civilization as a whole."[67] Perhaps the resemblance of such ideas on the Right and on the Left is due to a common derivation from the intellectual mood of the 1920s. Western Marxists of roughly the same generation and provenance are often striking in the extremity of their view that "bourgeois" society has somehow become the most wretched and hateful episode in human experience; Herbert Marcuse is an especially exotic example. A reflection of this is the conservative taste of many Marxist literary critics, for which Lukács is particularly notorious,* but which is found elsewhere as well. Walter Benjamin's sense of the present and the future is ideological and theoretical, but of the lost values of the past conservative and elegiac, so that in reading certain parts of his work, one has the impression of an old-fashioned German speculative cultural philosopher overlaid with a Marxist veneer. Bloch also often exhibits an elegiac, Neo-Romantic sensibility dressed up as Marxist, as when he in all seriousness offers the collecting of antiques as an anti-capitalist gesture against the "Bauhaus impotence" of modern design.[68] Claims made for the truth of literature grounded in a philosophy of history that sees only the lost values of the past and unrealized values of the future are built on a shaky foundation. If we cannot judge out of some respect for present values, any cognitive claims for literature become purely speculative. The loss of the present brings with it a constant threat of an unprogressive fixation on a mythical construct of the past.

Marxist futurism can lead to exhibitions of high metaphorical rhetoric. "True Marxist philosophizing," intones Bloch, "has the eagle's characteristic of flying very high, in order just so, with an achieved commanding view, to be able to penetrate at all times down into detail and to grasp it—with a dialectic simultaneity of commanding view and closeness of future perspective and the most intensive contemporaneity."[69] It is perhaps with such passages in mind that Jameson compares Bloch's view of futurity with Goethe's concept of the "demonic"; there is, for Bloch, "some powerful latency in existence itself."

---

* Lukács, to be sure, is not strictly or explicitly a Golden Ager; his powerful commitment to realism causes him to maintain his focus on real history, though in a characteristically schematic way, and enables him to see the Lost Paradise myth as a myth (see *Ästhetik*, I,132–134). But his acceptance of an unalienated *Urkommunismus* deep in the mists of time before the separation of the individual and the community (e.g., ibid., I,214) reopens the question.

Jameson goes so far as to claim that Bloch's whole work may be seen "as an immense commentary" on *Faust*.[70] This is an ingenious observation, but we should not lose sight of the specific latency of existence, located in the rising proletariat, in which all Marxists were once obliged to believe and which still can be found in the early phases of Western Marxist argument such as that of Ernst Fischer.[71]

Jameson denies that Marxism is systematically predictive of the future and remarks correctly that "the attempt to predict is but one of the symptoms of the failure to think in a situational way." Marxism is "a form moving in time."[72] But Jameson's Marxism—generally speaking, that of the "Fifth International"—is ultimately highly selective and domesticated, and hardly takes any notice at all of Marxism's political reality. Elsewhere he characterizes Max Weber's passionate resistance to teleological philosophies of life as "heroic cynicism," and, relating it to what he denominates "the reactionary political views of the majority of realistic novelists," ascribes to it a profoundly conservative allegiance to being-as-it-is.[73] I feel obliged to remark with some asperity that the insistence upon more or less resigned acceptance of the status quo as the only alternative to a belief in immanent progress in history is one of the demagogic incantations of the contemporary Left and is entirely without relation to the actual variety of possible political opinions and actions. My real point here, however, is that Marxist criteria for truth in literature are grounded in a philosophy of history that, while certainly not wholly implausible in the broad outline, is fundamentally speculative and tends to look somewhat quaint and simple-minded as soon as one takes any real historiography in hand.

Aestheticians of the strict observance normally argue that there can be no question of truth in art. Beardsley, in an argument turning principally upon the Sidneyan doctrine that there are no assertions in art, denies that fiction can assert anything. Of course there can be ideas in a work of art, "predications, the contemplation, and even the testing of which can be shared by different readers, and the writer too. But it is not a 'message,' and not in the ordinary sense a 'communication,' since it is not an assertion and therefore claims to convey no information." A corollary to this is that the falsity of a thesis cannot vitiate a form. Beardsley goes so far as to say that there is no indictment in a Kollwitz painting, "for there is nothing that can be read as an index pointing to anything indicted." There are, Beardsley says, "social and political aspects of the subjects of Courbet and Ben Shahn, of course, but they are simply set forth. It is we who compare them with the world and ask whether they represent it truly or misrepresent it. . . . But only by an ellipsis, and a misleading one, could we say that the [Daumier] cartoon is itself an accusation."[74]

Here is a case where one's common sense rebels against an apparently logical argument, and we are faced in the other camp with the question of whether a theoretical structure is always superior to unmediated experience. The failing lies, it appears to me, in the reductively bilateral relationship of work and contemplator. Of course a man from Mars would not detect an indictment in a Kollwitz woodcut. But we are not men from Mars; we live in a historical and social continuum of which Kollwitz and her work are also a part. We know what human suffering looks like, although our sensibility of it is undoubtedly the more intense because of Kollwitz. We know whose suffering this was, when, and under what circumstances. We know what Kollwitz thought was the cause of this suffering, and that this impelled her art. We may not agree that Communist explanations and solutions are the best ones, but Kollwitz prevents us from evading truths that made Communism seem believable to her. We cannot shut this knowledge out of our minds if we have it. M. H. Abrams has argued that our disinterested contemplation cannot extend to our recognition of engagement with the values articulated *within* the work, for then we would simply not comprehend; we would not know, for example, a villain or hero when one is intended.[75] It seems queer to assert that there is no critical link between the social and political aspects "set forth" in a work and our own apprehension of them; and it hardly seems a humanistic device to argue that artists may understand their own activity as making assertions but that we will insist they do not make them.

Modern literature brings us to a serious impasse with regard to the cognitive aspect of the poetic imagination. The Marxist record of literary evaluation makes it very clear that the veridical claims that sometimes emerge in the Marxist defense of poesy cannot be sustained without reference to criteria located outside the realm of literature. The agony over modernism has been a recurrent theme in Marxist discussion from the Bolshevik Revolution to the present. The Marxist tradition has incurred disastrous risks in cutting itself off from the profoundest achievements of modern art and literature; that it cannot permanently accept this impoverishment without harm to its overall intellectual eminence and persuasiveness is proved by the tendency for every "thaw" in orthodoxy to be accompanied by an effort to regain meaningful contact with modern art and literature. The non-Marxist, on the other hand, has to deal with the puzzle of the undeniable reactionary strain in much modern literature, not because it is an expression of "bourgeois imperialism" or the decay of "late capitalism" or some other ideological degeneration in Western civilization, but for the opposite reason, as Lionel Trilling has pointed out: that this strain is at odds with the increasingly liberal or radical tendency among educated people, the audience for literature.[76] The dilemma remains bewildering as long as any serious view of the cognitive truth of art is maintained. For the simple fact is (and it would be worth reminding Marxists of it from time to time) that most of us resist in our own order of life and commitment substantial parts of the vision of a long list of poets and writers who stand at the head of the modernist canon. A measurable space has opened up in our century between aesthetic value and the truths that we would wish to recognize, and I think it would be best to acknowledge this and try to find a critical posture for dealing with it rather than seeking ways to argue it out of existence.

Such arguments proceed from the reasonable effort to acknowledge the bright side of poetic integrity, to detect, as Trilling puts it, the values of "energy and fineness of life" even in modern writers of reactionary views.[77] The line is not dissimilar to Rosa Luxemburg's defense of Russian writers of reactionary views on the grounds that what is important is not their solutions but the depth, daring, and integrity with which social problems are grasped.[78] I do not think we can maintain a practical criticism in any way adequate to its object without some such attitude. But we need to be a little bit careful of it because of the lurking tendency of the modern critical tradition to ascribe prophetic gifts and comprehensive unity to the artistic imagination, which requires us to postulate a split between the author's real intellect or allegiances and an aesthetically relevant personality that can create out of a deeper wisdom than that of the individual consciousness, a view found among numerous modern poets and critics, and theoreticians as diverse as Croce and Lukács.[79] Despite its well-known usefulness for making criticism more austerely focused, I continue to regard it with suspicion. We can distinguish aesthetic value from communicated truth without wholly separating them, and the most rational modern critics have recognized that art cannot regularly be depended upon to tell the truth, the whole truth, and the best truth we can recognize.[80] I propose that we dispense with notions that literature as such, or even the great literary works, offer a reliable cognition into a higher truth unattainable by any other means, although there must be some degree of cognition and may be some partial, oblique truth in literary works; and second, that we keep our aesthetic and our moral, political, social judgment intact simultaneously. It is better to differentiate our response than to split off from the literary phenomenon political and ideological components without which it is incomprehensible. Much of the tendency of a great deal of current criticism out of social commitment (like many adaptations in the contemporary theater) is to dismantle literary works in order to separate out aspects that suit our present sensibilities. I propose instead that we leave the works intact while amplifying our categories of critical apprehension.

There are some great poets of clearly Fascist or reactionary leanings; we may say, therefore, that it is good poetry but the poetry is not unambiguously a good thing. Conversely, there is literature of less aesthetic achievement but of substantial social value or influence; this, too, we may acknowledge. The view of the recent past that only aesthetic values are discussible and to speak of anything else is a sacrilege; and the currently developing view that no aesthetic values are admissible, are equally destructive and threaten to drive the study of literature into irrelevance. We do not have to believe that our world is deteriorating into silence, even if the progress of Samuel Beckett's works suggests this; on the other hand, the echo and the fascination that Beckett arouses in us all suggests that he is on to *something* unnerving going on in our world, and we ought to question ourselves what it is, and whether it is as Beckett presents it. At root, if I read *Murphy* correctly, Beckett begins by measuring our present condition by fairly ancient, mystical, and atavistic standards, and thus a piece of our consciousness and discomfort finds a sharply circumscribed vantage point from which much of what we normally feel to be life's substance recedes to a·perspectival vanishing point. So we may detect a truth in Beckett's voice. Yet our lives as a whole are not perceived as Murphy's or Malone's, Vladimir and Estragon's, or Krapp's. Are we then, are our lives, the fictions? I think not; Beckett's visions are the fictions, particularly intense segments of experience, and we may retain our liberty to consider how much or how little of our experience they project and explain, without submitting ourselves passively to them. After all, Beckett served valorously in the French Resistance, and I cannot detect in any of his works an indication of why he, or anyone else, should have. A judgment that rejects Beckett on the ground that he is just the last gasp of a dying late-bourgeois culture and is therefore irrelevant to those to whom the future belongs makes the same error of passive submission to the artistic vision; it makes of an, after all, rather eccentric and narrowly focused mind the vehicle for a whole truth about a whole society. It is especially characteristic of much modern and contemporary literature that it symbolizes with great intensity biased and twisted perceptions; these are not, and cannot be, reflections of the "truth," yet, in view of their resonance and the degree to which they are shared in kind by substantial numbers of artists, they cannot be dismissed as irrelevant to truthful cognition. I should be inclined to call their kind of truth "segmental," expressions of one voice or group of voices among numerous possible ones. But we sometimes forget that they are not the only voices and visions in society, and there are no grounds, as far as I can see, for granting the "avant-garde" or artistic extremists a cognitive privilege. We tend to forget that art of a more familiar kind and much normal life continue to go on parallel to these developments; as Malcolm Bradbury has observed, we still talk to one another despite Pinter, like narrative despite Beckett, apprehend reality rather than transform it.[81]

Literary sociology, in my view, must get out of the habit of seeing writers and literary works as totally representative, "global" vehicles of social phenomena, falling into the temptation, as César Graña puts it, "of taking the unique eloquence of art as *proof* of its social representativeness,"[82] which only perpetuates in secular, "materialistic" form the old myths of the poet as magus and prophet. Elementary discrimination is needful here. We know very well that the nineteenth-century realistic novel is intimately bound up with the growing self-awareness of the middle class and there is much to be learned from it about social circumstances and their accompanying ideologies; to deny this out of hand would be mere bumptiousness.[83] At the same time, novels are fictions, and yield no authority without the regulation of knowledge gained outside them.[84] In many circumstances, the literary-sociological problem may be to examine "how literary stereotypes differ from other accounts of the same social realities,"[85] in other words, to seek a function of literature not in truthful correlation, but in ideological alternatives maintained, often with great stubbornness, in the imagination.

Literature is certainly one of the ways in which man has tried to understand himself and his circumstances, and Lukács seems to me right when he argues that art in general intensifies and clarifies the consciousness of human social existence.[86] If we believe that this process has, in the course of time, achieved some not inconsiderable results, then, in a general sense, we are acknowledging some truth in literature emerging through time. Christopher Caudwell has some not unhelpful things to say on this point. Even primitive magic, he points out, is in touch with reality: "No magician makes spells for a winter harvest."[87] But literature differs from magic and religion in that it can change, because it accepts

itself as illusion and does not pretend to reality: "we give to the statements of poetic art only a qualified assent, and therefore reality has no
vested interest in them."[88] * Caudwell does not deny that literary statements are assertions of a kind, but, because they are "illusory" or, as we
might better say, fictional, our assent to them is qualified—probing,
weighing, experimental. There is no mirror theory here, and, indeed, in
the latter Stalinist period, Caudwell's works were thrashed by orthodox
Marxists on this ground.[89] Thus, despite his excesses, Caudwell is one of
the defenders of the imaginative freedom of literature. This freedom is
not absolute; it is bounded by a world of real experience. But a similar
freedom is available to the critic, to test how adequate products of the
imagination are to the truth of real experience.

To say this requires a certain confidence in our own present judgment,
in our own moral stance. The danger of a parochial censorship involved
here is an old one, and it is one of the enduring accomplishments of
Romantic historicism to widen our receptivity to artistic phenomena that
do not grow out of our immediate social determinants. This is a great
achievement of the human consciousness, and any repeal of it would be
regressive. The practical critic must be able to bend without breaking.
But whether we admit it or not, we do judge out of present consciousness; and the range of our lives, our experience, and our learning is
usually wider, if often shallower, than the literary object we confront.

*Lukács gives a more philosophical and rigorous account of this development (*Ästhetik*,
I, 190–227).

IV

Value

HEINRICH HEINE observed crisply in the 1830s that, as soon as a religion turns to philosophy for aid, its ruin is inevitable.[1] It is a characteristic judgment in an age that was extremely sensitive to the decay of a unified social field in which the order of society could be identified with the order of nature. The struggle for the rearticulation of coherence is the clearest demonstration that coherence is no longer self-evident. A related observation could be made of the difficulties encountered by the philosophy of value in this century, particularly in aesthetics. To become philosophically curious about value statements and the evaluation process is natural enough. But the failure of axiological theory to deliver comfortable solutions to criticism is a symptom of the segmentation of the categories of value in a society in which universal canons can no longer be maintained or imposed. Undoubtedly the problem emerges at that crisis point to which Heine's generation bore anguished witness. Stefan Morawski has boldly and, I think, defensibly argued that, since the nineteenth century, civilization stands in a qualitatively different relation to the aesthetic object in that aesthetic value is no longer obviously subordinated to "utility value or fetish value."[2] Nor are the canons of aesthetic value any longer coextensive with the value systems of society as a whole or even the dominant classes in it. Under these circumstances, aesthetic value theory, just like the philosophy called to the aid of religion of which Heine remarked, becomes a defensive effort to construct an edifice of conviction in a context of doubt or indifference.

Modern analytic philosophy has devoted much attention to axiological theory. Its effect, it seems to me, has been to pacify dispute over values in modern society by refraining from establishing what values are or ought to be in favor of considering what we are doing when we evaluate. By developing careful distinctions between propositional and persuasive statements it appears to give a cachet to the forensic rhetoric of evaluative argument. The question remains how much use this, in itself, subtle and significant philosophy can be to the beleaguered practical critic, who is in increasing difficulty with the canon, its maintenance and transmission, the relation of aesthetic values to other values, the difference between valuing according to some experienced criteria and mere liking, and the problem of how and, indeed, whether to communicate aesthetic values to others. The modern ramification of society and the acceleration of historical change have obviously put practical criticism into a very difficult situation with respect to value. The effort of the New Criticism to turn poetry itself into an "ark of value"[3] has failed because of its misleading circularity. It tried to establish values as intrinsic that, in retrospect, clearly appear as extrinsic because they are related to life as a whole and therefore cannot escape the social and historical determination of consciousness. The development of a rational system of genuinely intrinsic values, such as we find in the work of Monroe Beardsley, is worthwhile but insufficient because it is dependent upon the canon and a body of minority educated experience; it therefore has no recourse against the stubborn resistance of personal or group taste, which is evidently so intimately involved with the deepest personal or group self-understanding that any form of contradiction of it is perceived as assault. It is this obvious circumstance that impels the literary-sociological search for new perspectives on literary value. Such solutions as it has offered have tried to take account of the actual or potential function of literature in our society and most are committed, according to various political standpoints, to a more democratic and progressive view of literature and criticism. But many have been purchased at an intimidatingly high price.

The thorniness of the value problem is highlighted by the evasiveness with which it has often been treated in modern criticism. It seems the better part of valor to step gingerly around it, or at least to get all the rest of our business straight before we confront it. Evaluation is said to be only the last cautious step to be taken after long, hard work of interpretation has been accomplished.[4] This is an important warning, but it gives us enough to do that we may conscientiously postpone evaluation to never-never day; furthermore, surely it is often true in practice that it is some initial instinct of value that attracts us in the first place to take the work in hand and perform interpretive operations on it, and it is far from clear that the process of interpretation can be kept separate from value assertions. Nevertheless, there has been a tendency on the conservative end of modern criticism to exclude the discussion of value altogether. Emil Staiger is notorious for this position. "Every genuine writer, and every reader endowed with some sense of artistic quality, will react to the problem of literary evaluation with intense suspicion." Why is this? Staiger replies with another question: "Does love ever ask for reasons?"[5] Apart from the likelihood that love that does not ask for reasons will often lead to bad marriages, the question shows Staiger's insistence upon an unmediated, unreflective experience of the aesthetic object, so that this experience becomes the subject of criticism. So extreme is this argument that one wonders if it is not in some way defensive, if it is not motivated by the fear that reflective questioning would weaken the privileged position of the canonical literature, the experience of which Staiger propagates. Northrop Frye is another consistent polemicizer against evaluation: "Such a phrase," he says, "as 'of course I don't like this *kind* of poetry' can never be uttered by a serious critic."[6] Why a critic, unlike all the rest of mankind, is not permitted to have preferences, even generic ones, evades me; it can more plausibly be argued that a strongly focused, pronounced taste is more likely to produce a strong criticism with a true affinity to its object.[7] But Frye does not believe evaluation is a legitimate critical enterprise: "When a critic interprets, he is talking about his poet; when he evaluates, he is talking about himself, or, at most, about himself as a representative of his age"[8] —as though the apprehending consciousness could be completely neutralized and dismissed from the critical process, and as though Frye in his criticism were not talking about himself unremittingly.*

Of course, these very postures and gestures communicate values. Staiger is dependent on Heidegger, whom Palmer has explicated thus: "When the art work is seen not as an objectification of human subjectivity but as a disclosure of being, or a window to the sacred realm, then one's encounter is a receiving of a gift, not a subject's act of grasping its subjectivity."[9] One's relationship to the work of art is feudal humility before an act of grace, a position that is illuminated by a passage in Schopenhauer, who tells us that we stand before a text as before a prince,

---

*Frye's position follows logically—perhaps more logically than that of some other modern critics—from his principles of organicism and aesthetic autonomy, "the view that the imagination is a law unto itself. . . . If poetry is truly autonomous, then Frye is right and critical discriminations are meaningless" (Gerald Graff, *Poetic Statement and Critical Dogma* [Evanston: Northwestern University Press, 1970], pp.75–76).

waiting to see what he will say.[10] Nothing illustrates so well the authoritarian aspect of Staiger's and Frye's capitulation before the canonical work or artist. Apart from being reactionary, the position is also misleading. Staiger has evaluative principles of notorious rigidity; they are centered on German Classicism and Romanticism and have led to a polemical repudiation of contemporary literature that did much to exacerbate the strained academic and intellectual atmosphere in his part of the world. Frye has poured enormous resources of imaginative criticism into an impassioned study of William Blake; why did he choose Blake instead of, say, Southey, for such an effort? Frye would, I should think, agree that Southey's poetry could not support such a critical work as *Fearful Symmetry*, that Blake is infinitely more exciting and absorbing, and this would seem by any normal standards to be a value judgment.[11]

Erwin Leibfried has put Staiger's criticism into the rhetorical category of *laudatio*, and argues reasonably that this is one possible stance of criticism among many.[12] * But since a literary work is not imposed upon us as a prince is, we can and do choose the object of our *laudatio*, and the question of the relativism of value and taste is only suppressed by the argument found in Staiger, Croce, and others that there is no such thing as bad literature, only literature—which we receive as a "gift"—and non-literature, a distinction which limits our critical contemplation as strictly as Lukács' principles did to the Greeks, Goethe, and the realistic novel from Balzac to Thomas Mann with little more than Scott in between. The only difference is that Staiger would leave us with the Greeks, Goethe, and Clemens Brentano. The mode of *laudatio*, the constantly reiterated claim that explication and description must be preferred to evaluation, assumes the canon. It is therefore flawed for practical criticism, which must be persuasive to those who do not assume the canon and must be able to show where excellence lies, how it can be perceived, in initially alien and opaque objects. Have we not all had this experience, either in our own process of acculturation from uncomprehending youth, or in mature years, that criticism has helped us to be appreciative and discriminating of an art unfamiliar, perhaps new to us? Perception must be either socialized or trained; art is not immediate to a *tabula rasa*.

Behind the polemic against evaluation lies a fear of relativism. Our historical awareness of relativism causes us to mistrust present values,

* It is not without interest in this connection to remember that Goebbels, whose instinct in such matters was usually, if not always, reliable, eventually banned all criticism of art. This is one way to institutionalize the mode of *laudatio*, with consequences that are well known.

not in a way that weighs them and reflects upon them, but that denies their availability for critical purposes at all. It is surely true that a livelier awareness of the historicity of our own present consciousness is needful; but if we are not to believe that the accumulated experience of literature and criticism leads to some evolutionary expansion of understanding and judgment, then those who suggest that we might just as well shut down our universities will be in the right. Empirical literary sociologists also tend to reject evaluation, although more for methodological than for ideological reasons. This caution about the intrusion of values in literary sociology[13] reinforces the questionable reserve of empirical study before the work itself.

The recognition that evaluation is a component of our immediate responsiveness to literature and in our choices and treatment of literary works as critics suggests that it cannot be refined out of the critical process, even if that were somehow desirable. Value statements appeal for conviction, and therefore their presence in literature and literary criticism exhibits a desire for an intersubjectively shared community.[14] But since axiological principles do not normally achieve immediate agreement, a pluralistic discussion of values must be kept open if we are to achieve any intersubjective sharing of response.[15] This line of argument leads to objections against the work of art as a totally enclosed structure and to Ernst Bloch's view that all great art is broken and open to something as yet unachieved.[16] The danger, however, lies in the disappearance of the work as a fixed object in any sense at all. It shows up prominently in Escarpit's total focus on reader consciousness and his concept of "creative treason." He says rightly that when a great gap of understanding separates the reader from the literary work, the reader (or public as a whole) will interpose a subjective myth; this is, Escarpit remarks, the way in which the literature of the Far East has been received in Europe.[17] He does not seem to regard at all optimistically the possibility that an education in literary history and criticism might help to close this gap.* While the work of literature in Escarpit's theory of

---

*An elementary example sticks in my memory. While teaching in an interdisciplinary course, we were confronted with some old Chinese poems that seemed, even in translation, to be of great delicacy. Our colleague in his lecture then explained that they were a prostitute's advertising copy, and explicated the conventions and nuances of their imagery in the light of the promise they extended. With a leap we were all closer to the poems, not as close as our colleague, who could read the Chinese, but much farther away from the provincial pattern of perception we had initially brought to bear on them. That the poems did not diminish, but expanded in stature and interest in this process, needs hardly to be said.

apprehending consciousness exhibits a Protean character, the consciousness of the respective public at any given moment appears quite fixed; "a successful book," he tells us, "is a book that reveals to the group its own image."[18] With that we are back to Lukács' reflection theory, though centered in the public rather than in the work, and bereft of Lukács' conception that the criterion of aesthetic achievement is the subjective constitution of an independent objectivity.[19] Taste for Escarpit is both involuntary and anterior to judgment: "The reader is a consumer, and like every consumer he is led by his direction of taste long before he judges anything, even when he is capable of submitting a reasonable justification for his direction of taste a posteriori."[20]

From the point of view of literary criticism, Escarpit's argument is defeatist. If he is correct, we can only study the vicissitudes of value; it would be futile to attempt to recover and transmit the values intrinsic to past works. This is correlated with his view, shared, it seems by a number of Continental theorists, that all criticism is "impressionistic," a term that appears to be synonymous with "arbitrary."* There is, however, in the theory of the preordered apprehending mentality a greater danger than this. If one believes, as Marxists are logically obliged to do, that one has some choice of the mental set with which one apprehends the world, and believes at the same time that this set determines the nature of what we apprehend, then some curious results may emerge. A sobering example is Benjamin's account of his visit to the Soviet Union in 1927. The problem here is not to allow the painfully acquired Communist faith to be distracted by disorderly empirical observations; or, to put it another way, one must defend oneself against falling into the bourgeois habit of denigrating the great revolution by pointing to such surface phenomena as shabbiness, human misery, economic incompetence, or violations of freedom. "Basically," says Benjamin, "the only guarantor of correct insight is already to have chosen one's stance before one comes. Especially in Russia, only the decided observer can see." And he goes on: "Only he who, in his decision, has made his dialectical peace with the world, can grasp the concrete. But to him who would judge 'in the light of the facts,' these facts will give no light."[21] Such a person would be one

---

*This erroneous view has emerged in an American populist version in Herbert J. Gans, *Popular Culture and High Culture: An Analysis and Evaluation of Taste* (New York: Basic Books, 1974), pp.121–22, where the experienced critics' judgments are denominated "private evaluations" entitled to no privilege over the opinions of others. More will be said of Gans in Chapter VI below.

of Bloch's "asses of induction."* Bloch, too, in his estimate of the Soviet Union before the facts finally forced some light on him, exhibited this pattern, as when he derived from his "principle of hope" the right to dispense with all "pedantic" considerations such as Marx's notion that the course of history required a society to pass through capitalism before socialism could be achieved.[22] Reading the remainder of Benjamin's essay today is a spooky experience. If there is anyone around who believes in the value of the ideological criticism of language use and yet is not hypnotized by the current Benjamin fashion, a close analysis of this text would prove fruitful.

The very freedom of literature is threatened by the inflexible application of the anterior theoretical mind-set, which is actually a cognate form of behaviorist psychology.[23] In 1934, Benjamin said in a speech in Paris: "The Soviet state will, of course, not, like Plato's state, exile the writer, but it will . . . set him tasks that will not permit him to display the long since falsified richness of the creative personality in new masterpieces."[24] Indeed. Christopher Caudwell came independently to much the same conclusion, defending the control of the artist in the Soviet Union on the grounds that the artist, being socially determined, cannot in principle be free and consequently must be consciously controlled like every other aspect of society.[25] Caudwell set as the motto to *Illusion and Reality* Engels' assertion that freedom is the recognition of necessity; for Caudwell there is only the choice between control of consciousness by instinctive, irrational, anarchic, unreflected determinants, or by rational, considered, collectively developed determinants. Naturally, he chooses the latter. These are the intellectual premises of censorship and the systematic terrorization of artists and writers. To appeal to Rosa Luxemburg, as modern Marxist humanists like to do, does not help very much here; perhaps it is even futile to call extensive attention, as Iring Fetscher has done, to Marx and Engels' continuous battle against and denunciation of censorship,[26] for that took place, seen "dialectically," in a different situation—at the end of the Golden Age of the bourgeois eschatology, when

---

*During the Time of Troubles at Yale, a graffito outside my office window caught this spirit perfectly: "If you know what's going on, you don't have to know what's going on to know what's going on." In 1927, the Frankfurt School, to the outer circle of which Benjamin belonged, shared this loyalty to the Soviet Union and its scholars muted or repressed any explicit critical thought they might have felt. See Martin Jay, *The Dialectical Imagination: A History of the Frankfurt School and the Institute of Social Research, 1923–1950* (Boston: Little, Brown, 1973), pp. 19–20. Jay continues to say that the Frankfurt line of argument is *implicitly* critical, and the same may be said of some aspects of Benjamin's essay.

concepts of constitutional liberty were not yet reified. Censorship and the control of art and literature derive from not one but two fundamental principles of Marxist, if not Marxian, criticism. One is the view we have just been discussing: that all perception is preordered one way or another, and therefore our intellectually responsible task can only be to get theoretical control over this preordering. The other is an issue of a totally different kind and has to do with the social efficacy of literature. It has occasionally been pointed out that it is easy to maintain freedom of expression in a society like ours where nobody cares what artists say anyway. The distinction between advocacy and action so important in our own constitutional practice is, if not a "reified" one, nevertheless one that is far from self-evident and easily operated to cut the link between ideas and their implications threatening to the status quo. What if the book is a weapon? Would it not then be apparent that it must be controlled like any other weapon? This was the tack taken by Karl Radek in 1930 at the outset of the Soviet campaign for Socialist Realism: "We never promised the 'freedom of art,' just as we never promised anyone the freedom of smuggling weapons or dealing in cocaine."[27] For Louis Kampf, this is sufficient justification for Mao Tse-Tung's system of thought control: "It is difficult for anyone in my comfortable situation, where ideas cost so little and rarely have any visible consequences, to understand that death may be the consequence of a wrong slogan chanted or drawn on a wall; that an incorrect line spoken in a drama performed before hopeful but doubting villagers may become the cause of defeat at the hands of the enemy."[28] The differing thrust of Kampf's last two clauses muddles the issue nicely, and he has evidently reflected too little not only upon the preconditions of his "comfortable situation," but also upon the question by what innate authority an idea has the right to immediate "visible consequences." Why not turn the argument around and say: in a modern society art and literature are likely to be of vast social import only where there are large areas of unfreedom? We might moderate some of our traditional salvationist view of art and confess that it is only one of the possible vehicles of freedom and that it probably will not suffuse a society in which other vehicles function also.

That fiction has substantial social efficacy is an intuition constantly encountered. It becomes more articulate in times of crisis. An interesting example is the interference of the Office of War Information into the ideological content of American movies during World War II, which has been thoughtfully chronicled by Richard R. Lingeman.[29] This policy reflects an unquestioned confidence that the ideologically meaningful symbols in a popular fictional medium are able at least to confirm or reinforce, or on occasion to weaken or turn in a more desirable direction, aspects of convictions, opinions, or prejudices held in common by a very large audience; their control therefore becomes a matter of domestic psychological warfare.[30] No one engaged in such an effort, it appears to me, really believes that fictional images and symbols thrust convictions and attitudes upon an audience, that they generate assent and belief; if anyone were to hold to such a conviction, it would be sufficiently refuted, I should think, by the most common category of popular criticism, that such and such a work or aspect is not "true to life," by which is meant that it does not meet preformed expectations of what is probable, real, or true. But there appears to be a sense that, in a complex society, prejudices and stereotypes are to some degree held in suspension, are likely to be mutually contradictory, and are therefore malleable. Perhaps all but the most pathological or mentally deficient racists sense in some part of their minds that their generalized and abstract feeling may not be wholly correct, or, even if correct as far as their experience and place on the social battlefield will allow, not wholly right in a moral or logical way. The scorned cliché, "some of my best friends are Jews," or the phrase that I remember with a shudder from my own upbringing, "high-type Negro," are not necessarily euphemisms masking a monolithic racism, but just as probably soft spots into which a wedge of experience and reason might conceivably be driven. The capacity of fictional images to reinforce or weaken such images in the consciousness of an audience is doubtless not trivial, and this raises the question of the social control of such images in a most grave way. At the same time, in a society that is not totally under ideological control there will be resistance and displacement, a tendency for the audience to exert a counterpressure and, despite all specific manipulation, to make of popular fictions, in Lingeman's words, "garbled echoes of the American collective conscience speaking to itself."[31] That we do not have much systematic knowledge of how this works is another example of the difficulty encountered by the sociology of art and literature in solving the most basic questions. The research that has been pursued indicates strongly that mass communication does not cause opinions or shape consciousness; rather, it serves as a reinforcement of existing states of consciousness; people tend, where choice obtains, to evade expressions of uncongenial opinion.[32]

There has been a vast amount of technical sociological study about the ways in which a text can affect behavior.[33] Most of it, however, is concerned with matters of information and opinion, that is, with credibility.

When this approach is extended to fictional texts, the matter becomes substantially more complex.[34] In order to make literary texts available to communication sociology at all, they must be treated, with greater or lesser subtlety, as declarative statements. The problem emerges in its most questionable form in the sociological method of "content analysis," a highly elaborated model of inquiry that nevertheless appears to the literary critic as a very blunt instrument.[35] From the point of view of criticism, these ways of treating a text will seem sadly regressive, though from the point of view of a sociology of reception, they may correlate with much empirical behavior. But it appears to be simply not known whether literary texts can form and generate behavior patterns in readers—apathy or rebelliousness, affirmative or critical views of the status quo, violence and prejudice—or whether they serve at most as codifiers and reinforcers of value dispositions. In any case, the familiar contemporary argument based upon the total manipulability of the populace by the "culture industry," found in Adorno and Marcuse, is impelled by a combination of cultural pessimism and canonical acceptance of cultural values, and lacks sufficient empirical verification. It is rather difficult even to know how to test the avant-garde claim that traditional realistic narration associates the reader with the omniscient author, thus obliging the reader to accept uncritically not only the narration but the world narrated. It is not known whether brutality in literature and the media serves as a safety valve, habituates to brutality in the environment, or increases readiness for aggression; and it is by no means clear that "trivial" literature and "finer" literature generate fundamentally different processes of consciousness. How far these questions are amenable to testing remains to be seen. That literature has the capacity for affecting behavior is assumed, or at least hoped, by all activist writers. An exceptionally brave and forthright writer will not repine at the unpleasant consequences but accept them. The militant German pacifist Carl von Ossietzky asserted characteristically: "Whoever, like the writer, believes in the immaterial power of the word hurled out into the world will not complain if this word, having gained substance, bounces back at him in the form of a rubber truncheon or jail sentence."[36]

It would be inhuman to expect such a level of courage from all writers; and while it may be suitable for the oppositional publicist, it indicates a bleak environment for the imagination, a world in which culture is in exile. Such conditions, while, alas, not infrequent in our century, are abnormal. Escarpit and the Marxists underestimate the flexibility of a properly educated mind, its ability to emancipate itself provisionally or experimentally from its own value system. Wayne Booth, the theoretician of the narrative second self, has also postulated a reader's second self, which can be very different from the "self who goes about paying bills, repairing leaky faucets, and failing in generosity and wisdom."[37] Literary sociology seems prone to the failing of making consciousness too monolithic, not only in relation to groups, but also in terms of the trained mind's own ability to suspend its normally governing principles. Perhaps this is because much literary sociology is a Continental phenomenon and Continental societies, even—and especially—on their oppositional wings, are more conformist than is the case in English-speaking countries. The degree, for example, to which new West German dissertations resemble one another in langugage, method, and opinions, is disquieting to an American reader, who is more used to scholarship as dialogue rather than as a recruitment of troops to march with the current manifestation of the *Weltgeist*. Any adequate principle of evaluation of literary experience that is not to be wholly parochial and presentist requires tolerance of foreign values as the foundation of understanding. The question is whether this tolerance is entirely without bounds. Marcuse's concept of "repressive tolerance" is a dubious paradox; but it is perhaps so, on the one hand, that there are insuperable limits of tolerance somewhere in our own value systems, of which it would be well to be aware; on the other, that complete tolerance demoralizes the literary experience to a distortive degree. Much literature appeals to moral judgment and values, and to refuse it this appeal is to reduce its inherent richness. Booth has asked whether there is "no limit to what we will praise, provided it is done with skill," and he says of Céline that "we cannot excuse him for writing a book which, if taken seriously by the reader, must corrupt him. The better it is understood, the more immoral it looks."[38]

I doubt that a reader both sane and educated can be corrupted by any work of literature. In order to hold a writer like Céline in unstinting regard without moral objections in some part of his mind, the reader must have been previously corrupted by some process in the social environment of which he is a part.[39] Ideological orientation tends to be the most resistant aspect of a strange literary work to most readers. Critical appreciation is much concerned with the suspension of this resistance, and readiness is required if a literary work is to "corrupt." The footing is slippery here. Can we establish limits to *literary* evaluation on the basis of our moral or political convictions? Judgments made in this way tend to inhibit intersubjective sharing with those who do not hold the same convictions. On the other hand, it seems peculiar to argue that we can or should suppress or suspend our moral and political selves while engaging in the humanistic activity of literary criticism.

Karl-Otto Conrady, in an introductory handbook for beginning students of literature, tried to draw the limits of the permissible this way:

> We should raise critical objections where literature puts itself in the service of totalitarian thought; where it works against the free play of forces in society; where it hinders the enlightenment of man, the possible guidance of man out of his self-caused immaturity [an allusion to Kant's phrase, *selbstverschuldete Unmündigkeit*], and instead mystifies forces and dimensions that are regressive and defame reason and critical thought as seditious and nihilistic; where literature helps to prepare the ground for chauvinism; where forces of blood, of soil, of race, of the folk are presented as eternal and exclusively valid; where war and soldiering are celebrated as the great moment in the life of a man and a people.[40]

Probably Conrady believes, after the experience of life and literature in this century, that these are criteria that all contemporaries of good will can share. His list is of course colored by special problems of the German tradition; Sartre made an argument similar in form on a quite different set of political premises.[41] But many will think the whole list oblique to the real problems encountered in practical criticism, and insouciant about literary works as statement. Does not the *Iliad* celebrate war and soldiering? Does not Dostoyevsky defame reason and critical thought? Furthermore, one must ask whether literature really can do all the things Conrady fears from it, and if it can, whether we are not putting ourselves into difficult combat with whole social groups, and whether censorship would not be in some sense justified if all these atrocities could proceed from literature.

My own view on this subject is derived from my respect for the formal discipline of liberal constitutionalism. I do not believe that any person or group in society has any grounds for legislating what others may or may not read. Consequently I regard any censorship, whether of pornography, or sedition, or of racist sentiment, as anomalous and impermissible. On the other hand, I am equally convinced that the expression, fictionalization, and propagation of certain kinds of views are morally, ethically, and politically reprehensible, and in consequence I would urge that literary criticism does have serious issues of socially relevant value to raise, and, being properly inhibited from propagating them under the aegis of power, the obligation to think them out seriously and argue them as coherently, convincingly, and unremittingly as possible is all the greater.

When we search literary sociology for usable theories of value, we find that the question is in a relatively primitive state, and that the only coherent theory of value is Marxist, which, as always, generates difficulties if one does not share the Marxist assumptions. The main line of Marxist aesthetics reveals the origin of Marxism generally in the intellectual atmosphere of early nineteenth-century Germany. On the whole, its literary values have been traditionalist, unfriendly to experimentation, and suspicious (as we all well might be, but not to this extent) of avant-gardism. Like German Classical aesthetics, to which it owes much, it seeks, as one observer has put it, the direct succession to Classical antiquity.[42] Some younger radicals in the West have grown impatient with this and have hard words for the old masters of Marxist criticism,[43] and perhaps the end of Marxist traditionalism is in sight; but the younger ones often have little to offer other than a call for the direct agitatory employability of literature. Lukács had a curious way of combining a Classical canon with a Romantic practice of injecting poetic values into reality and then seeking their recovery in literature itself. He welded this traditional practice together with the Marxist concept of dialectical conflict. "The inner poesy of life," he wrote in the thirties, "is the poesy of struggling man, the combative mutual relationship of men with one another in their real *Praxis*." A failure to penetrate to the true nature of this struggle will impair literary value by leading to the static naturalism of writers of lesser rank like Flaubert, whose prejudice, Lukács tells us, was to confuse life with the dullness and monotony of bourgeois life.[44] A canon of values that excludes Flaubert may seem to some of us excessively strict, although doubtless Goethe would not have cared much for *Madame Bovary* either. It can, however, open the canon in other directions. If one can make oneself believe, as Benjamin could, that "a work that exhibits the right tendency must necessarily exhibit every other quality," then we may assign outstanding value to a novel by Tretyakov that has arisen out of active participation in Soviet collectivization.[45] Thus the absorption of all possible values, aesthetic and humane, by a single set, could lead a sensitive intellectual to fall for the Stalinist hoax.*

*The usual grim irony came to accrue to this frantic struggle for partisanship. The following summer, Benjamin noted without comment a remark made in Brecht's presence that Tretyakov was probably no longer alive (Benjamin, *Versuche über Brecht* [Frankfurt am Main: Suhrkamp, 1966], p.130). A few months later, in January, 1939, Brecht, who had been befriended by Tretyakov, heard that he was being accused as a "Japanese spy" (Brecht, *Arbeitsjournal*, ed. Werner Hecht [Frankfurt am Main: Suhrkamp, 1973], I,36. The annota-

This suggests that literary sociology, like any other kind of criticism, has a need to keep the conflict of competing values alive.

Goldmann appears to me to be less clear on the subject of value than he is on most matters, and this creates certain difficulties insofar as he chooses the great writers for his subject and one would like to know how these are identified apart from inherited convention. By fundamental instinct, Goldmann is an essentialist; he is not interested in individual or eccentric deviations from the "world vision," which is an instrument for separating the essential from the accidental. In consequence, the question of aesthetic validity is also uninteresting, for in his view it is not only "arbitrary and subjective," but has also "the additional disadvantage of being quite inapplicable to works of philosophy or theology." On the basis of this judgment, one could say that Goldmann is not a *literary* sociologist at all, but a philosopher of culture. The amalgamation of philosophy, literature, and theology into a global phenomenon of common relevance may be justified for large-scale purposes, but it does not contribute to concentration on the special qualities of fictionality. Nor does the denial of the value of deviation correspond to our experience. Goldmann argues that dialectical studies show "that cultural events of outstanding importance—such as the *Pensées* and Racine's tragedies—are rarely linked with obscure and secondary social movements." [46] But one wonders whether there is not a hidden circularity in this argument, whether the "outstanding importance" is not a priori linked with the major social movement. When pressed by Alphons Silbermann, who, as an empiricist, argued that value distinctions are of no importance at all for literary sociology, Goldmann confessed that he, too, did not know what the criteria of value are; nevertheless he suspected that one of the values is "coherence defined as functionality," an obscure formulation, to be sure, but one that looks as though it might be building a bridge to a familiar critical criterion that other contemporary literary sociologists are inclined to deny. Against the empiricists, Goldmann argued in the usual fashion that if values are ignored, they creep into one's work in an unexamined way. [47]

Corresponding to the Classicist aesthetics and traditionalist canon of Marxism has been its rejection of most modern literature as the pessimis-

tion to this important publication is one of the political scandals of modern editing and will tell the reader nothing of what became of Tretyakov.) He was finally liquidated in August, 1939. Benjamin's original positive mention of him probably had some reference to the Marxist debates of those years, in which Tretyakov had served Lukács as an example of decadent deviation from his model of realism.

tic or nihilistic expression of a dying class. The recent history of Marxist literary theory has been largely a process of the gradual revision of this stance; a major turning point is often seen in the Prague Kafka Conference of 1963. This history is well documented and need not be rehearsed here; it is furthermore so intertwined with Communist politics that to treat it separately as a theoretical development would be misleading. The link with the concept of a dying class cannot, however, be cut without leaving the ground of Marxism altogether; evaluation remains dependent on the question of whether it is a good thing that certain oppositional or "progressive" bourgeois writers are documenting this decline. Benjamin took this position in the thirties. Avant-gardism is for Benjamin the long way around to a goal near at hand: "the way of the intellectual to radical criticism of the social order is the longest as that of the proletariat is the shortest."[48] Bloch, in his sharp criticism of the quarrel over Expressionism ignited by Lukács, while correctly pointing out the idealistic foundations of Lukács' values, stressed mainly on behalf of the Expressionists that they were good because they sped the process of bourgeois decadence.[49] These arguments all assume a total or nearly total assimilation of artistic expression to social process.

Where Marxist aesthetics is rooted in German Classicism, it tends to stress organic evaluative criteria. Among Western Germanists, however, there has been a tendency to warn against allowing such formal criteria to become self-sufficient in criticism,[50] or even sharply to oppose them on the grounds that formal perfection is just as likely to be the mark of the trivial and insignificant, while the richness of content ought to be our criterion for literary value and interest.[51] The argument of August Wilhelm Schlegel against Kant, that no geometrical figure can be any more beautiful than one similar to it, is revived to oppose the criterion of unity in multiplicity and to redirect attention to meaning as indispensable to aesthetic apprehension.[52] * In listening to German arguments of this kind, it is necessary to keep in mind the excesses of idealism, harmonization, and nationalism that are especially pronounced in the German tradition and account for the allergic reaction in that country to critical concepts that may seem to the rest of us more innocent because they have never borne such a heavy load of *Weltanschauung*. It is necessary to distinguish between an architectonic order that may well be a

* Cf. Ernst Fischer's argument that symmetry is a stable energy condition in which there can be no "will to form"; form is the conservative principle, while content is in motion and is thus the revolutionary principle (*Von der Notwendigkeit der Kunst* [Hamburg: Claassen, 1967], pp. 136–138).

characteristic of commonplace literature and the particular unity, complexity, and intensity in the texture of the work.[53] The claimed incompatability of coherence and complexity is not at all necessary and suggests that these theorists would do well to become better acquainted with Beardsley. Often one encounters the reduction of the criterion of coherence to a bland harmoniousness and fidelity to conventional genre. This cannot be sustained by a critic or literary historian of any sensitivity, who soon must entertain the possibility that artistic coherence can stand in a dialectical relationship to a rupture with a disharmoniously experienced reality,[54] a view that could easily be accommodated by more traditional principles of criticism. A certain puritanical, anti-aesthetic affect has become evident among some prominent contemporary Germanists, who do not actually appear to *like* literature very much. The result is naturally a failure to respond with any precision to the details of the text and the propagation of a rather low order of criticism.

More convincing are objections that arise out of a realistic sense of history and change, which can help to defend against the curious primitivism that accrued to critical value judgments earlier in this century. Robert Weimann has found an example in T. S. Eliot's desire to seek a "pattern below the level of plot and character," and comments as follows:

> What remains dubious here, despite all the obscurity of definition, is the evaluating undertone of the preposition "below": in what way do pattern and symbols in general lie *below* plot and character? And even if this were true, why is the lower level more valuable than the upper? The fact is that this distinction is untenable and distorts the actual architecture of literature. It arouses the suspicion that "below" relates here to the lower strata of consciousness (or to the subconscious), whose artistic correlates are then understood not to be characters and plot, but the use of images and symbols less controlled by *ratio* and ethics. If one were to apply this criterion consistently, then the representation of the least refined impulses, i.e., the configuration of the instincts, would be the greatest art.[55]

A touch of conventional prudery has gone into this formulation, and I have suppressed the following clause, which turns the argument in orthodox fashion against modern art. But it ought to be some cause of concern to us that it is Marxists who are defending the values of civilization in criticism, while our own recent tradition is shot through with primitivism and archaism (at the same time as some of us complain that our students are slovenly and uncivil). If it was the fault of the German idealistic tradition to dissolve the complexity and conflict of art into a hovering higher realm of eternal verities, some of our own critics in recent decades, with their stress on myth and instinct, have been trying to dissolve literature downward into the atavisms of the race. If literary sociology can do something to haul criticism back to the surface of civilization, it will help at least some value criteria to emerge that have a relationship to humane considerations of value in general.

The Marxist line of argument leads to a reopening of the question of the relationship of form and content. The New Critical postulate of the identity of form and content is a reaction against the naive apprehension of poetic fiction and a symptom of a characteristic pressure toward unifying the aesthetic object as far as possible. In practice, its effect has often been to deny a legitimate interest in referential aspects of content apart from their internal formal patterning, and it has often led to an ahistorical distortion of older literature; well into the nineteenth century the rhetorical tradition that the same content could appear in various *Einkleidungsformen* remained alive and affected formal considerations.[56] In neo-Marxist and other oppositional theory there is a clear tendency, as can be seen in some of our citations, to assert the priority—not necessarily temporally—of content over form.[57] This tendency is not always correctly understood by unsympathetic observers. It does not mean that fictional utterances are confused with propositional statements, although this may occasionally occur in what, in some quarters, is referred to as "vulgar Marxism" or "vulgar sociology." The main line of modern Marxist theory is not indifferent to form; its strong historical awareness generates attention to genre as form modified through time for ascertainable and significant reasons. Lukács was always oriented on Schiller's precept that form must dissolve or destroy at least the material content (*Stoff*). Nor do Marxists and speculative literary sociologists tend to think of form as a vessel into which content is poured. Rather the position is that content—which we may define for this purpose as the communicated apprehension of and judgment upon the world—generates form and in that sense is anterior to it. Perhaps what is meant is better expressed as "argument" in the old literary sense of the term, as the still inchoate *demonstrandum*, the thing worth expressing. It is the prior intentionality of any literature that is not a pure exhibition of formalistic experiment. Value can therefore reside in content, as being intimately involved with the purposiveness and the larger human relations of the creative process.

Despite the evident dangers in such a position to aesthetically adequate criticism, it would be unwise to reject it out of hand, for it may be due for a more sympathetic hearing after some forty years of insistently formalist criticism from which we perhaps have begun to learn as much as we usefully can. Two considerations suggest this. One is that a strictly formalist approach sets its face against the normal social process of literary reception. From the outset, this was clearly and explicitly its purpose. Richards' *Practical Criticism* documented the incapacity of educated people to comprehend poetic texts in any way adequate to their intrinsic character or even to their superficial sense. But, as a more refined sensibility to aesthetic structures was being pursued, the implied repudiation of the common understanding began to escalate into an insistence that, in contrast to what ordinary people might think, literary texts are not about anything, which in turn results in a denial of social relevance. Quite apart from the refinements of theoretical positions, practical criticism with a general educational appeal cannot be conducted this way. It is too remote from the normal experience of reading and the way in which literature functions in social situations. The initial educational purpose of giving literate people access to literary phenomena and thereby enriching and expanding their consciousness was lost sight of, and the result is the odd sense of absence from the *theatrum mundi* in much of almost any issue of a journal of scholarly criticism. The educational gap is consequently filled with synthesizing savants and charlatans often out of rational control.

The second consideration concerns the actual purposiveness of creative activity. It is still true, at least in my field, that much contemporary academic criticism in this country is written as though a poem or a drama or a novel should interest us as the achievement of a web of sounds, images, and other techniques of literary art. In a way, this is an attempt to recover in criticism part of the play of creation; there is a tendency among artists to see whether a certain thing can be done, and, having established that, whether the opposite can be done—thus we get holes in the desert, wrapped-up cliffs, piles of old plumbing, or denunciations of the theater audience as contemporary art. (Some boundaries of the principle that art is anything an artist does are gradually being reached; Piero Manzoni's offering of a can containing thirty grams of his own feces, which in the spring of 1974 managed to throw Bavarian cultural officials into a dither, may perhaps approach some sort of limit. "Decadence" is hardly an adequate term at this point.) There are also situations in which the solving of formal problems seems imperative. German poets in the early seventeenth century wrote sonnets, not in the first instance because of a content that demanded this form, but out of a felt need to prove that it could be done in German as well as in Latin or in the languages of more advanced countries, although in a short time it developed that the sonnet was well suited to the antithetical structure of the perception of a shattered world. But such examples prove the rule; they show that the formal aspects do not stand alone, but are impelled by wider considerations without which they become incomprehensible activities. It is more than a little doubtful that purely formalistic purposes generate memorable art. A novel such as Günter Grass's *Tin Drum* is formed of the most intricate kind of structural and symbolic patterning, but it is motivated by the challenging problem of trying to gain artistic control over the experience of Nazi Germany, and no interpretation of it that focused exclusively on its patterning without concern for this purpose would be adequate to its reality. Form is purposive and responsive, and thus relates to the widest human concerns. One can, for example, examine the formal structure of dialogue in the modern novel in order to become more attentive to changing social relationships; one can also query the content and implications of literary works as to the adequacy of their intelligence and vision. Such an awareness is the only possible way of coping with Hermann Hesse, for without attention to the shallowness of his vision and the reactionary complicities involved in the very features of his works that make him popular among students, the result is a drift into noncommittal registration of a superficial skein of formal relationships.

Here the danger of moralism keeps emerging, and I have found, especially in discussions with students, that the question is dogged by the speculative problem of the imaginary Nazi masterpiece. Even supposing sociological causality, the question raised by David Daiches as to whether origins can affect value[58] remains troublesome. Nor can purpose directly generate literary value; such a principle, as Beardsley has argued, would place *Uncle Tom's Cabin* higher than *Hamlet*[59] —although there is no serious critic in any camp who would make such a contention. It appears to me that for practical purposes value can only be conceived of intersubjectively, indeed, in respect of a socialized consensus that can, of course, be made more catholic and discriminating once present. It may be that literary value is contained in the work *in potentia*, permanently awaiting its emergence to the correctly attuned sensibility. But as an argumentative posture this will carry little conviction, as most of us know from experience. The readiness for literary value is surely linked to values perceived in the general context.

There seems to be no way out of it other than to admit that the values have to be ours, as well as "spread over a whole environmental situation."[60] They must, of course, exhibit a historical sensibility; Jost Hermand is right to remark that any boor can evaluate, but the elementary cognition of a literary work is dependent upon historical knowledge.[61] But it is also the historical sensibility that can create a crippling diffidence about our own values. Since we now hold in disregard many values that actuated criticism in past ages and believe them to be distortive of interpretation, we fear that an imposition of our own values will suffer the same fate. Probably it will, but we are critics, not poets, and we are not even pretending to write for the ages. We have our own work to do in our own time, and we do it best on behalf of the future by allowing the controlling imperatives of our own time—peace, liberty, justice, democracy—to permeate our judgment, in order to seek the amalgamation of critical criteria "with consciously articulated principles that correspond to what we actually believe."[62] At the same time, if we are not to be wholly captured in our own provincialism, one of the personal values of the critic must be a willingness to welcome values that challenge his own without necessarily yielding to them. The goal is to maintain the tension between the ideal of judging without presuppositions and our allegiance to the examined presuppositions that we bring to our task as citizens.[63]

Such a position is difficult to obtain in the present climate, which is divided between arguments that either deny evaluation, thereby obscuring the value systems employed, or apply values that are severed from those that otherwise guide our lives; and arguments that demand a Leninist partisanship that focuses all literary creation and critical thought upon a political goal. It is only out of the latter kind of commitment that one can defend the insouciant employment of terms like "progressive" and "reactionary" as dominant categories. The difficulty is, however, that a critical standpoint that would wholly ban such terminology from our usage often turns out, upon examination, to be generally committed against the idea of progress.[64] Literary critics often rightly scoff at the notion of progress *in* literature; where, they will ask, is the qualitative advance in the drama over Shakespeare? Marx naturally thought such a naive notion of cultural progress ridiculous.[65] But to put the question in this way is to hold fast to a concept of internal literary history; if we see literature *within* history, broader and more differentiated areas of concern emerge.

A pertinent discussion has developed around Paul Celan's poem about Auschwitz, *Death Fugue*. Adorno propagated the influential opinion that

this poem is unacceptable because it is too fine and therefore aes-
theticizes a reality of unmitigated horror.[66] The question of whether an
excellent and, in some degree, harmonious poem misdirects our proper
attention from a searing and disharmonious reality is a difficult one. It
seems to me that such a judgment is grounded in a presupposition that a
work of art must adequately encompass the totality of any reality, rather
than being one possible way among many of representing it and coping
with it, one voice among a variety of human answers. One might as easily
argue that bringing poetic and therefore humane values to bear on an
otherwise wholly unassimilable catastrophe is a necessary activity.[67]
Jeremiah's lamentation over the collapse of his world under God is, after
all, a cycle of poems in the form of an alphabetical acrostic. We are
certainly not the less moved by it for that reason. Adorno's opinion that
poetry is no longer possible after Auschwitz[68] is not the more credible
because it is constantly cited. What is terrifying about the phenomenon
of Auschwitz is not its newness but its apparently indestructible ancient-
ness.* If mass atrocities and genocide were to obviate the possibility of
literature, no poetry would have been permissible since the beginning of
time. The argument that aesthetic form is incompatible with rebellion is
perverse and explicable only out of unconsciously shared idealistic presuppositions; one would think, rather, that the reverse is the case and
that Celan's poem is an expression of humane reconstitution in the face
of barbarism. For Adorno, the aesthetic qualities of the poem are narcotic; but it would seem equally as plausible to argue that, in their display of
human mastery over chaos, they help us to regroup our strength before
a reality that is otherwise annihilating of hope. But it is nevertheless
useful that Adorno has raised the question. We are reminded that, in

---

* During the preliminaries for the celebrated "positivism" debate, Popper is said to have
written to Adorno that the difference between them was that Popper believed we are living
in the best world that ever existed, while Adorno did not. Adorno agreed and commented
that he found it hard to believe that "no [world] should have been better than the one that
hatched Auschwitz" (Theodor W. Adorno, et al., *Der Positivismusstreit in der deutschen
Soziologie* [Neuwied: Luchterhand, 1969], pp.141–142). This exchange is illuminating, not
only of the socio-political ground of intellectual standpoint, but also of Adorno's position.
First there is his assumption of the totality of the capitalist world, while Popper would
doubtless argue that his adopted country did *not* hatch Auschwitz, whatever one may say
about Great Britain's share of responsibility for the consolidation of Nazi power. Secondly,
the exchange exhibits the global hatred of the present that Adorno shares with his
associates, the tendency to see modern Western society as a moral unit, all aspects of which
are irredeemably fallen. Popper's liberal tendency is to seek out and build on the positive
potential for freedom and justice that our society contains. Insofar as this difference bears
upon literary criticism, I should think Popper's view more fruitful, though personally I
should be inclined to hold it in a more qualified and cautious way.

order to justify our canon of values, we are forced to reach beyond the internal qualities of the work of art.

An irrepressible example, one that can still stand some continued debate, is the case of Ezra Pound. It will be remembered that in 1972 the Council of the American Academy of Arts and Sciences vetoed its own committee's proposal to award an Emerson-Thoreau medal to Pound. Here is a case where the issues are clear, if the judgment we ought pass on them is far from settled. I must say I do not understand why the Pound dispute is occasionally adduced as a clear example of the unwisdom of involving political considerations with literary judgment. In 1949, after the Fellows in American Letters of the Library of Congress had awarded the Bollingen Prize in Poetry for 1948 to Pound's *Pisan Cantos*, a minor poet, writing in the *Saturday Review of Literature*, used a generalized charge of Fascism to mount an irresponsible, philistine, and jingoistic attack on modern poetry and criticism. Perhaps the worst part of this event was the calling of the cops, in the person of Senator Jacob Javits, on the Library of Congress; the Senator's behavior on the occasion was most questionable. The naturally outraged rebuttal of the Fellows and their supporters had, however, the familiar tendency to put poetry and politics into barely tangent boxes; all concerned were united in their disapproval of Pound's opinions and behavior (he was at that time under indictment for treason), but most seemed confident that this did not matter. Allen Tate dismissed the charge of Fascism by showing, in effect, that his own politics were to the right of Fascism, without any evident consciousness that reactionary fantasms are easily muddled by Fascism into delusory promise and therefore ought not to be solemnly indulged in by intellectuals.[69] Threading through the arguments is an apparent conviction that poetry, in a privileged way, is large, generous, and wise with respect to human life and the world, while politics is narrow, accidental, decisionistic, and constrictive—an intellectual abdication that may have something to do with the genesis of the political miseries we currently endure. My own opinion continues to be that a body sponsored by an institution of the United States government would have been unwise to confer an honor on Pound even if he had written the *Divine Comedy* and the Fifth Symphony, and it is a matter of concern that a panel of exceptional literary dignity did not seem more than peripherally uneasy about it.*

*For a succinct refutation of Archibald MacLeish's muddled defense of the award on strictly critical principles, I recommend Graff, *Poetic Statement and Critical Dogma*, pp. 172–179.

A lucid contribution to the Academy disagreement was made by Michael Wood in the *New York Review of Books* of February 8, 1973. Wood has much of subtlety and understanding to say about Pound's poetry and the relative force of his political views in it. But he will not let us escape the incontrovertible and unpleasant facts. "The texts of his broadcasts from Italy during World War II . . . ," he writes, "make very unpleasant reading, and will come as a shock if you have been expecting to hear a harmless crank preaching strange doctrines." [70] As for the poetry, Wood gives an example from Canto 30 of a firmly and finely expressed "frame of mind' that "fits well enough with fascism, whether it happens to be linked historically with fascism or not," and continues: "His ugly ethic of purity, repented of or not, is really there in *The Cantos*—not right in the middle, perhaps, but not off in some margin either." [71]

But I cannot agree with Wood on the subject of the medal. He thinks the Council's refusal is hypocritical, pretending to a verbal remembrance of concerns that in fact have lost their real urgency for us. This judgment seems to me excessively harsh—it is another instance of the undifferentiated contempt for the present—but the subjective motivation of those involved is not the central issue. The central issue is that with all the profoundest appreciation for Pound's poetry and with all sympathy for the pathos of his later life, we ought not to be giving him public awards, least of all such as are associated with names like Emerson and Thoreau. Such awards are given to a poet and a literary life, not just to a poem or a literary achievement; the difference is not trivial, and Pound would not have entertained the separation of the aesthetic and the political, which he, like other reactionary artists of his age, forcefully welded together. [72] Much of the counterargument is grounded in a sense of disgust at our own civilization, a feeling that our own moral basis is so unsound—one thinks of the barbarous treatment Pound received after his arrest (though he might quite properly have been hanged)—that we have no right to pass such judgment on a great creative spirit, especially in regard to events a generation in the past and upon a poet on the threshold of death. We are fearful of the stupidity and philistinism we encourage if we begin measuring artists by common moral standards. And doubtless it is true that, without the healing effect of forgiveness and forgetfulness, the human race would go completely insane out of hate, vengefulness, and guilt; there are examples enough in the past and the present. While granting all this, I would suggest two other considerations. There is a hierarchy of moral concerns, and therefore of practical critical values. The choice of an *intellectual* to generate public anti-Semitic and Fascist propaganda is no ordinary kind of political allegiance; it is qualitatively of unforgiveable gravity—*for us*. The enormity of it crushes the highly important inhibition against moralistic judgment on art. Anyone can be mistaken, and even an intellectual can be stupid in his hunger for wholeness. But, as Thomas Mann said in reply to Hesse's enthusiasm for young Nazis, there is a degree of stupidity that is no longer permissible.[73] As for forgetting, while it may be necessary to the survival of the race in general, the specific task of scholars, literary critics among them, is to remember; it is for them especially to keep the memory of past atrocity intact and not encourage its fading. There is an important difference between suppressing writers and literature out of moral and political considerations, and refraining, out of such considerations, from confer-ring special public honors. Such value as we have from the continued existence and availability of Pound's poetry is not impaired by the refusal to make the award, and it seems to me that we preserve another value of a different kind by refraining from a gesture that implies callousness toward boundless human suffering.

It seems clear that "value" is not a unitary category. Practical criticism obliges us to treat value as a relational category: good in terms of what, good for whom? Certainly there is a special set of values appropriate to artistic excellence; they can, up to a limit, be described and taught, and they are real human values whose denial can only be the result of an ideological puritanism whose attention is absorbed by an entirely differ-ent set of concerns. But it is one of the peculiarities of modern criticism to insist that artistic criteria are the only kind of value predicable to the literary object of which we may legitimately speak. Under the cover of this claim all kinds of unacknowledged value criteria of other types have been smuggled into criticism, with the result that much contemporary critical discussion has acquired a cast of disingenuousness. It is empiri-cally true that whenever the charge of irrelevance is raised against literature or the study of literature, a defense is always mounted in terms of the values of our lives as a whole; even Beardsley concludes his account of aesthetic values with reference to such desiderata as the relief of tension, the resolution of conflicts, empathy with others, an aid to mental health, and so on.[74] Literary sociology has an, as yet, largely unrealized potential for helping us see, on the one hand, that the experience of literature is not exhausted as an anodyne or narcotic, and, on the other, that our canons of judgment are necessarily and properly involved with our whole estimation of man's life in the world.

V

Endurance

KARL MARX made some trouble for modern Marxist literary theory when in 1857, in the abandoned draft of an introduction to a *Kritik der politischen Ökonomie*, he set down his musings on the imperishability of Greek art, which did not altogether seem to accord with the historical dialectic. After having raised the "difficulty" that, although "Greek art and epos are bound up with certain forms of social development . . . , they still constitute with us a source of aesthetic enjoyment and in certain respects prevail as the standard and model beyond attainment," he ventured a precritical solution that gives us a glancing look into his cultural presuppositions:

> A man cannot become a child again unless he becomes childish. But does he not enjoy the artless ways of the child and must he not strive to reproduce its truth on a higher plane? Is not the character of every epoch revived perfectly true to nature in child nature? Why should the social childhood of mankind, where it had obtained its most beautiful develop- ment, not exert an eternal charm as an age that will never return? There are ill-bred children and precocious children. Many of the ancient nations belong to the latter class. The Greeks were normal children. The charm their art has for us does not conflict with the primitive character of the social order from which it had sprung. It is rather the product of the latter, and is rather due to the fact that the unripe social conditions under which the art arose and under which alone it could appear can never return.*

*The passage was originally published by Karl Kautsky in 1902–03. See Peter Demetz, *Marx, Engels, and the Poets: Origins of Marxist Literary Criticism* (Chicago: University of Chicago Press, 1967), pp.72, 242. It is not carried in the official Marx and Engels, *Über Kunst und Literatur*, ed. Manfred Kliem (Berlin: Dietz Verlag, 1967–68). I quote the text from Maynard Solomon, ed., *Marxism and Art: Essays Classic and Contemporary* (New York: Knopf, 1973), p.62.

Unhelpful as this not wholly lucid passage may be for a Marxist or sociological view of literature, loyal Marxists frequently feel obliged to refer to it admiringly and even programmatically, though not always with notable precision. Ernst Fischer tells us that, while art is subject to determination by time, it also contains a permanent "element of humanity" that transcends the historical moment and represents a continuum of human values emerging out of various classes and social systems.[1] The solution is an old one, with roots in Plekhanov, Trotsky, and the literary-sociological discussion in the Soviet Union in the 1920s,[2] and it is constantly being resuscitated in modern Marxism.* It is not far out of accord with common critical views that see literature as an illumination of human nature, and, although all of us must grant this to some extent unless we wish to deny any objectively adequate cognition of a work of the past, one would not think this a point that either literary sociology or Marxism would be chiefly concerned to stress. A younger neo-Marxist typically deals with the problem by becoming what Caudwell called a "Golden Ager," and argues that ancient culture retains for us the lost sense of the totality of society.[3] What is characteristic of these and similar commentaries is that they have no relation to Marx's text. He does not talk here about the continuity of human nature, nor does he set up Classical antiquity as an example of prealienation, though his later allusions to Greece, especially in *Capital*, show that he believed it was.[4] Rather, he equates Greek culture with the childhood of the race, and compares our pleasure in it with the continuing pleasure we have in childhood or childlikeness. Of course, there is nothing childlike about Classical Greece; it is a mature and self-conscious culture, looking back on long memories and rent by defects that we do not associate with the innocence of childhood. There does not seem to be much that is dialectic in a metaphor of history that would equate it with the ages of human life, not to mention that extending the metaphor would result in a view of the coming utopia as one of decrepitude and decline. Marx is employing a venerable trope of cultural philosophy, as Lifshitz already noted, and to be intelligible in his context it requires at the very least an additional cyclical or dialectical term of rejuvenation.[5]

---

* The Marxist David Craig differentiates this way: "Cultural change is bound to act upon our more intimate as well as our more social selves, yet the deeper the experience the more rooted it must be in the scarcely (or very slowly) changing human organisms. Presumably, therefore, the view we take of our passions changes more in the course of history than do the passions themselves." (*The Real Foundations*: *Literature and Social Change* [New York: Oxford University Press, 1974], p.17).

The difficulties generated by Marx's text are illusory and result from the Talmudic need to regard every utterance of Marx and Engels as a revelation of canonical standing; even Lukács felt obliged to take over the "childhood" notion.[6] There are still powerful inhibitions against saying that in one place or another Marx or Engels was tossing off a casual comment of no binding theoretical force or was just plain talking through his hat. It is characteristic that there are still people around who think it possible to "refute" Marxism by pointing to contradictions in the sacred texts, thereby acknowledging its universal pretentions, just as there used to be people who thought it possible to undermine religion by pointing to contradictions in the Bible. In fact, if Marx had been more introspective by nature than he was, he should have had no difficulty understanding his problem with the Greeks on his own principles. It is conditioned by the intellectual environment of his time, by what E. M. Butler called *The Tyranny of Greece over Germany*;[7] it shows up as well in Engels' argument that the Greeks had discovered dialectical reasoning, which had become lost in the metaphysics of the intervening centuries.[8] Indeed, as Peter Demetz has shown, Marx's literary taste (in contrast to that of Engels) seems to have been curiously out of touch with his revolutionary philosophy.[9] It was, after all, Aeschylus, not critical and doubting Euripides, who was Marx's life-long favorite. Marx in these matters simply accepted the valuations of the culture in which he was educated, including the myth of Classical antiquity as the human norm that is fundamental in Hegel as well. Had he cared enough about the question to pursue it theoretically, which he did not, he would have been forced, I should imagine, to a revision of his view, confronting the historicity of the high prestige accorded the Greeks in his time and perhaps analyzing its relationship to the general consciousness of alienation, which Marx codified but certainly did not discover. The acceptance of the German Neohumanist myth left him with contradictions he could not resolve.[10] If, as has recently been done, one takes the statement more seriously as an idealistically derived acknowledgment of an imperishable substance of art, viable in antiquity and perhaps again in a utopian future, but throughout intervening history subject to the deformities of alienation and ideology,[11] then a chain of paradoxes emerges, not the least of which is the modern Marxist attempt to restore the validity of the intervening artistic tradition in a utopian continuity that threatens to sever basis and superstructure. The trouble is that Marx inherited the Romantic confusion about "primitive" societies, in which "the early stages of Greek civilization, the society depicted in the Old Testament, contemporary Arabian society, the feudal Middle Ages, and the dim time in which Ossian was supposed to have lived are all considered the same."[12]

However, the problem of the endurance of literary works is not only important for literary sociology; it is probable that only a socio-historical view will help us to a rational grasp of it, although this has not yet been achieved. It is of considerable importance for practical criticism and the teaching of literature, and it is one of those aspects of literary sociology that carries for us the potential of acute discomfort. For a long time, cultural education has been informed explicitly or implicity by an Arnoldian faith in the best that has been thought and said; or, as David Daiches put it, "that which can be seen to have served [a human need] for most people over the longest period of time."[13] which is a variation of Samuel Johnson's phrase in his *Preface to Shakespeare* of 1765 that in judging works "appealing wholly to observation and experience, no other test can be applied than length of duration and continuance of esteem."[14] (It is not without interest to add that Johnson immediately goes on to oppose a judgment canonized by long continuance and esteem concerning the dramatic unities.) The question of what can possibly be meant by "most people" will concern us in the next essay. Here we are faced with the question of whether our confidence that literary quality will insure permanence in the cultural memory is justified. Historically, we must face the fact that, if endurance is inherent in literary works, in its present canonical breadth it has been acknowledged only relatively recently— since the Renaissance at the earliest, more exactly since Romanticism broke beyond the culturally parochial horizon of one's own time and place. Most of the ancient classics, with few exceptions, were held in no regard for centuries; their revival in the Renaissance was accompanied by major social changes, and at present it is a hard question whether they are still alive in any specific sense in our present cultural consciousness. The French in the eighteenth century could not make head or tail out of Shakespeare; it took the frustrated and shackled Germans, in search of images of freedom, to remind the Continent of his greatness. Taste has continued to fluctuate since Romanticism but, up until recently, at least, in a less violent way; Heine's stock may be rising at the moment and Hemingway's declining, but these are adjustments within the canon rather than major upheavals that can reach to the limit of total oblivion—or so we think. It is true that most educated people are likely to find the canon fairly reliable; at least I do.

But if taste is culturally and historically determined, this may mean nothing at all other than that most of what seems enduring to the culture within which I was educated seems enduring to me. The temptation to believe that quality determines endurance is strong and is not to be dismissed out of hand, although it is hard to square with history. Jean Starobinski has made the appealing suggestion that the memory of man retains certain works because they demonstrate the most expert, accomplished, felicitous uses to which language can be put, mastership relating to our common apprenticeship in language use.[15] But surely we must recognize the vast synchronic and diachronic gaps in this process. The trouble already begins as soon as one tries to reach beyond one's culture. I remember a conversation with a German-born American physicist and philosopher of wide cultural learning who stated with assurance that Goethe's *Werther* is an effusion of silly sentimentality that no one could take seriously; having read and taught *Werther* many times, I am certain that this is not so, but the example, which could be easily multiplied, shows to what extent literary endurance is dependent upon the cultural readiness of readers as well as upon some liberating, educational insight into context. There is every reason to doubt that endurance is safely intrinsic to the literary work alone, that what the sociologist Vytautas Kavolis calls "the formal 'compellingness' of a substantively alien perception"[16] reliably generates its own impetus.

That endurance is not self-explanatory is at present daily being brought to the attention of literary scholars and teachers. We are told that Shakespeare, whom we have come to think of in our culture as the most imperishable writer since Classical antiquity, cannot and should not be taught to American Black students.* Louis Kampf, in his assumed

---

*This excruciating problem is basically not one of literature but of literacy. *The New York Times* of August 15, 1972, reported on a project for teaching urban high school [!] boys to read with sports magazines. One of the pupils commented: "At least here you can understand what you're reading about. Reading about sports is better than literature and all that." Endurance does not have a fair test when huge segments of a society have been shut out from the most elementary access to culture. Western Europeans, judging from their less anarchic and more conformist societies, will express shock at this state of affairs; for example, the Austrian cultural critic Wolfgang Kraus remarked in wonderment that some of our world-renowned universities are surrounded in their immediate neighborhoods by tens of thousands of functional illiterates, a condition not unlike that of the medieval university (*Die stillen Revolutionäre*: *Umrisse einer Gesellschaft von morgen* [Vienna: Fritz Molden, 1970]), pp.68–70. This gap of centuries in our society is indeed shameful beyond bearing. But European societies, though less spectacular in this regard, often seem, despite their large apparatuses of publicly supported culture, to be generally undereducated. One can sometimes be surprised by how little an ordinary European seems to know about anything outside the purview of his immediate life. I remember a sardonic Swiss television program on the myth of Wilhelm Tell in which it appeared from random street interviews that hardly anyone could tell who or what Friedrich Schiller was.

role as the apostle of the deprived to the gentiles, asserts that "force-feeding people on a rich diet of Western masterpieces will only make them more sick."[17] Many German scholars, oppressed as they are by the special rigidity of the canonical values of their past, are trying to make us read alternative writers on the ground of oppositional ideology or reception history; but most of the *poetae minores* and propagandists brought to light in recent years seem to my unregenerate bourgeois sensibility excruciatingly boring. But Kampf touches on a sore point, though perhaps not entirely from the right angle, when he says that "literature seems barely to survive outside of schools."[18] That endurance of literary works is not an automatic process, that historically it is bounded in the past and perhaps in the future, seem to be facts with which we must contend. From a pedagogical point of view, it can be argued that the resistance of the underprivileged to learning the literary code is due to its incapacity to communicate beyond its class determinants and that literary experience ought to be nourished in that sort of writing that minorities or working-class people find inviting and accessible, even if in aesthetic terms it is discriminated against as subliterary.[19] On the other hand, we may ask ourselves also whether the continuing value some of us believe we are aware of in literature of the past is entirely delusory or class-determined and whether literary criticism is not under an obligation to keep this value intact and alive.

Part of the fascination of pursuing almost any problem in literary criticism is that someone can always be found who denies its existence or legitimacy altogether. So it is with value, with intentionality, with the form-content relationship, with literary sociology generally, and so it is also with endurance. For it seems to some literary sociologists, empiricists especially, that there is no such thing as endurance over an indefinitely long term, that literary works fade in their significance as social change progresses, and an important corollary to this view is that the preservation of literature in literary history and literary education is purely antiquarian and of no living relevance. Robert Escarpit, though, as we shall see, not yet prepared to deny endurance altogether, has developed studies that point the way to that result. Escarpit has observed that people of any given time generally know about as many contemporary books as books of the past, which suggests a continuous recession of literary works in the cultural memory into oblivion. He has computed that, within one year, ninety per cent of the new books on the market have become unsaleable, and, in the course of time, another ninety per cent of the remainder disappear: "If we count the names of all the

writers retained by the historical memory of a given nation—that is, the
writers mentioned in the histories of literature, the encyclopedias, the
school or university curricula, the academic theses, the erudite articles
published in specialized reviews, the papers read in symposia and con-
gresses—we find that they represent about 1 per cent of the number who
actually wrote and published literary books."[20] Escarpit argues that it is
always the upper or ruling class that shapes literary opinion; all literature
not conforming to this opinion is regarded as subliterature until a
change in the opinion-making class brings a change in standards. The
endurance of literature is therefore tied to the endurance of a group,
class, or nation; Molière continues to survive because his culture continues to have something in common with ours and his satire remains
socially relevant; when this ceases to be the case, Molière will die.[21] One
might ask here how it is, then, that all of Molière's contemporaries do not
survive along with him with the same force. Escarpit appears to me to
have difficulty with this kind of question. In a footnote he says that his
empirical argument has nothing to do with the inner or historical value
of the work,[22] which has the surprising effect of severing endurance
from value. But he does not mean quite to do this, either, as we shall see a
little later on. Despite these modifications, the main thrust of his argument is a denial of indefinite endurance.

Indeed, as one pursues the factual side of the matter, as did Karl Erik
Rosengren in his *Sociological Aspects of the Literary System*, it begins to look
rather more bleak. The implications of this remarkable book have not
yet been sufficiently pondered. Although Rosengren presents his work
as a technical investigation in sociology, it is, in fact, an inquiry into the
cultural memory of literature. His ingenious method was to take reviews
of new books and count the mentions in them of authors other than the
one under review. In other words, it is an investigation of the consciousness of past literature in the minds of a literate although non-academic
segment of the population. Rosengren's study is technically complicated
and cannot be treated in adequate detail here, but what he found was
this: "the mentions tend to concern writers that are some 60 or 70 years
old, that is, in most cases, they are the writers who were leading the
development some 30 or 40 years ago. . . . The reviewers, who might
choose among writers for a huge time period, some 3000 or 4000 years,
prefer to move within a span of some 50 or 60 years." Moreover, this
result was the same for reviews taken from two widely different periods:
the 1880s and the 1950s and 1960s. Rosengren concludes from his
analysis of the data that all classics, ancient and modern, "are less and less

remembered. . . . At last they will be dropped for good into that base-
ment storey of the literary system inhabited by the historians of literature."[23] The process described by Escarpit has a vanishing point; all
authors eventually die. We scholars, meanwhile, are mouldering in the
cellar, vainly attempting to breathe life into our quaint and curious
volumes of forgotten lore.

Objections can easily be raised to Rosengren's results. One critic of his
book complained that a study of reviewers was distortive because they
would have a natural bias for the moderns.[24] Presumably a reviewer
confronted with a new work of Ibsen would not normally think of
adducing Horace or Chaucer for comparison. But there is something to
be said for the selection of book reviewers as representatives of the most
cultivated and literarily sensitive non-academic part of the population
that one is likely to find apart from writers themselves, despite the bad
reputation reviewers have in academic theory.[25] A more serious theoretical difficulty turned up by these studies is the evident time lag between
modern literary life and public consciousness. In Rosengren's study, it is
not the most contemporary authors who primarily come to mind, but
those of the preceding couple of generations whose success has meanwhile been canonized (by whom?). Escarpit, who made a study of the
authors that a batch of army recruits—a random social distribution—
were able to name, found that regardless of class or educational status
of the respondent, almost no current, avant-garde writers were mentioned and the youngest author named by any of the nearly five
thousand recruits was forty-six years old![26] This result—which, incidentally, does not seriously conflict with our common-sense expectations,
and which corresponds to other studies suggesting that books thirty to
sixty years old have the strongest fame in the present[27] —is very disturb-
ing to any literary-sociological view that would see literature and its social
environment as a synchronic totality. As Hans Robert Jauss has said, the
sociological insistence on the congruence of a work with reader expectations "always puts literary sociology in an embarrassing position
whenever it wants to explain later or continuing effects."[28] One might
argue that writers are a more advanced segment of the culture, more in
turn with the future; but what happens then to the argument that
literature is the expression of a ruling and, at present, dying class?

In general, however, these results of empirical literary sociology present a significant challenge to the contemporary literary enterprise and
particularly to its status in education. One fact that empirical studies
constantly underline is the relatively peripheral importance of any litera-

ture in our society. Rosengren, in another essay, determined that not even students specializing in literature read poetry voluntarily,[29] a result that has not surprised any of my colleagues to whom I have mentioned it. Of Escarpit's 4,716 recruits, three-fifths could not name five authors they had heard of, and 986 named none. Nor can one be very optimistic about the extent to which the authors that were named represent a living experience. The most commonly named was Hugo; he and six others accounted for half the mentions: La Fontaine, Dumas père, Molière, Daudet, Voltaire, and Saint-Exupéry; these were followed by Racine and Lamartine.[30] Except for Dumas and possibly Saint-Exupéry, the list smells of school curriculum, and Escarpit shows how closely the choices correlate to the sharply angled French educational pyramid; the results for those with higher education differ considerably from the overall results in favor of more modern literature and higher quality.[31] The striking absence at the top of the total list of any foreign writer, or any writer at all whom we would number among the greats of modern literature, looks as if it reflects a combination of nationalism and antiquarianism in literary pedagogy. By recruits with only primary-school education, the names of authors were often misspelled, suggesting a hearsay acquaintance, and Flaubert's astonishing location in sixty-seventh place may be due, as Escarpit depressingly speculates, to the fact that no film was ever made of any of his works.[32] All in all these results, which for the most part only codify what we already know, but often suppress, create difficulties for any view of the permanent endurance of literature or of any natural importance accruing to it that is itself proportional to the gigantic enterprise of literary education in schools and universities. Even the extensive claims made for the importance of literature by speculative literary sociologists and Marxists look a little queer in this light.

Thus Geoffrey Hartman's question—"How do we ground art in history without denying its autonomy, its aristocratic resistance to the tooth of time?"[33] —may not be correctly put. For it appears that the resistance to the tooth of time is not as inherent in the work of art as we thought, that it is not a process of natural momentum, but a result of something we do; it is an action within civilization, and it involves choices. If the will to remember should collapse, then no aesthetic force could keep appreciation of the literary past intact, except as an even more peripheral and eccentric pastime than it is at present. The argument from antiquity, that it is "not likely that what has been long and widely esteemed should be worthless," is as old as Sir Philip Sidney,[34] but it begs too many questions as to how long and continuous this esteem has actually been and by whom the works have been esteemed. The argument from antiquity is circular, and endurance is only an index of value that is an aid to judgment.[35] There is a probability that value will be found in enduring works if we are interested in that kind of value, but the process of evaluation must be taken in hand ever anew and cannot be made to rely upon the fact of the canon. It implies further that our motives and purposes in rediscovering the qualities of endurance must be reexamined, especially at a time when there is not only passive but articulate resistance against such rediscovery. Since we are talking here about involving groups in an intersubjective experience, a sociological aspect to the problem is impossible to evade.

From this point of view, it is curious that some literary sociologists themselves are willing to allow the argument from antiquity to stand. Laurenson and Swingewood solve Goldmann's problem in this regard by stating flatly that, in choosing the great writers to discuss, our criterion is "persistence, that great literature *survives*,"[36] but this is precisely what remains unproved. It is especially startling to find a version of this argument in Escarpit himself, who has done so much to undermine the foundations of endurance. Escarpit's statistics, unlike Rosengren's, do not lead to the vanishing point, but leave a residue intact somewhere in the cultural memory, if only in literary history and pedagogy. He contends that a writer whose work survives his death by ten, twenty, or thirty years will make this canon; he does not, as Rosengren does, see a continuing deterioration in enduring status. (Rosengren, on the other hand, cannot explain any more than Escarpit why some authors endure longer than others, even if only a couple of generations.) Escarpit goes so far as to say that endurance *is* the characteristic that distinguishes the literary work from other kinds of utterances. His instrument for relieving the apparent contradiction between endurance and the determination of literature by a ruling class is his often reiterated concept of "creative treason." It is only through a kind of meaningful violation of a work's intentionality that it can be appreciated in a society for which it was not meant.[37]* But the concept of creative treason threatens to sever

*Escarpit implies that literature deriving from differing social environments is in some sense incomprehensible. A version of this view has now emerged in a much noted East German compendium, Manfred Naumann, et al., *Gesellschaft, Literatur, Lesen: Literaturrezeption in theoretischer Sicht* (Berlin: Aufbau-Verlag, 1975), pp.313–314. Diana Spearman, in her critique of sociological criticism, asks: "If literature is tied to a particular social setting, how is it that no literature which is incomprehensible has been found?" (*The Novel and Society* [London: Routledge and Kegan Paul, 1966], p.5). This stand-off shows the ease with which incompletely argued issues can be raised in these matters. Escarpit fails to consider

present apprehension of a work from its historical and objective intentionality and meaning, raising the hermeneutic problems that E. D.
Hirsch has been tirelessly pointing out. Murray Krieger has elaborated
on the fairly obvious difficulty that a theory that sees a work's existence
only in the reconstituting subjective consciousness of the reader or critic
will tend to result in making all apprehended works to some degree
alike; Georges Poulet, according to Krieger, makes Balzac appear to be
the same sort of writer as Mallarmé, an effect that practical criticism
should surely want to avoid.[38] Furthermore, Escarpit keeps circling
around the possibility that endurance may, after all, be an inherent
quality. He raises the question "whether the likelihood of being betrayed
is due to some specific quality of the work and not the audience. Such a
surmise is quite plausible and points to one of the ways in which the
sociology of literature might help to found a system of literary values."[39]
But the empiricist suggestions he makes in this regard are not wholly
convincing, and it seems as though here, as elsewhere, he is giving
ground to aesthetic criticism. How else shall we account for his statement
that, for connoisseurs, "there is no aging or dying of a work"?[40] If,
ideally, education or, for that matter, the abolition of alienation, could
make all people into "connoisseurs," would that not bring us back to
where we were on the question before the sociological inquiry began?

Jauss's reception theory is related to Escarpit's stress on readers and to
the concept of creative treason, but he shifts the stress. His assertion is
not that there must be some quality in the work that accounts for its
endurance in changed social circumstances, but that "it can continue to
have an effect only if future generations still respond to it or rediscover
it—if there are readers who take up the work of the past again or authors
who want to imitate, outdo, or refute it."[41] In other words, it is the fact of
endurance that is the empirical given; from it derives, as it were, the
continuing existence of the work. Yet, from Jauss's hermeneutic position, something in the work must impel the process of changing horizons
of receptivity, and his criteria on this point sometimes seem like a
complicated way of talking about novelty or originality. How long many
people will continue to believe with enthusiasm that reception theory can
help us out of the impasse of literary studies is hard to say; it is a difficult

how far education can create access to otherwise alien literatures. His argument, like the
stronger East German one, suffers from what I am inclined to call the "fallacy of immedi-
acy," which not only assumes the competence of any reader whatsoever, but implies that this
is the only competence that is possible or useful for literary-sociological consideration.
Spearman is much too insouciant about the immediate accessibility of any literature, as the
whole history of criticism sufficiently shows.

and problematic matter. It has the virtue of sharpening our concern for the reader's reconstitution of the literary work as a fact of the literary phenomenon, and can expand our sense of the resonance of texts. Literary history from the point of view of reception often will look very different from canonical literary history and contains the potential for exploding certain myths about the true communal significance of revered cultural monuments. It serves to remind us that there can be a kind of subterranean endurance of which literary criticism has taken little notice until recently. A good example is Gustav Freytag's classic bourgeois-nationalist novel, *Debit and Credit*, an international best seller after its appearance in 1855, which has maintained a continuous respectable sale down to our own time, long after literary criticism had ceased to take any notice of it.[42] There are many examples like this—one might think of the surprisingly vast community of *Gone With the Wind* buffs—and reviving attention to them is as useful to recovering the rationality of literary studies as the sobering results of studies of the vicissitudes and limitations of the true cultural significance of Goethe and Schiller.[43]

But reception theory, insofar as it has an empirical aspect and is not restricted to a hermeneutic examination of textual potentiality, encounters difficulties, some of which appear to be insuperable. The most serious is probably that, despite its ambitions to a scientific study of literature, even in its recent, highly sophisticated semiotic variant (which also tends to cause the original text to vanish),[44] it is bound to be in some degree accidental. There is no way of recovering the experience of a total readership, and the older or more significant a work is, the less this ideal can be approached. Only if we believe in a highly conformist coherence of social groups can we make safe extrapolations from the material we can recover. Publication and sales figures are helpful, but they not only become harder to estimate as we go farther back in time; they can also be misleading about actual readership. Certain kinds of books, especially those of an oppositional character written under oppressive circumstances, may have a much larger readership than publication figures indicate. On the other hand, if one were to judge from the publication and sale of editions, one might conclude that Goethe is one of the most popular authors of the last hundred years, but other evidence indicates that this is far from true. The Bible, of course, is the perennial best seller of our culture, yet today it is hard to find a university student who can tell Elijah from Ezekiel. Reception history is almost totally dependent upon written records: memoirs, essays, critical studies, publishers' recollections, anthologies and school texts, but, more than any of these, upon book reviewing and journalistic response. The purpose expressed by Norbert Oellers in his study of Schiller's immediately posthumous reputation of examining *everything* pertinent of this nature[45] is a somewhat alarming prospect for the scholarly life and, in any case, can only be achieved relatively. There is much of interest to be learned from such studies, but they cannot yield a sociologically exhaustive picture of reception. Not only is the documentation restricted to an especially literate and articulate subclass; even in the educated class a vast amount of reception goes undocumented. All of us have "received"—that is, consumed, thought about, responded to, and judged—many books in our lives of which we leave no record other than perhaps a purchase or borrowing statistic. There is also a constantly reiterated prejudice, especially among literary sociologists, that journalistic book reviewers are wholly group-conformist and only express for the common reader what he will think of the book, a principle that apparently permits large-scale sociological extrapolation from book reviewing and journalistic discussion. But, while there may be some truth to this in certain kinds of historical and social situations and in certain kinds of publications, I know of no evidence that has ever been adduced for it as a general principle and it seems to run counter to much experience. Where reception theory turns to the response to literary works found in other literary works, it encounters another objection: when one penetrates the difficult terminology with which these studies are sometimes encumbered, one usually finds a familiar old friend—influence. Literary influence is a respectable topic, but all the old objections against it reemerge when it is pursued, under the guise of reception theory, without any differentiated sense of literary structure, technique, or imagination. Furthermore, reception history cannot wholly silence the voice of criticism. Unless we believe that the literary work has its *only* existence in the totality of various reader reconstitutions, reception history is likely to appear as a chronicle of misreadings and misunderstandings that yield an argument for rather than against criticism more precisely focused on the details of the work. I am persuaded that there is such a thing as critical competence, but it is to be found only in a readership that has been educated to it.*

* An important contribution to this question within the terms of communicaton theory is the essay by Hannelore Link, "'Die Appellstruktur der Texte' und ein 'Paradigmawechsel in der Literaturwissenschaft'?" *Jahrbuch der deutschen Schillergesellschaft* 17 (1973):532–583, in which she builds upon and criticizes Wolfgang Iser's views on the indeterminancy of texts, a theoretical position related in kind to Escarpit's concept of "creative treason." In brief, her thesis reads: "Texts are readable as long as a certain degree of determinacy is preserved.

For these reasons, it appears to me that reception study cannot carry as much of the burden of literary scholarship as some people at present hope. It is, however, a very useful if extremely laborious endeavor, and it seems especially promising for a renovation of literary history. It contributes much information to the question of endurance and, like empirical literary sociology, will make us less certain that we know what we are talking about when we speak of timeless or enduring works. It also raises the question of whether the process of canonization is not excessively destructive of the total literary heritage. There is a limit to the amount of literature a culture can keep in view, and the severe process of selection described by Escarpit is natural enough, as is the not necessarily parallel formation of a selective critical canon, for we cannot, after all, read everything, and there is a natural tendency, which is no different in Lukács than in the traditionally-minded world literature experts in our English departments, to live only with acknowledged masterpieces. But scholarship, if it is to serve civilization, is often obliged to leave the path of what occurs naturally.

Marxists, as one would expect, relate endurance to their philosophy of history. Bloch's utopian principle of hope makes this especially easy to do; for him works survive simply owing to the latent futurity they contain. But one wonders whether this is a discovery made by Bloch from work to work, or whether it is not a rather complacent way of accepting the received culture. He seems, for a Marxist, to make a rather cavalier separation of social basis and the transtemporal utopian element: "The Acropolis belongs, to be sure, to a slave-holding society, the Strassburg Cathedral to a feudal society; nevertheless, as is well known, they have not perished with their basis and carry . . . nothing lamentable with them."[46] I find this total acceptance of art insufficiently critical and would be inclined to disturb it with Benjamin's more somber view that

---

This occurs especially for historical texts, by continuities of tradition of an objective or reception-technical [a hard word for the learning or educational process] kind. Such continuities can, in certain circumstances, be replaced by an independent but analogous cultural custom. Continuities or parallels are the more probable, the richer and more complex the work in question is. They can be entirely lacking, when the texts are insufficiently complex or too decisively fixed upon a narrow historical context" (p.559). The meaning of the work is not wholly open to historical relativity, for the work itself has to be the measure of concretions of it and our judgment on them. The intentionality of a text is not in the reader, but in the text (and, by extension, in the author). Indeterminacy can be an intended strategy of an author to awaken the reader's imagination, but this is a characteristic of Romantic and some modern literature. It appears to me that it is only from such a position that one can speak at all of misapprehensions of a text and retain the integrity of interpretation.

"there is no document of civilization which is not at the same time a document of barbarism."[47] It is curious how Bloch, like Lukács, continues to hold fast to traditional German values (the Strassburg Cathedral will seem curiously paired with the Acropolis here unless the reader happens to know that it was a significant experience in Goethe's youthful aesthetic development). Nowhere is Lukács' Classicism more evident than in his insistence upon a category of the generally or universally human, which, though qualified through history by alienation and the division of labor, preserves itself in aesthetic form for the day when Communism will have achieved the unified humane society.[48] The younger contemporary Marxist may see the link with the past in a more negative light. Since the present is a realization of history, transtemporality is a reality; nature is not yet overcome, nor is man's past, for there is still oppression as there was in the past.[49] But if this argument is part of a general revolutionary hope, as it appears to be, it suggests that endurance is only temporary; that once the atavisms of man are truly overcome, art will cease having an enduring significance or will serve at best for the gratifying contemplation of conditions that cannot reoccur. More genuinely Marxian is Robert Weimann's expectation that only in the classless society will truly aesthetic reception be generally possible. Thus it would seem that the classless and unalienated society would at last create the possibility for Kant's disinterested contemplation, which is only misleading and reprehensible in a bourgeois context. But, despite these fancies, which contrast so bitterly with the actual political effect Marxism has had on cultural life, Weimann is seriously concerned to maintain a viable hermeneutic link between past and present, and he argues persuasively against both antiquarianism and that kind of frantic struggle for the up-to-date that can treat past works only as parody or travesty. In this sense we may, I think, accept his formulation that we examine great works of the past in the light of present consciousness that these works have helped to produce. Weimann grudgingly admires Eliot's effort to keep the "timeless" and the "temporal" in view at the same time, and he makes perception into the historical situation the criterion of truth and therefore, presumably, of endurance: "In view of the fictional nature of aesthetic structures, the criterion of truth is not the agreement of fictional events with reality, but the historical veracity of artistic feeling and perception."[50] This veracity, however, is only assessable by means of Marxist "science," which can lead to the view that the discoveries of the imagination exercise the same kind of fascination upon us as the discoveries of natural science.[51]

It appears to me that this line of argument, although it has the virtue of stressing historicity, does not *explain* endurance, sociologically or in any other way, but sets up a new criterion for it. With a few radical exceptions—those who would have us read Georg Weerth instead of Mörike or Jack London instead of Faulkner—literary sociologists and Marxists do not normally attack the canon or demand radical revisions of it. They appear, on the whole, to accept endurance, although of course without idle talk about timelessness or eternity. Except for the occasional iconoclast, they seem to share the willingness of educated people since the beginning of Romanticism to believe that works of the past arising out of widely differing circumstances can have an enduring value for us; this is true even of Escarpit. Therefore it is the fact of endurance that requires an explanation. It is evident that it cannot be found in the global identity of a work of art with the social group that brought it forth. That literature preserves insights into historical truths or human discoveries that are still critical in our present lives seems unconvincing to me and leads either to a drift into defenses of poesy that operate with concepts of the timelessness of human nature, to a dubious and opportunist hucksterism sometimes encountered in the teaching of literature in the name of relevance, or to the kind of process regularly encountered in contemporary German literary studies of trying to turn writers of the past into companionable patron saints for present action, which inevitably cripples the possiblity of criticism at all.

Rather, it seems to me that enduring works of literature exhibit a critical resistance to determinants within a historical situation, offer alternatives (which may be utopian, but may only be a matter of taking the ideals that purportedly govern society more explicitly than they are regarded in reality), and measure reality against a more complex vision of the authentic potentialities in it.[52] Enduring literature is inside history and inside society, but works across the grain of convention, so that as critics we are obliged to have a historical and sociological awareness of the grain, but as evaluators we participate in the victory over what otherwise comes to be ossified as unalterable. The recognition and appreciation of the creation of alternatives does not in any way oblige us to associate ourselves with them in present judgment or to believe that they must conform to our present evaluation of what ought to constitute a progressive alternative. Much dubious, foreshortened judgment in contemporary oppositional criticism would be avoided if this principle could be accepted. It would also help to meet, without submitting to it, the rationally uncontrollable utopian element in contemporary neo-

Marxism, with its tendency to see all fiction-making and myth-making as a universal movement of the imagination toward the enriched recovery of some primordial unalienated state.

Much of the difficulty in the argument about committed literature lies in the question of what one might call extroverted or introverted perspective. The issue becomes: "Which side are you on, brother?" The terms are those of a binary dialectic of allegiance and opposition. The language of radical criticism and literature is often that of solidarity— with the poor, the oppressed, the internal or external proletariat, against capitalism, imperialism, bourgeois reification, and liberal mys- tification. Once this perfectly legitimate position is taken, it follows for some that subtlety and a love of aesthetic pleasure, "a concentration on the individual and his psychology; a preference for the private as op- posed to the public, for the microscope rather than the telescope,"[53] exhibit a conservative allegiance, an evasion masking as a liberation. In other words, he who is not with me is against me. How difficult the position is to maintain emerges in practical politics, where differences and internal criticism immediately splinter a movement, generating sects and heresies; if such politics have any relation to real power, the solution can only be found in that which was initially to be transcended: the application of brute force. I would raise the question whether strong art that can continue to command our interest is not more introverted, subsisting within its own universe of allegiance (with greater or lesser self-awareness), but anatomizing it, measuring its contradictions and mendacities, exploring its strengths and inner repulsions. In all art, especially of the past, a certain willingness to accept context is demanded of the critic. Dante and Milton cannot be disposed of because they were partisans of Christian doctrine, and a sufficiently erudite Marxist analysis can accept and recognize Sophocles' social prejudices and affirmative morality while laying stress upon heightened awareness of value conflicts.[54] Even Socialist Realism discovered that monolithic parti- sanship in literature is tedious; thus emerged the theory of "non- antagonistic contradictions," not only to make plot possible, but to give narration a modicum of staying power. The canon of complexity is not a mystification of bourgeois aesthetics; rather it is involved with the ethics of creativity, contributing a subtle moral dimension that, far from being incompatible with art, feeds a lasting human hunger and therefore is indispensable to endurance.

Wolfram von Eschenbach's *Parzival* is not a reflection of feudal society or of any group in it, although Wolfram's status as a footloose knight-poet may have contributed to that dissociation from social rootedness that makes literature possible. He does not, in a historical sense, communicate new truths and hopes to be realized in the future; he is, if anything, oriented on the past. What he does is to take seriously the Christian, feudal ideology by which his world was allegedly governed but in fact was not. Against the conventional and for that reason strikingly comic hero Gawan—to whom nothing can happen, apart from a cycle of adventures, because he is already the perfect (socially conditioned) knight—he sets Parzival, who must begin outside society and internalize for himself the fundamental ideal governing principle of that society, which is not heroism but compassion. What constitutes the enduring quality of *Parzival*, in my view, is not that it embodies the value of compassion, but that it brings this value to bear against clichés—including Parzival's own amusing tendency to transform principles into formulaic clichés—with such imaginative intensity that, far from accepting a social situation, we begin to rethink it from the ground up.* Similarly, the *Nibelungenlied* is gripping, despite occasional *longueurs*, not because it mirrors a social structure or a conception of it, but because it relates what happens when the acknowledged linchpin of that society, the authority of the king, breaks through a failure of character and intelligence. Not the fabled monumentality of the medieval structure, but a fantastic display of its fragility is the source of the gradually mounting excitement and terror in the poem. Modern novelists of stature who derive from an unambiguously upper-class background rarely reproduce unmediatedly the ethos of that class; they are much more likely to put it to the question in a more or less inquisitorial manner, to exploit the artistic virtue of disloyalty, as Graham Greene has put it.[55]

This kind of probe of the imagination into the possibilities of reality need not always be a negative or revolutionary process, for it often only militates against the clichés that have separated us from our own values. Most of us know and believe that there is a joy and pride of parenthood in the progress of a child, and in our culture there are many commonplace representations of it, but it takes Picasso to get us down on the floor with the baby taking his first steps and make us feel the exuberant

---

*According to Hugo Kuhn, even Chrétien de Troyes "acquires the impulsion, form, and doctrine of his poetry directly out of the criticism of this courtly society," and courtly literature is "the effort critically to secure society through a new metaphysical reinsurance," which is, of course, quite a different thing from an affirmative or purely reflective literature (Kuhn, "Dichtungswissenschaft und Soziologie," *Methodenfragen der deutschen Literaturwissenschaft*, ed. Reinhold Grimm and Jost Hermand [Darmstadt: Wissenschaftliche Buchgesellschaft, 1973], esp. pp. 457–459).

daring of this triumph in the framework of the mother's overarching power that is protective and liberating at the same time. We do not revere Shakespeare's histories for what they tell us about the kings of England, for we know more about them than he did. Nor do we, or should we, admire them for what they tell us about "kingship," for there is no kingship of this kind that is of any interest or importance to us any more—which is not to say that we cannot grasp to some degree its meaning for the context of the plays. Rather, we see an imagination, operating within a certain socially determined understanding and a certain political allegiance and intentionality, probing the implications one after another and demonstrating at the highest intensity the stress of social givens and human judgment. The task of literary sociology would seem to be to put what Shakespeare cared about and what we care about into a relation that is centered upon a common, emancipatory, flexible, and fluid freedom of the imagination.*

I am trying to find a language here that incorporates some part of the insights we know under the headings of "the negation of the negation" and "the Great Refusal" while myself refusing the tactics of insurgency often associated with these concepts, as well as their tendency to dissolve the differentiated levels and functions of art and literature into a single socio-psychological category of the human condition. Nevertheless, I am aware that my argument here pertains primarily to the mechanism of endurance as it operates among those with an educated experience in literature. Helmut Kreuzer has observed wisely that there can be differing reasons for endurance: "Intellectual complexity, inner tensions, ambivalence—according to Boas and Wellek—can be factors when a work is taken up across several epochs under ever new aspects. The long success of other authors seems to derive from, among other things, their capacity completely to renew and to individualize elementary models of

---

*I should think that this position need not be incompatible with a liberated Marxist criticism; one current American practitioner, Donald Wesling, in an interesting exercise, "The Dialectical Criticism of Poetry: An Instance from Keats," *Mosaic* 5, No. 2 (Winter, 1971/72):92, remarks: "Works of art are charged with significance not because they take sides, but because they are manifest contradictions—dialectical conflicts between opposing social forces." A more finely tuned formulation is given by Stefan Morawski, *Inquiries into the Fundamentals of Aesthetics* (Cambridge, Mass.: MIT Press, 1974), p.311: aesthetic experience "is contemplative and yet opposed to inertia, to that mode of apprehending rote response which deadens us to the rhythm of life and to persons and things as they authentically are. The aesthetic response would be impossible if it were not linked to our entrenched scheme of familiar perceptions. However, its effect is to freshen, to vivify our encounters with the world." In this argument Morawski has the considerable advantage, rare among Continental Marxists, of respectful cognizance of John Dewey.

narration, 'archetypal' motifs, and forms of apprehension."[56] The two possibilities appear to be parallel to the Prague structuralist Jan Muka-řovský's distinction between the "non-normed aesthetic," characterized by originality, unexpectedness, liberation from conventional language use, and the "normed aesthetic" that includes the tendency to generality, system, and perfection characteristic of both Classicism and folk art.[57] Doubtless there are more than these two possibilities. Jauss, in endeavoring to schematize the possibilities of aesthetic identification with the hero on the reader's part, distinguishes five modes: associative, admiring, sympathetic, cathartic, and ironic.[58] If my own suggestions here tend to a preference for the ironic, it appears to me the most mature response, one that admits an allegiance to the level of conscious literary experience that the accumulated tradition of criticism has reached. Without taking over the whole theology of negativity, I would accept Adorno's (by no means original) view that art is "a force of protest of the humane against the pressure of domineering institutions, religious and others, no less than it reflects their objective substance."[59]

Almost all who have wrestled seriously with critical problems in modern times have come to the conclusion that "the artistic structure as an objective phenomenon can develop more energies than the author believed were in it."[60] Yet it is hard to disengage oneself from the belief that the potential for this expansion of energies is located in the text without falling into mystical manipulation. The critic with some respect for rationality must believe that he is discovering and not inventing. Enduring texts have often been felt to be those that yield discovery and rediscovery continuously. Perhaps this is so, and it is perhaps the reason why those texts that have maintained themselves in the canon are often presented as the most profitable for sociological or Marxist analysis as well. If endurance is a fact, literary sociology and Marxism have not, as yet, been very successful in accounting for it without recourse to a philosophy of history that is itself hypothetical at best. The empiricist denial of endurance has the defect that it describes only a natural course of events, not one that can be made subject to intellectual governance. It is fair to ask whether civilization ought to accept the automatic displacement of one set of values by another, whether it should not rather be expansive and cumulative and in that sense conserving, if not conservative. For surely the profound experience that has led to the assumption of endurance is also an empirical fact.

But if literary sociology cannot satisfactorily account for endurance, it can make us healthily skeptical of what we mean when we talk about it. It works sharply against the process of complacent antiquarianism that inhibits the relevance of our activity and leaves us talking to one another, convinced of our unexamined values and grouchily wondering why hardly anyone will listen to us. It teaches us that literary works do not speak by themselves, but require from us as individuals and as social beings a continuing dialogue. It turns our attention to the question of how a canon is made, on what its claim to permanence is based, and whether it does not impoverish the benefits we might have from a less exclusive literary history. It raises the question of the audience of past and present literature, and this leads to the further question of by whom and for whom the canon is made. This last question is of the greatest importance for practical criticism and literary education, and we shall inspect it in the following essay.

VI
Elitism

NEAR THE beginning of the renovation of literary criticism in our century stood the hope that access to literature could be democratized. The notion that literature is a special possession of those with an instinctive sensibility was to be combatted by methods of interpretation that, at the outset, were rational and therefore learnable. Literary criticism was to be, if not necessarily a *Wissenschaft*, at least a subject of study that could be mastered to a point that would allow an educated person a non-naive apprehension of any literary work that might capture his interest. Although the New Criticism began in large measure with poets and other intellectuals impatient with traditional academic treatments of literature, I. A. Richards placed profound hopes in education as a means for civilizing mankind, and the education he had in mind was primarily one in language and literature. Out of these beginnings grew what now may be the vastest single educational enterprise in the history of man: the gigantic business of the teaching and study of literature in Western educational institutions and, at least until recently, its enormous hold upon the center of the curriculum.

The failure of these original hopes for a close interrelationship between literary study and the development of a democratic civilization is now coming to be generally recognized. The reasons, as I see them, are several. In the first place, we have not succeeded in educating the populations of our modern nations. This failure is especially bitter in the United States, which has undertaken the greatest effort at mass education in human history. Yet, at election time, analysts speak of those who "study the issues" as though they were a peripheral group of eccentrics like moon-worshippers or rutabaga farmers. The question of the permissibility of teaching evolution crops up in state after state, and even educational officials campaign against it. The local film censorship junta in West Nyack, New York, was recently headed by a blind man, a North Dakota school board organized a book-burning, and a very President of the United States hobnobbed with an evangelist of old-time religion. In West Virginia, religious enthusiasts have dynamited schools in order to shield children from contemporary writing, and in some schools there is currently a revival of the bleak nineteenth-century McGuffey Readers, a reissue of which my father presented me with when I was a boy for the sake of a good laugh. The claim of intellectual defectors that our society suffers from an excess of rationality is surely without any relation to reality.

In Europe, the effort at mass education has hardly begun. Universities, which are in any case mainly institutions for professional training, are collapsing under the weight of numbers of students that, by American standards, are not very large, while the school system still rather encourages working-class people to leave at an early age rather than stay in. We recall here Escarpit's results when asking army recruits merely to name five writers they had heard of. The Enlightenment faith in education is withering; in practice one has to fight off feelings that there is not enough natural curiosity or mental ability in the human race to sustain general education in a society of free choices, as F. R. Leavis has been insisting; or that social atavisms and class structures are still too strong to allow education to pursue a civilizing goal. The general failure to accomplish this encourages the acceptance of such phenomena as Father Ivan Illich running up the black flag of anarchy over the ancient reactionary purpose of inhibiting the enlightenment of the people.

Secondly, the original democratic impulse of modern criticism was to a large extent dissolved in the elitism of modern Western intellectuals. Literature, and poetry in particular, prided itself on being esoteric and exclusive,* and intellectual claims to special privilege rose up in resis-

---

*On this subject, see the recent essay by Haskell M. Block, "Some Concepts of the Literary Elite at the Turn of the Century," *Mosaic* 5, No. 2 (Winter 1971/72):57–64. Doubtless there has been a historical tendency for the intellectual caste generally to seek the succession to aristocratic privilege; César Graña asserts that "we must regard the demands of the modern intellectual not only as the product of aristocratic antecedents but also as an appropriation and peculiar re-creation of these antecedents" (*Fact and Symbol: Essays in the Sociology of Art and Literature* [New York: Oxford University Press, 1971], p.7). It may indeed be argued that our concept of fine arts and the doctrine of liberal education itself are part of this process. See Thomas Munro, *The Arts and Their Interrelations*, rev. ed. (Cleveland: Press of Case Western Reserve University, 1969), pp.33–48.

tance to the democratic challenge. Ortega y Gasset maintained that modern art is "antipopular" and "compels the average citizen to realize that he is just this—the average citizen, a creature incapable of receiving the sacrament of art, blind and deaf to pure beauty."[1] Along with this resistance came the wave of irrationalism among European intellectuals, an appeal to intuition, which, as H. A. Hodges has remarked in commenting on Lukács, is an "aristocratic theory of knowledge."[2] An aesthetics based upon an initial, intuitional apprehension of art implies a directness and universalism of this experience that is empirically not the case; therefore it cannot deal with the fact that the *Divine Comedy* is not a value for a Zulu, and consequently there is a silent assumption that "higher values and higher human beings belong together."[3]* Some have come to feel that the modern critic's criteria of value themselves are elitist and exclusionary; it was not a Marxist, but Wayne Booth who wrote that "ironic narration lends itself neatly, far too neatly, to disguised expression of snobbery, which would never be tolerated if expressed openly in commentary. . . . A frequent explanation of the snobbish air that sometimes results is that there is no serious audience left for art except the precious, saving remnant"[4] —an idea that Nietzsche developed nearly a century ago.[5]

The departure of Western modern literature from a stance of direct and realistic social responsibility is undoubtedly intimately connected with the critical development. Edmund Wilson, looking at the situation at its crucial point in the early 1930s, concluded that the First World War and its consequences resulted in "impoverishment and exhaustion for all the European peoples concerned, and in a general feeling of hopelessness about politics, about all attempts to organize men into social units —armies, parties, nations—in the service of some common ideal, for the accomplishment of some particular purpose," with the result that "the Western mind became peculiarly hospitable to a literature indifferent to action and unconcerned with the group." It seemed therefore that the poets who had avoided such allegiances "had maintained an unassailable integrity."[6] From the present perspective, this appears as an acute and important observation; but it also suggests a historically local situation of

---

* In this, as in other matters, one wonders whether literature is more bound to a specific culture than the visual arts. Vytautas Kavolis summarizes: "Recent cross-cultural work has suggested that universal standards of aesthetic quality are adhered to—at least by artistically sensitized persons—in societies as diverse as those of the Fiji Islands, Greece, Japan, the United States, and the BaKwele" (*Artistic Expression: A Sociological Analysis* [Ithaca: Cornell University Press, 1968], pp.2–3; references p.211). I should imagine a similar claim for literature would be most difficult to establish and maintain.

literary reaction, and should encourage us now, after forty more years of experience, to ask if it is right to maintain indefinitely the ideological hold of Yeats and Eliot, of aestheticism and symbolism, over the practice of literary criticism.

A third consideration is graver and more fundamental to the questions of literary sociology. The close relationship of culture with class division makes it appear that all traditional culture is elitist; which accounts, it would seem, for the increased difficulty in maintaining cultural institutions the more democratic a society is. The sociologist T. B. Bottomore thinks it would be a natural consequence of a truly egalitarian society "that the conservation of culture, which is bound up inextricably in present-day societies with the maintenance of class privileges, would be less strongly emphasized—or at least change its aspect—and come to be taken much more for granted; while the power to create new forms of culture, to make new discoveries in the arts and sciences, would be more highly regarded and encouraged."[7] The latter part of this hypothesis is Marxist-inspired and it is hard to judge because it is suppositious. One can only observe at present that in those societies that are the most democratic, much modern art is unpopular and esoteric, perhaps, from a Marxist viewpoint, due to the division of labor or the heightened sense of alienation to which the bourgeois writer is especially sensitive but to which he can see no solution.* But that a truly egalitarian society might become hostile to new creative forms and extremely repressive and restrictive in its cultural symbols seems an equally plausible supposition, especially as sociological research suggests that, while cultural participation may be class determined, appreciation and evaluation are relatively homogeneous across class boundaries.[8] The very word "Classical" is, etymologically and historically, a concept of class distinction.[9] If high culture is a creation or expression of superseded ruling classes, then its conservation may appear to be a form of conservatism; and, in a time of high political passion, such as we have been experiencing, claims made by or on behalf of new and wider groups may require a repudiation of

---

*The relationship between literary quality and popularity no doubt differs in different national traditions. A recent student of German popular literature has observed that, historically, German *Dichtung* "exhibits only in exceptional cases popular success similar to that of English and French" quality literature (Albert Klein, *Die Krise des Unterhaltungsromans im 19. Jahrhundert: Ein Beitrag zur Theorie und Geschichte der ästhetisch geringwertigen Literatur* [Bonn: Bouvier, 1969], p.3). An interesting comparative inquiry might be mounted on this point. I doubt that it applies to West Germany today. It might be added that the more rigid caste system in literary evaluation in the German past accounts for much of the special vigor of the attack on elitism in contemporary *Germanistik*.

any such conservation at all, just as the utilitarian Benthamites attacked literature itself on the grounds of social privilege in the early nineteenth century.[10]

The creation and study of indigenous cultural expressions is demanded in place of the transmission of those that have become irrelevant. This has happened in whole societies, in the past ordinarily as a natural process, in the present more often as conscious policy, and it becomes a hot issue in the civil strife besetting our own society. Who actually cares about the literary canon? Richards' confidence in its implicit universal value was strong enough that he thought a generalized education in criticism a goal worth pursuing, but perhaps he was mistaken in this. Perhaps the canon is so much the possession of a protected, historically determined class that new generations cannot be broadly led to it except under duress or by means of a violent up-dating of the meaning of texts in order to forge an immediate link with present concerns—and even the latter effort may be a disingenuous way of protecting traditionalist canons. On the other hand, do not both the persistence and the conservatism of popular culture at any time suggest—insofar as they are not put into connection with a dying class—that there is a contrasting, irreducible component of deviant excellence in progressive and innovative achievements that is not wholly explicable by a socio-historical scheme? It is always necessary to distinguish between two separate though connected senses of elitism, one referring to an art wholly accommodated to a ruling class and imposed upon society as a whole, and the other to art as deviance from the inertial norms of society as a whole and therefore repudiated by it on the grounds of elitism, a tack commonly taken by bestselling writers and producers of box-office hits who have done badly with the critics. Of course there are situations when writers and readers belong homogeneously to an elite community and come into strict ideological partnership with one another, sharing their literature and intellectual skills, and collaborating in a Classicism grounded in a myth of stability, of the permanence of norms and the vision of human nature of this class. Sartre has written eloquent pages about this condition in seventeenth-century France.[11] The Augustan Age in England is doubtless another such episode.

The question of whether the exclusiveness of culture has been increasing as we approach modern times is one literary sociology might attempt to solve with more precision than it has heretofore, as it is of great importance to the practice of literary criticism. It can frequently be that assertions made about a cultural situation actually suggest that something contrary to them is the case. The eighteenth-century revolt against the ossification and insensitivity of conventional society is not a sign that society was in fact becoming more ossified and insensitive than it had been in the past, even though Rousseau or Schiller or the German Romantics might have believed this; it is rather a sign that a new humane sensitivity (I leave aside the question of its relationship to changes in the modes of production) is developing more rapidly than changes in social convention can accommodate; what is new is not the rigidity of convention, but the emancipated self-awareness. Similar cases are Marcuse's claims that modern Western man is living in the least free and most oppressive of all possible societies, or McLuhan's contention that the printed word is dying out; both apparently believed by a surprising number of people in the face of massive evidence to the contrary. Arguments of this kind must be met with alert skepticism and the greatest possible attention to actual social processes, for in their contrariness to real developments they contain the potential for reactionary allegiances.

This caution might fruitfully be kept in mind when considering whether the segregation of culture was less pronounced at some observable time in the past. It is doubtless true that in the most primitive societies culture and society are a unity, and there is often a substantial degree of primitivism detectable in those who would have us recover this communal unity. At any level that we would call civilized, such unity becomes more difficult to detect. German Classicism alleged substantial cultural unity to be true of Greece, despite her foundation on a base of slavery and the obvious internal strains pulling sharply in different directions. Such models can do little more than mythical service. The question has more literary-sociological relevance when it is directed at a more recent past. A prominent example is Q. D. Leavis' *Fiction and the Reading Public* of 1932, which is an instructive combination of the intellectual elitism of that time with nostalgia for a cultural past in which these divisions had not yet appeared. The book, although it contains a good deal of pertinent and worthwhile empirical information, is a single, long lamentation over the decline of public taste in modern times. One of the tell-tale characteristics of cultural critics of this type is a profound contempt for detective stories (more recently, science-fiction) without exhibiting much inclination to understanding the genre itself or having made any effort to form evaluative distinctions. Mrs. Leavis notes as a result of her researches "that the author of detective novels consulted receives letters chiefly from 'schoolboys, scientific men, clergymen, lawyers, and businessmen generally.' . . . The social orders named here as forming the backbone of the detective-story public are those who in the last century would have been the guardians of the public conscience in the matter of mental self-indulgence." It is, as we see, the elite itself that has gone flabby and has betrayed its obligation to impose a cultural taste on the public. The best service a novel can perform, she asserts, is to allow "the reader to live at the expense of an unusually intelligent and sensitive mind, by giving him access to a finer code than his own." In her account, the fall from grace began sometime in the eighteenth century, and it is no accident, as Marxists are fond of saying, that this is the age of the emergence of revolutionary and democratic forces. Before that, in a generally finer society, there was true community between the writer and his public, though she leaves no doubt that the one is the leader and the others the followers: in the age of Shakespeare, "the masses were receiving their amusement from above. . . . Happily they had no choice."[12]

Mrs. Leavis' influential book is throughout a curious document and could bear a more detailed analysis than would be appropriate here.[13] By making direct inquiries, she found out a number of interesting things about the way popular authors and their public relate to one another. But it is literary sociology pursued without the slightest critical skepticism toward her own ideological stance and grounded in evaluative principles that see the function of literature exclusively in the improvement of the mind and character toward affirmative, therefore rather conservative ends. She does not, for instance, ask what might account for the remarkable popularity of detective stories among intellectuals and especially academics; whether it might not have something to do with fantasies about righting wrongs in the world through lonely, individual action and mental perspicacity, and thus be a reflex of the academic intellectual's own frustrated relationship to society and especially to power. Richard Hoggart, though an admirer of Mrs. Leavis, raises a related question when he observes that "most sociological analyses of crime-and-violence series on television leave you wondering whether their authors have ever *felt* the appeal of one of them."[14] Mrs. Leavis' idea of the public, though it encompasses the whole bourgeoisie, is still exclusive, and even under the alleged conditions of community in the past it is still under the tutelage of the great writers. I doubt that a literary history that understands itself as a segment of real, general history is likely to come up with any past age of total communal harmony with the best literature. Even Mrs. Leavis' substantial examples of Shakespeare or Bunyan are not convincing in this respect; they confuse a historically growing heritage of critical perception with the more direct use value of texts in their own time. Literary criticism lives on a margin of value that is not necessarily congruent with the reasons for wide public resonance.

Still, the problem she attempted to deal with is one that must continue to concern literary sociology. The power of commercialized ideology in a democracy for confusing egalitarianism with anti-progressive and anti-intellectual flattery of common complacency is formidable, but the question of whether the modern development of literature for popular consumption is a process of debasement is one that must be pursued with some subtlety of value distinctions and a realistic sense of life in society. Mrs. Leavis' inflexible attitudes lead only to ineffectual railing at one's fellow man. That the question can be approached in a way that expands our understanding is shown by Hoggart's excellent book, *The Uses of Literacy*.[15] Because Hoggart comes from the English working class himself, he has a strong, though rather conservative, sense of the dignity and survival function of its values, as well as of the narrow horizon from which these values derive, and consequently he is able to analyze the changing nature of the literature consumed by the working class and measure it against more liberated standards of value without losing his respect for the humanity of its audience, insisting that it ought to be elevated to the seventeenth-century grocer's standards, as Mrs. Leavis does, or generating fantasies about a capitalist plot for the ideological oppression of the working class via commercialized literature. Hoggart's acute knowledge of the difference between "vulgar" and "debased" is quite beyond Mrs. Leavis' reach, and, although his critique of progressivism is overstated and tends occasionally in the Leavis direction, and he appears to me to be rather outside the working-class culture of the 1950s—not so much by reason of his own increased literacy as by a generation difference (born 1918)—his analysis is judicious and instructive and his attitude carefully self-critical. His background also protects him from the pessimism into which the sheltered upper-bourgeois theorists of the Frankfurt School eventually fell.

A student of the German development has dated the emergence of a complete distinction between elite and mass public from around 1800, when the idea of a universally educated person was already becoming impossible, and sets the completion of the process at 1848.[16] The failed revolution of 1848 is a cultural as well as historical boundary in a number of respects, but for all of this scholar's useful observations on the changes in the role of reading in family life, the historical claim is schematic and unsound. The distinction between elite and mass public is very clear in the seventeenth century, where it separates whole genres. The trivial novel, mass-produced for mass consumption, is a creation of the eighteenth century.[17] Goethe, Schiller, and the Romantics were very much conscious of being in combat with what they regarded as a recalcitrant, backward, and shallow mass taste. The literary periodicals they founded to affect this taste failed one after another. They set their teeth against the continuing Enlightenment tradition in literature and it is not altogether clear that the cause of progress was thereby best served. They invented the "Philistines," who, it turns out upon examination, were all the members of the bourgeois class or aristocracy other than themselves. Friedrich Schlegel, who thought about everything, also thought about the difference between trivial and artistic literature and concluded sensibly that the trivial author analyzes and computes his reader in order to conform to him, while the artist synthetically constructs a reader as he should be; his brother August Wilhelm Schlegel anticipated Marxist theory by distinguishing between the true artist who is ahead of his time and the writer who only reproduces a passive apprehension of the present.[18] Goethe, whose remarkable confidence and equilibrium were not infrequently shadowed by moments of doubt, brooded as he worked on *Iphigenie* that his great humanistic mystery play had to be written as though the stocking weavers in near-by Apolda were not starving.[19] Meanwhile, Wordsworth, who set out to reverse the direction of poetry away from the elite towards the common man, was by 1815 obliged by the opposition to his poems to distinguish between a fallible "public" and a universal "people,"[20] a specious distinction that still finds tendentious employment today. All this indicates that the birth of modern literature was already accompanied by the problem of cultural elitism in clear delineation. Even the plausible theory recently adverted to by W. H. Bruford that printing caused literary art to emancipate itself from society, substituting private authorship and private readership for communal story-telling,[21] seems to me not to hold up well in the light of literary history.

   There is a fairly obvious way of cutting through this whole complex of concerns, by attacking the explicit or implicit value system upon which most of this cultural criticism is based. This populist, egalitarian approach, which is adumbrated in Hoggart, has recently been given an animated defense by Herbert J. Gans.[22] This version of the opposition to elitism differs in an important respect from the radical critique. The latter, while deploring the elitism of culture as a function of class dominance, is inclined to see in it a conspiracy of deprivation; in this way the value system of high culture reasserts itself in what abstractly might be seen as a gesture of pity toward the victimized masses. Gans, however, sees the various classes *choosing* their culture and vigorously defends their right to have it without intimidation from the classes of creators and connoisseurs. He regards the terrorism of the intellectual critique of mass culture as a symptom of the decline in influence and status of the intellectual caste and a counterattack against the rise of egalitarianism. The real class difference lies in the importance assigned to culture. Gans is wholly unworried about the alleged deleterious effects of mass culture—whether they are thought of as narcotic, encouraging escapism, or of transmitting behavior roles and ideology on behalf of the dominant class—simply because he believes the mass public does not pay that much attention to cultural media, but rather uses them for entertainment and relaxation in a utilitarian manner, so that they do not create but accommodate to social values.[23] Consequently, not only is there no reason why all classes should not have their own culture without any nagging by us; it should be a principle of public policy to supply all classes with the cultural fare they like and want most.

Gans's theses have become a center of controversy, and there are a number of objections in detail and in principle that I could raise to them if it were not that such a critique would be too digressive here. Radicals would of course immediately identify Gans as an empiricist and socially affirmative "positivist" in that he appears to accept the condition of consciousness of the mass public as a tolerably true and free consciousness; he is clearly a logical kind of liberal and takes liberal democracy as a paradigm for the political evaluation of the cultural situation. Gans is aware of such objections, but he does not see the cultural level of society as an essential priority compared to the basic questions of human welfare and consequently can see little profit in a cultural criticism that denies the legitimacy of the cultures preferred by the various classes of citizens. I sympathize with Gans insofar as he resists the notion that "the vast number of Americans exposed to popular culture can be described as atomized, narcotized, brutalized, escapist, or unable to cope with reality. . . . Most people are not isolated atoms, but are members of family, peer, and social groups, and . . . , within these groups, they tend to be moral, kind, pragmatic, and sometimes remarkably altruistic."[24] I think this is absolutely right and it is important to say it in the face of the familiar radical account of the parlous state of social relations in bourgeois society, which cultural philosophy proposes to relieve. Even if Gans somewhat underestimates the aspect of deprivation in mass culture, it is my observation that the radical objection to escapism, to literature and art as entertainment and respite, is grounded in an imperative that modern man should remain unremittingly and analytically conscious of his miseries by remaining as miserable and angry as possible all the time. Could a society remain sane in such a state? Can one be certain that the upheaval that might result from such a condition would be the progressive revolution envisaged by the radical imagination?

The species of tragic literary history propagated by Q. D. Leavis needs to be confronted with a consideration of a different kind. For cultural criticism attempting to delineate a historical process cannot be fairly undertaken without attention to the political forces that manipulated the development of the reading habit between Mrs. Leavis' predemocratic Golden Age and the deplorable present. Two major studies of this history have come to comparable conclusions with regard to England, Germany, and France. One is a classic of literary sociology, Richard D. Altick's *The English Common Reader*, the other a massive monograph by a contemporary oppositional German scholar, Rudolf Schenda's *Volk ohne Buch*. They make it clear that in all three countries, the political authorities, in the wake of the French Revolution, became highly suspicious of the reading habit in the population at large and pursued policies either to inhibit it altogether or to direct it into harmless channels; that is, away from literature or from the best or most interesting literature of the time. Altick is far from deploring the spread of the reading habit to the masses; he refers to it rather as the "democracy of print." [25] He tells an engrossing story of the efforts undertaken to inhibit this democracy, to keep the masses illiterate or, failing that, to "elevate" their taste while attempting to draw them away from fiction. He also describes the social factors that made the acquisition of the reading habit difficult: the (sometimes intentionally) wretched schooling, the workingman's lack of leisure, his weariness, the substantial cost of books or of candles to read them by.

Schenda finds similar conditions in Germany and France; after the French Revolution the authorities moved against reading, starved the schools, and discouraged fiction. Both the finer literature and the emancipatory thrust of the Enlightenment were actively discouraged: "What the readers between 1770 and 1870 could learn from their reading material was to think piously, act practically, only dream of adventure, be satisfied with their lot, and carry out orders." Schenda makes the interesting point that much of this trivial stuff fed to the folk was written by upper-class ladies or clergymen. He speaks of "all this fine, sublime,

frigid, snobbish, beautiful, Dürer-German, monarchist, virgin-pure, German-patriotic, aristocratic, plain and honest 'girls'' literature."[26] *
The results of Altick and Schenda make the lamentations of Q. D. Leavis and other deplorers of mass taste appear rather quaint; they reveal the danger of doing any kind of general literary history without the political equation. They show, moreover, that the problem of elitism has two sides. One is the question as to whether the canonical works can appropriately be urged on the public at large. But the other is the conscious and programmatic manipulation of the reading habit and literary taste for political ends.** Historically, it is simply not true, as the Jeremiahs would have us believe, that great effort has been expended to interest the mass of people in the best literature, but to no avail; in some times and places, at least, the effort has been quite the opposite. These two sides of the elitism question are obviously contradictory and one task of literary sociology would be to sort them out.

On the first point there has been a good deal of sociological assertion, based usually on the Marxist principle that at any given time the ruling opinions are the opinions of the ruling class. Ferdinand Tönnies argued that "in modern society [why especially modern society?] . . . Public Opinion tends to be actually the opinion and political will of the propertied, urban, and educated upper classes. It is, however, presented to the less wealthy, the rural, and the uneducated classes with the claim of authority, as the correct opinion which every respectable citizen and loyal patriot is expect to share."[27] Perhaps this was still true in an older kind of European society in the early part of this century, but it is a principle that one would have great difficulty applying, for example, to the contemporary United States. The question of whether one can easily transfer to the United States concepts based on the class development of Continen-

---

*Schenda's book, though rich in information, is weakened by some contradictions and confusions, one of which concerns the question of value. He polemicizes against the distinction between "higher" and "lower" literature, remarking that by 1984 it will only be a curiosity in the history of literature; in a sense he wishes to turn Escarpit's observations on endurance around and recover that reading matter that did not survive in literary histories. But the above diatribe, along with many other passages, shows that Schenda certainly does make value judgments, and so he finds himself in the same dilemma that besets any critic who denies evaluation.

** A parallel phenomenon is that of the systematic expurgation of books, which has been chronicled with great good humor by Noel Perrin, *Dr. Bowdler's Legacy: A History of Expurgated Books* (New York: Atheneum, 1969). This would not qualify as a work of literary sociology, as Perrin is unwilling to entertain very far a socio-economic explanation for this extraordinary phenomenon. However, it is vastly entertaining as well as instructive and, as I am surrounded here by an apparatus of solemn and often dreary studies, I cannot forbear recommending it to the reader.

tal Europe is one that I have not found addressed very thoroughly in our branch of sociology. Sartre sensed the difficulty when he remarked in an aside that he doubted whether there is a bourgeoisie of the traditional French kind in the United States.[28] Even in older cultures the class situation becomes more complex on inspection. In the Elizabethan age, "that class which was likely to dispense patronage, and certainly held the keys to preferment . . . was extremely mixed. It had all the surprising variety of a menagerie rather than the amazing sameness of a herd."[29] Dialectical class concepts seem only to maintain themselves in a historical perspective of some distance, as the contrast between their employment in *Literaturwissenschaft* and the complexity of actual social history tends to demonstrate. Binary or triadic schemes have difficulty accounting for the minority culture that develops within an upper, urban, or educated class and whose representatives are as much at odds with their class comrades as with the rest of the people. The relatively conservative Eugene Goodheart remarks correctly that "high culture has in fact been the long suffering counter culture in America" and argues that "in the current feeling that high culture is irrelevant, we have unwitting expression of the triumph of the dominant culture."[30] Raymond Williams distinguishes between the minority culture of the great artists with their supporters, and the use or misuse of it made by "particular minorities [who] confuse the superiority of the tradition which has been made available to them with their own superiority."[31] This is a distinction that a rigorous Marxist would not make and that is not altogether easy to sustain theoretically, but may have some practical and heuristic value.

The more traditionally rooted Marxist intellectual is likely to protect the values of the great tradition and put stress on its misuse. This is the official line in Communist countries, which profess to recover the true significance of the tradition for the people. In less orthodox fashion, Walter Benjamin complained of a lack of negative dialectic in the transmission of culture, which "increases the load of treasures that pile up on the backs of mankind. But it does not give mankind the strength to shake the load off in order to get it in hand."[32] But Benjamin himself, of course, is saddled with the weight of elitism; Ernst Fischer has said of him that he fled from the "overpowering banality of the mass bustle. . . . For him thinking becomes an unsociable pleasure in which only a few take part, a little circle of the elect who know how to protect what is rare and prefer the most precious fare." In consequence Benjamin became lonely and pessimistic,[33] a stance not unlike that of the more conventional world-weary critic.

Where the link to tradition is not so strong, however, both confidence and destructiveness increase. It is not uncommon for contemporary literary sociologists to suggest that the literary scholar lives off literature without asking whether he is not merely a museum official in a society that would just as soon do without museums.[34] Louis Kampf claims that, in our society, we study literature only to be certified, "and when it performs this function, literature is an instrument of social elitism."[35] The truly radical German, meanwhile, requires of literary study merely "the smashing of cultural privileges."[36] All of this argument lacks any of the subtlety of modern sociological study that distinguishes between various elites in society and the ruling class proper. Among sociologists, the subject of elites has been debated for decades, generally with explicit or implicit ideological complications. Even the modern Marxist Bottomore, however, is obliged to observe that "in the case of the modern capitalist democracies . . . , the notion of a distinct and settled ruling class becomes dubious and unclear." Of all the elitist subgroups that can be distinguished with greater or lesser sharpness from the ruling, because property-owning class, "the intellectuals are the most difficult to define and their social influence is the most difficult to determine"; they are "in most countries and at most times . . . , one of the least homogeneous or cohesive of elites"; and the situation varies widely from country to country.[37] In the light of this, it is certainly somewhat daring to speak apodictically of the congruity of elitism in the artistic realm with the power and ideology of the ruling class. Still, the true zealot will assert, in the jaw-breaking diction that has become his weaponry, that "culture is a concept for the idealistic paraphrase of those institutions that are erected by the respective ruling class for channeling the productive force of imagination."[38] One must at the very least concede that there are some limits to what a "ruling class" can accomplish in this regard. An example is the string of embarrassments that befell the cultural policies of the Nazis. Levin Schücking tells the nice story that the Nazis had to abandon the practice of recommending the six best books of the month, for the recommendations effectively ended the sale of the books.[39] When politicians attempt to wrestle with this dilemma, it can easily exhibit a comic side; one sociologist points out that "a good example of the perpetual confusion about art in the modern state occurred at the opening of the Paris Salon of 1865 when the Minister of Fine Arts admonished artists to 'resist public taste.' The year before he had told them to 'trust the public.'"[40] Indeed, the problem of elitism does not seem to lie in the imposition of a "ruling class" culture on the population as a whole, for this rarely if ever succeeds under modern conditions; the difficulty is rather to be found in the lack of communication between literary or intellectual culture and the population as a whole and what our judgment on this circumstance ought to be.

Cultural criticism based on a pattern of decline, whether conceived in Spenglerian gloom or in terms of Habermas' scheme of the decay of the ratiocinating bourgeois public, tends to operate with a kind of Gresham's Law of culture, as though mass or commercialized culture replaces and overruns refined and challenging culture. But this is clearly not the case. Proportionally the exclusive command of higher culture in the much larger literate segment of society may be less and its socially organizing force correspondingly less, but it has not vanished and in absolute terms its public is larger than ever. Neither has the commodity character of literature wholly penetrated content, as is so often asserted, nor is the public totally manipulable by media suggestion. Habermas himself notes the paradox that paperback offerings, despite the highly commercial form of their marketing, retain the original emancipatory function of culture, without, it seems to me, integrating this consideration into his argument as a whole; his assertion that television inhibits the "Räsonnement" of the public, derived in part from American discussion on this unhappy topic, has at least in part been refuted by the revolt of a substantial part of the public against the "media," suggesting that socially determined ideology, not its manipulation through communications media, is the primary force.[41] Evidence mounts that the media supply more "Räsonnement," i.e., news and discussions of public affairs, than the public wants, and that public opinion is not altered by it.[42]

Current political developments indicate that the very concept of elitism should be employed with some restraint. Recently, repressive political forces have been exploiting it in a campaign directed initially against the press, but by extension against any form of criticism emanating from what can properly be called the "intelligentsia" in the largest sense. Historically, such attacks have been a constantly recurring feature of preparation for right-wing totalitarianism and must be regarded with the gravest concern.* Some will object that there is a crucial difference

---

*The situation of Left totalitarianism is more subtle. Being aware of its revolutionary sources in philosophy, as well as of the power of the intellect and imagination in appealing to the generalized awareness that human affairs might be different than they are, its tendency is to organize and harness the intelligentsia with a great show of privileges, "education," and culture, while making sure that no results critical of the current apparatus of political power shall emerge. Probably there is truth in the interpretation of Raymond

between radical struggle against a culture that, by its very social situation of genesis and reception, must be affirmative of existing power relationships, and a petty-bourgeois anti-intellectualism exploited with the purpose of cementing those power relationships. But I am not convinced that in the question of elitism this distinction can be made practically without political risk. Insofar as elitism is understood, or denounced, as a consciousness that has set itself apart from communal norms, whether this liberation is due to a social privilege or a mysteriously acquired revolutionary consciousness, it is the same problem of the activation of human intelligence in socially deviant directions. If this is so, then Spiro Agnew and Louis Kampf have been fighting the same enemy, and since Kampf owes his slender base of influence only to the hierarchy of advantage he deplores, while an Agnew can represent large and potent political forces, their political relevance is highly disproportionate and far from suggesting that revolutionary anti-elitism is the more likely to succeed. Both appeal to the "people," but an Agnew can mobilize more battalions of the people than a Kampf, and if our choice is to decline to one between Agnew and Kampf, the future will be very bleak for the humanitarian cause. A really crucial question of freedom is involved here, on which may depend the evolution of the human race toward a condition consonant with its own best imaginings; and I believe it would be best if literary sociology would not press the critique of elitism to the point where it would repress the elements of freedom found everywhere in the exercise of the imagination, whatever the nature of the surrounding power relationships may be.*

One consequence of the contemporary resistance against the elitism of culture has been the demand to widen the purview of literary study. This is all to the good, insofar as it tends to the restoration of literary history and a widened context of interest. But it becomes problematical when it involves the kind of claim insisted on by Schenda that all kinds of literature—canonical, popular, and trival—should have equal rights,[43]

Aron, *The Opium of the Intellectuals* (London: Secker & Warburg, 1957), that the susceptibility of intellectuals to Communism or Marxist projections is due at least in part to the longing to be taken seriously in the organization of the social order.

*The nineteenth-century German critic Theodor Mundt took the position that all art is emancipatory and that therefore oppressive rulers who patronize art are in contradiction with themselves, for they are releasing the same forces they are attempting to suppress (*Aesthetik: Die Idee der Schönheit und des Kunstwerks im Lichte unserer Zeit* [Berlin: M. Simion, 1845], pp.24–25); cf. my comments in *Six Essays on the Young German Novel* (Chapel Hill: University of North Carolina Press, 1972), pp.59–62. It is an engrossing subject for meditation, as is the question of whether the efficiency and clarity of purpose of modern techniques of political repression have or have not made it moot.

for the result is evaluative muddle and a probable dilution of the most emancipatory elements of the human heritage. In German studies there has been for some time a campaign for the abolition of the exclusive concentration upon fiction and poetic creation and the inclusion of all kinds of writing under the heading of literature.[44] As a kind of polemic stance that has helped to unfreeze the canon of traditional German literary studies, this argument has been helpful. But, taken on its own merits, it tends to look back to that kind of literary historiography of which the most notorious German exemplar was Josef Nadler, for whom every conceivable kind of written artifact was the province of the literary scholar; if it were really pursued to this extreme, it would block the possiblity of literary criticism, as it was long blocked in Germany, and impoverish our potential experience. One might ask these scholars: If every writing activity is to be subsumed under literature, why not count house painting among the visual arts?

We find ourselves once again in a situation where we need to be careful about allowing one category of evaluation to dissolve all others. Conor Cruise O'Brien, in discussing Yeats, has argued, no doubt somewhat across his own grain, that progressive politics so constrain the artist as to inhibit his style, while "right-wing politics, with their emphasis on the freedom of the *élite*, impose less constraint, require less pretense, allow style to become more personal and direct."[45] Even Lukács once remarked, with wry self-irony, that talent is always right-wing deviationism.[46] One possible response to this observation heard occasionally is to denounce good style itself as elitist and evil, a form of egalitarianism satirized by Heinrich Heine long ago.[47] For all that literary culture in its creation and appreciation may be restricted to a privileged segment of society, it is nevertheless, as Raymond Williams has said, "a court of human appeal, to be set over the processes of practical social judgment and yet to offer itself as a mitigating and rallying alternative."[48] Literary sociology and radical criticism will not be able to deal fairly with the problem of elitism as long as they insist upon rigid and exclusive schemes that deny any oppositional space between the literary imagination and the class consciousness with which it is associated.

Christopher Caudwell wrote that "great poetry can only be written by the free."[49] He meant by the "free" the ruling class, in which skepticism and disbelief have established themselves. Of course, from a sociological point of view, or from Caudwell's, no one is totally free, but it is plausible that literary art is more likely to thrive where there is a relative freedom from material oppression and narrow horizons, so that it is to be expected that literature will form around the privileged pole of society.[50] It may be that this freedom from reality and practicality will reach a point where relevance is lost, where no link between the elite and the majority is sought or achieved, and artists regress to the forms of a priesthood[51] —Caudwell called this stage parasitic[52] —but when and if that is so will have to be weighed in each case and situation. Perhaps the question is sometimes picked up by the wrong handle, and ought properly to be one of the extent to which the best civilization of an age is diffused through-out society. Coleridge remarked in his criticism of Wordsworth's appeal to the language of the common man in poetry that "the best part of human language, properly so called, is derived from reflection on the acts of the mind itself. It is formed by a voluntary appropriation of fixed symbols to internal acts, to processes and results of imagination, the greater part of which have no place in the consciousness of uneducated man."[53] In this argument, Coleridge may overestimate the inarticulate-ness of the common man as well as the inability of the relatively inarticu-late to make "connections of things" and "relative bearings of fact to fact"; but it seems plausible enough that the best poetry is likely to occur at the most civilized and liberated level of society, where the gift of language has been the most attentively refined, and therefore the issue of elitism may redound not to the poetry itself, but to the organization of society, to the extent of the access to civilization and language itself within it.

This is not to say that, in a sharply stratified society, poetry will not tend to become enclosed within the privilege of the highly civilized minority and even to make privileged isolation thematic. We are at a juncture in civilization where this comes to seem no longer acceptable. "We look back at Pound and Eliot, at Bridges and Yeats," writes Geoffrey Hartman, "and we realize that their elitist view of culture is dead. Though their art aimed for the genuine vernacular, it could not resist the appeal of forms associated with high culture, forms which remained an ideological reflex of upper-class mentality."[54] To what extent this disappearance of elitist privilege is a net loss, as Harry Levin has argued,[55] is still an open question. I should not think that we may complacently accept that art be purchased at the price of injustice, and, of that art that has been pur-chased at the price of injustice, we must always be ready to say aloud to what extent it is so. Not even an *Iphigenie* may sanely be written *as though* the stocking workers of Apolda were not starving (and Goethe certainly did not think so); the awareness must somehow affect such a literary work, even if only in a subterranean or oblique fashion, making of it some kind of answer to a perceived situation that cannot morally or even rationally be excluded from consciousness. A work of art may naturally deal with only a segment of reality, with only one kind of vision, but any pretense that the remainder of reality is non-existent or unimportant is incongruous with the humanistic sensibility that informs the critical enterprise to begin with. We may search for the elements of freedom, emancipation, and opposition in any refined work of art, but it is obscurantist to argue that these elements wholly transcend or erase the social components of its creation and the social implications of its symbolism, for these are part of its meaning in its time, and that does not change. A valid literary criticism combined with sociological awareness would link the widest possible tolerance with the most alert possible skepticism, especially when dealing with the canon of the great works.

If, from the point of view of practical criticism and literary education, the charge of elitism were taken more seriously, it might become more difficult for those who raise it to drive it to iconoclastic extremes. The idea that the same literary canon must necessarily affect all people in roughly the same way is demonstrably wrong, although our vast enterprise of literary education is based upon it. We are gradually losing confidence in the original New Critical denial of a special readiness for the appreciation of literature that some people do not share. Leonard Forster has remarked: "It seems to me that we are now, in universities all over the Western world, virtually compelling students to exercise a talent [of critical appreciation] which very few of them possess."[56] There is much reasonable aesthetic theory to the effect that responsiveness is not a natural, universal given, but a result of acquired discrimination, not to speak of a willingness to work at it that cannot pragmatically be required of all individuals without exception. Literary sociology associated with cultural criticism tends to assume that literature ought to be universally relevant in society; this is due to the communitarian bias that binds Right and Left in these matters. But a thing that is of limited interest or accessibility is not for that reason irrelevant or censurable. You and I may understand nothing of nuclear magnetic resonance and most of us could not be taught anything precise about it, but this does not mean it is not a subject deserving of intense pursuit at some considerable cost to society. Aesthetic experience has a much broader claim on human attention, but I believe that, under modern conditions, the demand for a literature wholly relevant to society and a society universally participating in its reception is excessive and a massive time-waster in literary theory. Similarly, it is not elitist to insist that there is such a thing as critical competence that develops in learning, experience, and the special concentration of the attention on the subject of literature. As Walter Hinderer observes, just because aesthetic judgments are not shared instinctively by all does not in itself prove that they cannot be codified: "Just as the universal validity of a mathematical proposition does not imply that everyone can understand it, 'but merely that everyone who understands it must agree with it,' so the universal validity of aesthetic values does not necessarily mean that evidence of it is felt by everyone."[57]

But we will become confused if we persist in thinking of all this as a matter of natural personal endowments. Certainly the readiness for literature among educated people varies, and criticism, while being concerned to keep the lines of communication as open as possible between this and other areas of intellectual endeavor, has no need to deplore the fact, for there is no sound evidence that it was ever otherwise. But it is also true that there are whole classes in our society to whom literature is inaccessible and, if we believe in its value, this we must deplore. The literary scholar has the strongest possible interest in opposing an educational system that reinforces class differences, and this means that he has a political commitment that is at least two hundred years old and must be pressed in the face of enemies who have not changed very much in their purposes and strategies during that time. Consequently the claim that we are attempting to impose an elite product and the values associated with it upon classes for whom they are irrelevant must be taken seriously. If we proceed as if we were the guardians of a bounded culture to which every person must aspire if he is to have full social dignity, then the complaint will be justified. But Caudwell's association of elitism with freedom gives us unexpected help. The ruling classes may be oppressors, but they have also set a standard of freedom to which mankind has always aspired, as innumerable fairy tales and all kinds of folk literature, with their images of freedom set in imagined royal houses and princely marriages, sufficiently demonstrate. Writing that only reexpresses what ordinary folk have in their own heads is redundant, and a literary sociology that would identify the great writer as the one who does this with the greatest precision of reflection and the greatest skill with the material of language guts the interior of literature, which at its best unsettles our tendency to see through one common, general-issue type of spectacles. In all literature, including anything imposed on the public in print, there is a lurking quality of arrogance, of knowing something better; but as critics we are free to determine what justification there may be in this imposition without shutting out the possibility of uncommon experience by considering it elitist. If we are alert to these elements of freedom in the canon of great literature, the charge of elitism will be less destructive of cultural values, and we will not have to stand mute before claims that inarticulateness, ignorance, occult mumbling, and loutishness are just as good as fine literature.

VII

Extrinsicality

IF ONE FOLLOWS the quarrels in contemporary literary criticism from afar, one can get rather the impression that there are two large camps in opposition to one another. One insists upon the radical autonomy of the work of art, independent of any external determinants or implications, seeking all meaning and value from the internal relations of the work itself. The other maintains that the work is the product of historical and social determinants, and both its meaning and value are inextricably bound up with these causative processes. One camp is convinced that it is defending the freedom and multiplicity of the creative imagination against reductive attempts to degrade literature to propaganda or the direct communication of statement via content. The other is convinced that it is defending the humaneness of literature against attempts to idealize it and sever it from wider moral, political, and social relevance, in order to falsify it into the service of conservative or reactionary purposes.

All this is prejudice. Like most prejudice, it is loosely related to a real background. Evidence can be found that suggests the existence of both positions, as well as for justifications of the charges made against each by the other. But both, in the bald way I have set them out, have the appearance of being untenable, and no one who tries to educate himself about criticism is able to hold either one of them for very long without qualification. The multiplicity and complexity of these qualifications is fascinating, and it would be a valuable task to attempt to bring some order and judgment into them. I wish here only to point to some examples, in order to support the assertion that the complex of issues I have subsumed under the heading of "extrinsicality," though in itself difficult, does not separate the modes of criticism as profoundly as is sometimes supposed. If I am right about this, not only could some of the exhausting blood and thunder in contemporary critical discussion be dispensed with, but a more practical view of the potential of social theories of literature, without erecting them into a means of salvation or demonizing them as a conspiracy against the good and the beautiful, might appear potentially possible.

One profound difficulty that stands in the way of a radical ontological claim of the autonomy of a work of literature is the nature of its artistic material. In this regard, literature exhibits a difference from the other arts that has long been troubling for general aesthetic theory. A stone has no meaning, other than a geological one; the sculptor imposes form and meaning upon the stone that was in no way inherent in it before. The result will have a mimetic relationship to reality, its form will repose in some way or other in culture and therefore in society; the character and texture of the material will be a determinant; but the artistic object as a whole has still to some extent been created where the thing had not been before. Not quite so with literature. Its material is already freighted with meaning before the author takes it in hand. Grammar, lexicon, and social usage impose a degree of form on the material anterior to its artistic use that is much more constraining than with any other medium. The explicitness of the socially shared symbol system is much greater and more extensive. Language is formed of "conventional symbols understood only in a given community, loaded with a semantic content and organized according to syntactic rules valid only for a definite body of population."[1] Yet, at the same time, language in its social dispersal is diffuse, "a corpus of prescriptions and habits common to all the writers of a period . . . a kind of natural ambience wholly pervading the writer's expression, yet without endowing it with form or content."[2] Modern linguistic thinking suggests that language is less malleable than pigment, stone, or metal; not only is it restrained by the conventions of *langue*, which literary experimentation can only partially escape; our very capacity for making the world intelligible is supposed to be delimited by linguistic structure and even by the particular *langue* at our disposal. It is true that writers from time to time have endeavored to escape these constraints through abstraction or a poetry of pure sound, but in the history of literature generally these are marginal phenomena, impelled by the tendency of artists to attempt whatever can be conceived of. There have also been critical efforts to treat language like any other medium and to see texts as structures of purely formal relations. But such strictness is rarely maintained except in the most highly specialized academic exercises. Practical criticism is almost never able to evade the fact that language is talk about something and that it retains this quality in a literary work, which does not dissolve the meaningful referents the words bring with them from their existence anterior to the work, though it may narrow, expand, or otherwise alter them. No serious critic of any school, including the New Critics, is unaware of this. W. K. Wimsatt stated plainly that "the purpose of any poem cannot be simply to be a work of art, to be artificial, or to embody devices of art."[3] A fact so obvious that its implications are often overlooked is that literature cannot be understood unless the language in which it is composed is known; auditory experiments with poems recited in languages unknown to the hearers have demonstrated this. Iconic arts also have a culturally determined language that must be learned if they are to be fully understood, but they clearly yield more immediate accessibility than a printed work or even a recitation or performance in a foreign language. Thus it would seem beyond debate that a substantial part of the meaning and indeed the being of a literary work is delivered into it from the outside. Since language is a medium of interpersonal behavior, the meaning is of a social nature. However one may wrestle over the details of the Hegelian-Marxist subject-object dialectic, the social substantiveness of language itself implies the objective elements of the world formed, re-formed, or imagined in subjective consciousness.

There has been much discussion in modern theory of language's "abbreviation of reality" that leaves spaces and ellipses to be filled by the kind of receiver projected by the sender, but which another kind of receiver has to find a way of recovering, filling in, or inventing.[4] The conclusion that the text, even a fictional or poetic text, therefore lacks specific referentiality seems to me very much contrary to experience. Rather, Searle's argument that fiction contains real as well as pretended acts of referring[5] is not only preferable but necessary to an account of how fictional texts can be comprehended. Yet it is just these real referents—whether material or social and moral—that generate disparities in reception. The more cultural and social experience is shared between author and reader, the more precise will be the reconstructions in the reader's apprehension. Let me give two personal and elementary examples. Heimito von Doderer's novel *Die Strudlhofstiege* (1951) takes place largely in a district of Vienna in which I was living when I read it. There can be no doubt that my concretization of the streets, edifices, and neighborhoods described in the novel—not to mention its central image, a complex of steps and ramps between two street levels—is more precise and closer to the author's own intentionality than if I had not known this scene. This is an extreme case, for Doderer's novel is drawn intimately from life, and Viennese acquaintances have told me that some of its characters can be encountered walking about to this day; for such readers the concretion is even more precise, perhaps disturbingly so. As much as one might wish to argue that what is important in the novel is its highly refined formal structure and the internal significance of persons, places, and events, the reader cannot expel his knowledge from his consciousness, and therefore such a book will be rather differently perceived by different readers, depending on the extent of this shared experience. The alternative would be to argue that the reader who knew nothing about Vienna or about Austrian society between the world wars would have the most adequate access to the novel, a position no one could take, for the very comprehension of its language is partly proportional to such knowledge.

The other example is Peter Handke's recent novel, *Der kurze Brief zum langen Abschied* (1972), which begins in the city of Providence and recounts a journey westward across the United States. Handke has been to an extent under the influence of the French "new novel," and he inserts a number of commonplace factual details as a lattice of micro-observations into his narration. Now, as it happens, I know both Providence and part of the route described in the novel very well, and a number of the details do not correspond with reality. This worried and distracted me as I was reading. It seems hard to believe that their relation to reality is indifferent, for other such details, like the route numbers of highways, correspond exactly, and both Handke's mode of fiction and such internal evidence as there is suggest that they are meant to so correspond; they are not passing details of scene-setting, but are prominently thrust upon the reader's attention. Perhaps they are slyly meaningful deviations from reality inviting interpretation, like Kafka's Statue of Liberty brandishing a sword in *Amerika*; but this, too, would be an extrinsic device apprehendable only by someone sharing the knowledge. On the other hand, it would not be generally regarded as critically sound to speak of these deviations as mistakes, for such a judgment would violate the stressed fictionality of Handke's text, which furthermore moves steadily into a realm of fantasy. Nevertheless, incorrect naturalistic devices, if that is what these are, always have a perhaps gratuitous tendency to preoccupy the attention of the informed reader. Here the alternative would be to argue that, when Handke puts toll stations at regular intervals along the Pennsylvania Turnpike, rather than at the exits, this cannot be called a mistake at all, for what we find in the novel is not the Pennsylvania Turnpike, but a fictional "Pennsylvania Turnpike" that has no relation- ship to the real road at all. The phenomenologist may wish to take this view, but it would introduce an arbitrary indeterminacy into the text, for there would be no reason why the author could not have spoken instead of a "Pan-American Highway" or a "Martian Canal," or, for that matter, a "giraffe." In practical terms of reception, there can be little doubt that the European reader who has never been in the United States will read the book somewhat differently than I do, my concretions in this case being more philological, as well as more distracting.

My teacher Heinrich Henel used to point out that those scholarly critics who insisted upon the irrelevance of literary history or biography or other "extrinsic" information to interpretation nevertheless had all these things in their heads, and it is hard to imagine that they do not continue to inform apprehension and critical judgment. From time to time there was a dark feeling about what would happen to literary understanding if this traditional cultural learning were in fact to disap- pear. Some idea of the answer is given by the occasional student one encounters nowadays who refuses to learn anything of a factual or objective nature. The consequence is not so much that he falls promptly into the affective fallacy—this may not be as serious a misdemeanor as it was once thought to be[6] —as that he offers so little possiblity of an intersubjective literary experience. Such a student will exhibit in an extreme form those features for which the New Criticism has (often unjustly) been criticized: total impressionism, a lack of control for the validity of interpretation, and eventually a private, unsharable response that tends to the inarticulate. A person who is immovably insistent on such a response is wasting his time as a student of literature; he is irrelevant to literary criticism.

As there is no escaping the fact that there are extrinsic aspects of the literary work anterior to it, so there seems to be general agreement that the work in isolation cannot yield meaning. Monroe Beardsley defines meaning as "a semantical relation between the work itself and something outside the work." [7] Ingarden stresses the social nature of every language and asserts that the literary work can contain *both* statements that refer to objects or events outside the work as well as the kind of mimetic utter- ance that Richards called "pseudo-statements";[8] Ingarden's more difficult term elsewhere is "quasi-judgmental character of statements," which one explicator renders simply as "quasi-statements." [9] These ex- amples could be multiplied and show that intrinsic critics do not, generally speaking, have so mystical and radical an idea of the isolation of the literary work from history and society as their enemies often allege. Harry Levin, who speaks on the matter with more authority than I can, has vigorously protested the Marxists' "oversimplified impression of New Criticism, which they take to be antihistorical. A firsthand look at our critical output should assure them that historicism is still preponderant and that some of us pay serious attention to sociology, to ideology, indeed to Marxism."[10] Of course, when Levin numbers *himself* among the New Critics, he is perhaps widening the category more than one should. But it was not Levin or even Friedrich Engels, but T. S. Eliot who observed: "Any radical change in poetic form is likely to be the symptom of some very much deeper change in society and in the individual" and "the development of poetry is itself a symptom of social changes."[11] On the whole—and I recognize the danger of generalizing across so vast a field—while there is a substantial and sometimes confusing insistence in the New Criticism on the non-referential character of poetry, the concern of modern criticism has not been to insist upon an ontology of the individual work uprooted from any real extrinsic ground or referent, but rather to focus on those aspects of the imaginative, poetic utterance that differentiate it from any other kind of utterance. The emphasis is on the new dimension of creativity rather than on the borrowed, extrinsic dimension.[12]

Furthermore, as soon as the admissibility of literary history is granted, then the intrinsic critic must at least go so far as to acknowledge that the literary work was made by *somebody*; R. S. Crane admits to literary history "elements of two kinds: terms signifying actions, characters, habits, aims, and circumstances of writers, and terms signifying attributes of literary works; without the latter the history would not be a history of literature and without the former it would not be a history."[13] Crane's language is typically austere here; what the first set of "terms" "signifies" is that there is a human being at the source of the work, and if he is of any interest, he will promptly involve us in a complex web of relationships of life and reality. Moreover, from Richard Foster's account of the progress of the New Critics, we learn that they themselves moved from an intrinsic formalism; for Allen Tate, for example, Foster says that "from literature considered as art the critical intelligence must move into the broader human issues," and these are holistic, organic, and reactionary.[14] At this point we are no longer engaged in an altercation over intrinsicality, but with the question of whether the extrinsic concerns toward which the

New Critics moved were not unfortunate and whether we cannot turn our attention to better ones.

At the other end of the altercation lies the question of causality or determination. Among those who reject the possibility of literary sociology or the Marxist view of literature one can often read that these latter believe that social or historical circumstances "cause" literary works in some mechanistic fashion. The fact that there is little or no evidence for this anywhere in contemporary work does not seem to trouble these polemicists, who, like the critics of the intrinsic approach, have a tendency to harden and radicalize the position of their opponents in order to dispose of it more easily. There may have been, in the nineteenth century, sociological dreams of a strictly determined linear causality, but there is no trace of it left in any literary-sociological argument that I know of. The sociologist oriented on the terms of natural science may argue that "a necessary if not a sufficient condition for asserting a causal connection between an event B and an event A is the assertion of a regularity statement to the effect that whenever events of kind B take place, then events of kind A occur,"[15] an axiom hardly susceptible to application to the history of art and literature. But Hans L. Zetterberg has argued that such truly deterministic relations are actually uncommon in sociology; more common are stochastic propositions (if X, then probably Y). "They range," he observes, "from the quite strong to the highly attenuated."[16] Literary sociology certainly deals in relatively attenuated stochastic propositions, often escalated into assertions; nevertheless, to recognize this is not a license to deny the presence of causal linkage. The rigor of determination can also be eased by reference to Popper's distinction between the relation of a fact to a universal law, and the relation of a fact to "specific initial conditions."[17] That we can give contextual reasons for events, including imaginative ones, that follow upon or relate to other events, is fundamental to any historical discourse and does not involve us in the logical conundrums of deterministic causality. We have had occasion before to speak of Crane's rigor with regard to causality; he quite rightly calls illicit the "assumption that we can deduce particularized actuality from general possibility."[18] The question is whether there is anyone who maintains such a deduction. Certainly not the empiricist Fügen, who stresses that the same situation can yield differing results and that literature is a dialogue of the author and his world among various possiblities. For him, the strict sociologist, literature is more illustrative than documentary.[19] Fügen accuses rather the speculative "social-literary method" of tending to a dogma of strict causality, but the evidence does not support this, either.

Constantly we find among the more general literary sociologists as well as among Marxists a resistance to direct or "mechanistic" causal relationships or to a naive view of mimesis. For all the wide currency that Lukács has given to the concept of reflection, he will be found to be atypical on that point, and for him as for any Marxist, the reflection of reality is a form within a, to be sure, socially ordered consciousness and not a direct correspondence between reality and artistic phenomenon. Indeed, Lukács mounts an eloquent argument against regarding the text from the outside, for example, as a document to be measured against the truth of history, except as a methodological inquiry aware of its limitations.[20] There is even caution concerning the bourgeois novel, perhaps the most mimetic of genres with the exception of the realistic and naturalistic drama. Jean Duvignaud, for example, asserts that the novel is not at all the "reflection" of the values of a class, but expresses the surprise and excitement of living in a society of multiple possibilities and relations,[21] a view that could without difficulty be made congruent with that of Ian Watt.[22] Most Marxists can be found arguing against mechanistic "sociologism"; frequently they find recourse to Marx's fundamental conception of work as the peculiarly human projection of the creative imagination into the world, dynamically transforming reality.[23] They will insist that the aesthetic autonomy of the work of art should never be lost from view, and stress that Marxist literary theory does not imply a simple determinism, although art is "to a high degree" dependent on material determinants.[24] Nor does Lukács himself, of course, believe that reflection is anything like photographic reproduction; he points out that the most elementary sensual responses to reality require a process of selection and organized emphasis in order to serve the subject's survival,[25] and, in his highly complex argument on his favorite subject, reflection is mediated and modified in any number of reciprocal ways. It is as plain to Lukács as to anyone else that selection, exclusion, and concentration are fundamental to art; this process, however, he connects with *Praxis*, so that it also reflects reality.

It is easy to see that there are serious logical difficulties in these positions. They are quite similar to the difficulties caused by the elder Friedrich Engels' qualifications of the basis—superstructure relationship. Engels, indeed, was among the first to protest against mechanistic determination and towards this end mounted a famous argument that the basis determines the superstructure "ultimately" (*in letzter Instanz*) but there are all kinds of complex mediations, reciprocal relationships, and temporal inconsistencies in the working out of the process.[26] Peter Demetz went so far as to call this late position of Engels revisionist.[27] Many Marxists are not sufficiently emancipated from their bibliolatry to weigh this question judiciously and tend to fall back on empty abusiveness when confronting Demetz' argument. It does seem that Engels has solved one problem while creating another. His formulation is an effort to deal with the contingency, complexity, and general bad fit of empirical reality, but it deprives determinism of any rigor to which it might otherwise aspire and opens up a space that seems wide enough to accommodate almost any kind of rational historical argument. The same difficulties apply to our examples of repudiation of determinism and direct mimesis. Some people are inclined to argue that a cause is either a cause or it isn't, while others may feel these admissions entitle us to leave determinism aside as the uninteresting part of the literary phenomenon and actually give us a mandate to examine that remnant of creativity or autonomy here admitted.

There is, of course, a large body of argument under the heading of dialectics that is directed toward this problem. I confess I find dialectical theory difficult, and I do not quite understand its view of, or alternative to, causality. I grasp the point that the materialistic dialectic makes of the human mind a productive force, working back on the material and social determinants that initially shape it, so that change and progress through human agency are possible. But I cannot see that this is much more than an experiential observation, a formulation born of necessity. I still do not understand the ground of creativity, as the category of work seems too imprecise to define it, nor have I been able to become clear about what the actual range and limits of creativity are understood to be. An explicator of Lukács has argued that in his "undogmatic" Marxism change is not predetermined (or, of course, spontaneous), and he illustrates this by a quote stating that reality "combines a consistent following of an unchanging direction with incessant theoretical and practical allowances for the deviousness of the path of evolution."[28] But it would seem to me that an "unchanging direction" implies that change is predetermined, that the subjective end of the dialectic—repeatedly *asserted* by Lukács—has again fallen out of the case, and that we are back with Engels' modified determinism. Kenneth Burke calls dialectical materialism "idealistic materialism" because of its necessary stress on human "agent" in interaction with material "scene,"[29] which adumbrates the problem without, to my mind, wholly clarifying it.

Clearly a Marxist philosophy would have to set its face against a pure, mechanistic notion of linear causality, with life and the universe, experience and history an infinite mass of billiard balls clonking with infinite kinetic energy. Under such a doctrine humanism could hardly survive, and the whole appellative character of Marxism would be lost, an awareness that continually revives in every Marxist rebellion against its own ossification, as well as in Marxists' dislike of truly deterministic doctrines such as B. F. Skinner's or of the anti-humanistic iconoclasm of some of the more eccentric offshoots of French structuralism. Therefore dialectics appears to me to be a strategy to retain and account for variability, choice, and perhaps even morality in a materialist context. The practice of Communist politics makes it too easy to forget that Marxism is a doctrine supportive of Western civilization. Not surprisingly, therefore, one encounters formulations that the non-Marxist critic could accept without too much difficulty. Jameson, for example, writes that "the best dialectical analyses show not so much that external social reality *causes* a particular type of thought, as that it imposes basic inner limitations upon it, in an almost a priori fashion." [30] Jameson's "almost" troubles us in this context as much as Goldmann's "à peu près" (see above, p. 28) and makes us wonder whether there is not a weakness in the argument. But I shouldn't think the statement as a whole need be rejected by any reasonable person; it does not oblige us to believe that the "basic inner limitations" cannot be transcended or that within them there cannot be a highly variegated set of options and creative possibilities. As for structuralism, it is said to avoid the paradoxes of causality by rejecting cause and effect in favor of laws of transformation;[31] this rather makes structuralism sound like an empirical science. But in interpreting Lucien Goldmann, Laurenson and Swingewood have a rather curious argument with regard to extrinsicality. "Unlike literary psychoanalysis," they write, "which freely infers the significance of myths and symbols from outside the text in order to understand the text, structural analysis infers nothing which cannot be related to the actual literary work itself or its environment." They keep insisting that the sociological approach "does not set out to read into an author's work but to relate his text to verifiable human experience, and not to go beyond the text in order to understand it." [32] These statements themselves are hard to understand. One would think that, as soon as one looks at the environment of a text, one is going outside it; and certainly literary psychoanalysis believes that it is relating the text to "verifiable human experience"—indeed, it must, since the dialogue situation of psychoanalytic therapy is necessarily absent from it;

nor can one understand how anything in a text except formal relationships can be verified without going beyond it. The dilemma stems from
Goldmann himself, with his concentration on the great works, which
itself makes determinism impossible to sustain.

The point I am trying to make here is not that these dilemmas are not
resolvable in one philosophical way or another. I am merely trying to
suggest that modern critical attitudes may not be as mutually exclusive as
they are often made out to be, and, from the point of view of practical
criticism, we may be dealing with differences in emphasis or in the kinds
of questions put to literature, at least where criticism is relatively free and
is not obliged to serve the dictates and ends of established political power.
If this has not always been so, the gap is certainly closing today. One can
see this in all camps. Phenomenologists and textual critics acknowledge
the ground of reality and authors as the human source of fiction.[33] E. D.
Hirsch, for his part, argues that there have been extrinsic components in
the most puristic criticism. He points to the limits of evaluation that we
have mentioned before: "Not even Croce, I think, would judge a work
good which perfectly achieved some perverse or idiotic aim. So I conclude that although Croce's theory is the only one capable of providing
truly intrinsic criteria, this theoretical purity is almost entirely irrelevant
to serious criticism." "The Coleridgean mode of criticism practiced by
the New Critics," says Hirsch, "is, for the most part, extrinsic, despite its
pretense of being otherwise. . . ." The sanction of its criteria "comes
entirely from the religious, moral, and aesthetic standpoint which spon-
sors such criteria as estimable values."[34] Hirsch goes on here to say that
the introduction of judgments grounded in extrinsic considerations is
the very reason that these critics have produced significant criticism.
That may be, but from Hirsch's position to an ideological and social
critique of criticism is only a small step. Furthermore, in view of the
constant appeal of modern intrinsic criticism to Coleridge and Wordsworth, it is somewhat piquant to open Wordsworth's preface to the
Lyrical Ballads and find there in the third paragraph the statement that an
adequate account of his kind of poetry would require, among other
considerations, "retracing the revolutions, not of literature alone, but
likewise of society itself."[35]

The Marxists, meanwhile, leave wider latitude in their positions than is
commonly assumed. Ernst Fischer is perhaps not the best example to
adduce here, for, in the history of Marxist criticism, there is hardly
another so sensitive to literary values; and, in viewing his career and his
own interpretation of it, one gets the impression that Marxism was an

ethical obligation he imposed upon himself rather than a total intellectual commitment. It would be hard to deny that he was a kind of incipient revisionist from the outset. Still, as the most successful and influential Communist cultural politician in the recent history of Western countries, he is not a negligible quantity. So it is not without interest that from that vantage point (well before the events of 1968 resulted in his expulsion from the Austrian Communist Party) he was one of the warmest defenders of the freedom of art. "The law of its freedom," he wrote, "binds it with gentle force to the social, the common, the humane. But only art itself, in free choice, can effectively impose this bond upon itself."[36] I should think that this is a formulation with which most critics could associate themselves, and Fischer's gently binding force is a long way from the Moloch of determinism to which Marxist critics are believed to sacrifice literature. As for Lukács, perhaps the other pole of this issue, René Wellek keeps complaining that he counted over a thousand adversions to the reflection of reality in the first volume of the aesthetics. But since that, after all, is Lukács' subject, I should think he would be permitted to mention it, and anyway it is grounded in larger dialectical considerations; so large, perhaps, that they lose any threatening precision. Roy Pascal, in a sympathetic account of Lukács' concept of totality, explains that the "'mirror' does not denote surface-reflexion, as the image seems to imply, but means any type of formulation of the relationships in which man stands to the experienced world, so that a flint arrowhead or a scientific formula are 'reflections' of reality."[37] What is reflected, according to another commentator, is real, non-metaphysical essences selected from the aggregate of sensory experience.[38] Thus we need not fear any threat of reductionist determinism in this kind of "reflection" theory, for it can encompass every kind and nuance of mimetic or reactive relationship that can occur.

The dissolution of conflicting viewpoints into eclectic resolutions is especially annoying to radicals and other possessors of whole truths, and it should not be overlooked that sufficient difficulties remain in the area of extrinsicality. One of these is that in talking of "inside" and "outside,"* one runs the risk of reifying one's own metaphors. A charmingly comic example of this is found in Christopher Caudwell, where he has mounted an argument that the activity of criticism, in contrast to that of

---

*The terminology alludes to Karl Mannheim's difficult concepts of *Innenbetrachtung* and *Außenbetrachtung*, now influential in German criticism. See Mannheim, "Ideologische und soziologische Interpretation der geistigen Gebilde," *Jahrbuch für Soziologie* 2 (1926): 424–440.

creation or mere appreciation, requires one to pass outside art. Then he reaches for an illustrative simile, with disastrous consequences: "Art is the product of society, as the pearl is the product of the oyster, and to stand outside art is to stand inside society." [39] Can he mean that to stand outside the pearl is to stand inside the oyster? More important than this kind of solecism, which arises out of Caudwell's *légère* assertiveness, is the question usefully raised by Viktor Žmegač "whether the categorization into immanent and external phenomena yields any tolerable meaning beyond its admittedly heuristic extent." He argues that externals can become immanent and formal aspects external impulses. "A social—moral, legal, or other—norm can call forth a formal decision of the artist in affirmative or polemical reaction and thus flow into the aesthetic shape, become 'immanent'; on the other hand, any topos, once completely integrated, can freeze into an external flourish that hardly has a claim to aesthetic validity and consequently does not deserve to play in the 'inner' history of literature a more privileged role than an impulse called for by changes in social conditions." The value of this observation lies in its capacity to put to rest once and for all the question of an internal literary history as an alleged alternative to a literary history understood as a segment of general history. To the frequently encountered arguments that it is literature that generates literature in the author's confrontation and struggle with the challenge of his cultural heritage, Žmegač opposes the view that literary tradition is actually an *extrinsic* determinant. With legitimate recourse to Marx, Žmegač asserts that "there is no natural history of artistic rhetoric, only a social history." [40] I am convinced that this is right and, if so, that it brings down a major structure that has been erected against extrinsic determinants of literature and its local embeddedness in social and historical reality.

However, certain other Marxist principles may exhibit a tendency for partial observations to ossify into fixed phrases. One prominent example of this is the tirelessly reiterated slogan of the work of art as a commodity. It derives from Marx's axiom that in the cash nexus of capitalist society all values become exchange values. This is a polemic hyperbole that has been transformed into a "scientific" truth; it seems to me both historically unsound and an inadequate account of the conflicting value systems and impulses in society. The postulation that the work of art is a commodity is an observation on the disappearance of the aristocratic Maecenas and his replacement by a large, mainly anonymous public, often maddening in its recalcitrance and "false consciousness," and supplied by the author through a publishing enterprise that must struggle for its commercial existence. The harmfulness of this state of affairs has not yet been convincingly demonstrated. It is true that there is a large body of literature generated by purely commercial considerations, from the mass-produced pure junk of subliterature and "confession" magazines through the short-story market up to some best sellers. It is also true that this literature is wholly or partly conformed to the expectations of its readership, affirming its generally conservative consciousness or distracting it with escapist fantasies, and that the need to maximize sales can lead, even in more ambitious writing, to the lowest-common-denominator effect so notorious in American television. But it is certainly doubtful that, if the public had access only to a literature of a high degree of refinement and difficulty, or one that ran coarsely against the grain of its convictions and prejudices, it would accept such literature instead and derive social benefit from it. The history of popular literature suggests very strongly a priority of popular demand for cheap and trivial fiction forced upon commercial endeavors initially concerned with instruction and cultural elevation.[41]

The commercial aspect of publishing is an important object of literary-sociological study. Control over the means of literary production is a power position highly susceptible to manipulation, corruption, and abuse. This circumstance, however, is not peculiar to capitalism; it applies equally to aristocratic or ecclesiastical patronage, public cultural support by democratic governments, and, to a much grimmer degree, to exclusive political control wielded by the state in the name of the "people." One current alternative is to displace the authority of the publisher by that of an authors' collective. What the consequences of this will be remains to be seen; the traditional capacity of authors for critical insight and objectivity is not notoriously great, and the present literary situation suggests that authors' collectives might exercise even greater oppressiveness through cliquishness and modish ideological conformity. Already one such endeavor in West Germany, the Wagenbach Verlag, has fissioned in an ideological quarrel, while other groups have indulged themselves into bankruptcy. The economic status of authors is certainly a serious issue and has an effect upon literature that is too often underestimated. It has been calculated that a European writer, in order to reach the income of a linotypist, would have to produce every eighteen months a work selling eight to ten thousand copies.[42] In England, for a novel with a printing of 3,000 copies, 80% of those sold will go to libraries, and one case is recorded of a highly praised novel that sold but 2,243 copies, of which only 193 were purchased by individuals.[43] These are sobering statistics, and in Europe, the growing economic dependency of authors on the mass media and other public institutions is driving them into unionization—with what results, it will be interesting to observe. On the other hand, one might argue that at the present time there is a closer correlation between literary quality and at least a modest degree of success (except in poetry) than at any time in modern history; and the tolerance for experimentation and provocation has grown large enough that, especially in West Germany, where the outrage over the capitalist corruption of literature is loudest, it is not easy to imagine a literary work so bad, silly, or subversive that it could not be published somewhere, although undoubtedly the majority of what is written is not published. Effective alternatives to the commercial production of literature are not clearly in view, for, if the public is not to decide who is a writer, who shall? Should writers be identified and salaried by the state? We have an example of this in the Soviet Union that does not invite imitation. Escarpit, who has weighed in great detail the problems of the "murderous system" of book distribution, concluded flatly: "We are now sufficiently well acquainted with the mechanics of literary life to appreciate that the writer proposes and the public disposes—and so it must be."[44]

To say that a literary work is nothing more than a commercial commodity because it is sold is a little like saying that a book is a dirty book if it has been dropped into the gutter. How the relationship of the cash nexus displaces the communicative one between text and reader is wholly unclear; while its effect in actually constituting literary content is, I believe, overgeneralized by contemporary theorists. The collapsing of genesis, mode of production, and use is excessively violent. For example, it may be plausibly suggested that a book loses its commodity character when it is in a public library.[45] How then could that character have suffused the work in the first place? Is it true that commercial publishing has always been a baneful influence on literature? Even Jürgen Habermas, in his admired analysis of the historical shift in the structure of what we mean by "public," argues that the transformation of the literary work into a commodity was initially an emancipatory development, dissolving the sacral authority of the work and making it an object of critical discourse.[46] If the educational system may now have largely institutionalized the once spontaneous activity Habermas ascribes to the Classical bourgeoisie, the quantitative and qualitative results are perhaps not so decayed as he believes. Nor is it characteristic only of the Classical age of the bourgeoisie that publishers have assumed the Maecenas role out of a commitment to cultural responsibility contrary to their commercial interests; the relations between many major writers and their publishers supply some of the most moving chapters in the literary history of the nineteenth and twentieth centuries, alongside of examples of exploitation and neglect. It has been established that the prestigious Swedish publisher Bonnier loses money on one hundred per cent of the poetry volumes it publishes, yet it continues to publish them,[47] and a skeptical probe into the motives for doing so would not alter the end effect. It appears also that it is the queer, "Adam Smith" economics itself of the publishing trade in the United States that allows so many literary works to be published at a loss;[48] the costs of publishing are not reckoned on the profit of the unit product but on the total overhead of operation, and the fierce competition in this last of classically capitalist industries encourages risk publication in the hope of once in a while hitting the incalculable jackpot. Indeed, in many respects a book (by which is normally meant a novel) is a peculiar sort of commodity. Success with one product does not give the producer an advantage with another; a purchaser who likes the product nevertheless will not return and buy another copy of it; and the customer does not know he will like the product until he has consumed it. Altogether, it is an ornery commodity; while it is possible to orchestrate the writing and promotion of a best seller, the assumption often encountered on the Left that this is easy to do or frequently successful does not accord with the almost aleatory character of the publishing business. It is, of course, true that best sellers can be manufactured; a recent successful example is Peter Benchley's *Jaws*;* though failures are certainly as common. But in other cases, such as Erich Segal's *Love Story* or Richard Bach's *Jonathan Livingston Seagull*, meretriciousness is the consequence of an individual stroke of genius; no commercial institution could have inspired or imagined trash of such delicate simplicity. Indeed, Bach's infantile and retrograde homily was rejected repeatedly before it was published, indicating that publishers can still lose money by overestimating the intelligence and taste of the public. That no publisher can profess to be confident about public taste weakens the foundation of the Marxist view of commercial publishing.

Nor are the radicals, as they sometimes imply, in exclusive possession of a secret about the relationship between art and commerce; writers themselves in the literary system usually know the difference. Authors of

*An instructive account of the splendidly successful and businesslike planning of this novel is given by Ted Morgan, "Sharks," *The New York Times Magazine*, April 21, 1974, pp. 10–11, 85–86, 88–91, 95–96.

truly trivial literature rarely are under any illusion that they are producing something worthwhile.* Although the more venal best seller authors may proclaim publicly, perhaps as a public relations stunt, that they
think of themselves as authors of good books, many are probably literate
enough to know better. One thinks of Horatio Alger's frustrated, life-
long dream of one day writing a serious novel. Alistair MacLean, the
author of best sellers like *The Guns of Navarone*, describes himself as a
businessman rather than a writer, thus showing that he knows the
difference between "a good story" and a work of literature, apparently
with some wry self-irony.[49] Writers of this kind will sometimes tend to fall
back on a static, populist concept of democracy by asserting that they are
giving the public what it wants, thus defensively but not irrelevantly
raising the problem of elitism that painfully crosses the argument about
the work of art as a commodity. Here is an excellent example of an issue
that falls into the purview of literary sociology and that is of sufficient
importance for the understanding of literature that we would like to be
able to get it into focus; but this is hindered by the undifferentiated
application of insufficiently flexible categories. The question needs also
to be answered on pragmatic grounds. One may say all one likes about
the commercialization of art and the filtering process of the market
system, but when one considers the results, the magnificent literary
achievements of the Western world in modern times, the force of the
complaint begins to fade. Slowly the ongoing Marxist discussion begins
to discover the inapplicability of such terms as commodity, use-value,
and consumption to the work of art and to detect the resemblance of the
employment of these categories to conservative cultural criticism.[50]

For practical criticism, extrinsic considerations raise several familiar
difficulties unrelated to the commodity problem; their recurrence, how-

---

*Richard Hoggart argues that trivial literature is "produced by people who possess
some qualities in greater measure than their readers, but are of the same ethos," and
"presumably most writers of fantasy for people of any class share the fantasy worlds of their
readers" (*The Uses of Literacy: Changing Patterns in English Mass Culture* [Fair Lawn, N. J.:
Essential Books, 1957], pp. 174, 175). But he does not seem actually to have studied trivial
authors, and those who do often come to different conclusions. See Walter Nutz, *Der
Trivialroman, seine Formen und seine Hersteller* (Cologne: Westdeutscher Verlag, 1962), and
Marion Beaujean, *Der Trivialroman in der zweiten Hälfte des 18. Jahrhunderts* (Bonn: Bouvier,
1964). Hoggart refers to Q. D. Leavis on this point, but her researches were more
concerned with authors of best sellers and of popular literature rather than of subliterature.
Probably cases differ here; there were, especially in the late nineteenth century, popular
writers who lived in a profoundly intimate symbiosis with their public; in Germany, the
authors of immensely successful sentimental and melodramatic bourgeois novels, Hedwig
Courths-Mahler and E. Marlitt, would be examples, as would Sir Walter Scott in England
and James Whitcomb Riley in the United States—all in literary borderline cases.

ever, and the tendency to try to find middle-ground solutions to them suggest that extrinsicality has not been legislated out of the purview of concern. One such difficulty is that extrinsic considerations may obscure the focus upon literature in its difference from other kinds of utterances. This is particularly likely to occur when stress is laid upon literature as a superstructural epiphenomenon;[51] because of the negative evaluation placed on the "superstructure" by Marxists, the logical result is a view of literature as a vehicle of content, thus erasing the boundaries that mark it off as a defined object of consideration. It is not only literary sociology that has brought the distinction between literary and non-literary writing under suspicion; some contemporary scholars wish to construct a spectrum without a fixed boundary, while for others "fiction" is from the outset a bourgeois, suspect category.[52] A related problem with extrinsic considerations is that they may obscure precise distinctions of literary works from one another. This accounts in part for the fact that literary sociology has produced so little major criticism of specific works; its wider focus and its sometimes allergic reaction to any notion of individuality inhibits an interest in literary detail. The result is that periods or the corpus of a single writer are treated without regard to their inner differentiation, thus often violating both the intentionality and the observable character of literary works.

Then there is what I would call the argument *ex silentio*. The concept of false consciousness has heightened our awareness of what an author does not say, what he does not get into view, what is veiled, obscured, or deflected in his communicated apprehension of the world, his failure to be conscious of social commitments and class complicities. Much of the current discussion of nineteenth-century German realism, for example, makes much of the fact that the proletariat is largely absent from it or is presented in an archaic or euphemistic manner; thus it is seen as a flawed, even ideologically corrupt, certainly imperfect realism. It is most useful and necessary to draw attention to such matters. But the danger is to lose track of the positive specificity of authors. Michel Zéraffa asks: "How does the non-awareness of Balzac differ from that of Eugène Sue, the non-awareness of James from that of his friend Paul Bourget, the non-awareness of Virginia Woolf from that of her 'enemy' Galsworthy?"[53] These are very just questions. My own experience in reading contemporary literary study is that, while the sociological argument *ex silentio* is helpful in blocking out the gross location of a writer, it does not carry very far into criticism, which at some point or other has to accept the ideologically limiting boundaries of a text and turn its attention to what goes on within them. The alternative is a literary history that consists primarily of expulsions.

By middle-ground solutions I mean those that acknowledge extrinsic considerations hovering around the genesis and reception of literature but that try to delimit their significance for criticism. In their famous essay on the intentional fallacy, Wimsatt and Beardsley argued that internal evidence is public, as it is grounded in shared language discoverable from the public text, while external evidence is private because it is personal and idiosyncratic.[54] This is an ingenious twist on the argument and I would not at all associate myself with it, but it may help to point the way to solutions by calling attention to the social nature of language and inviting us to differentiate among extrinsic concerns that are private and those of wider relevance. Beardsley is elsewhere concerned about the intrusion of personal resonances, nostalgic associations, or professional enthusiasms into evaluation, and observes: "It is easy for a Scotsman to overrate Burns, a liberal Democrat Whitman, or an old French scholar *Le Chanson de Roland*."[55] But modern theory is becoming increasingly less convinced that it is possible or even desirable to wash out the associative resonances of the receiver in favor of a neutral contemplation, and in any case I do not think private predilections ought to be put in a series with the question of the democratic evaluation of Whitman, which is a matter of larger public and historical relevance and requires a less off-hand kind of approach. Ingarden, attentive to the problem of dissolving the specificity of the work by bringing external information to bear upon it, goes to the other extreme of asserting the total individuality of each work, which threatens to atomize literary experience into monads* and contributes, I think, to making criticism idiosyncratic and unshareable.[56] David Daiches has tried to solve the problem by saying that we need no extrinsic information "in order to assess the written work as it exists, an independent and self-existent work of art, but we may need such information in order to see the work properly before we begin to assess it."[57] The sharp distinction between the processes of cognition and interpretation leads to the same objections as the distinction made by empirical sociology between pre-work and post-work phases and the work itself. If extrinsic information is needed to know the work, then it is not independent and self-existent except in a purely heuristic sense. The newer attitude in these matters is captured by

* Lukács' traditionalism shows up again in his insistence upon the singularity of the work of art (*Ästhetik* [Neuwied: Luchterhand, 1972], II, 158, 205). He goes so far as to call the individual work a "windowless monad" (ibid., III, 55).

Ronald Peacock when he argues that "the other interests are built into the art-object, are internal elements of it, not external relational objects. [Claudel's] *Partage du Midi*, or *Le Soulier de Satin*, or Eliot's plays, do not 'have a relationship with' religion; it is built in." In a fable, "the moral point is not neutralized by an aesthetic object but sharpened into a work of art called a fable."[58]

The impossibility of talking about literature and its meaning without extrinsic referents when coupled with a denial of the propriety of such referents has led, I fear, to some mysterious ingenuity. Northrop Frye supplies an example in *The Critical Path*. He begins this queerly subtitled "essay on the social context of literary criticism" with a familiar restatement of the claim that literature has nothing serious to do with anything outside of itself and by condemning "the impulse to find the ultimate meaning of literature in something that is not literature."[59] Yet he does make some extensive if rather recondite claims for the relation of literature and society, and since he denies any connection between literary history and real history, he invents two concepts, which he calls a "myth of concern" and a "myth of freedom," from which he develops some not unmeaningful insights, but in a wholly essayistic manner of free association. So Frye has it both ways: he is able to propagate his own social views while assuring us that his view of literature is free of extrinsic considerations. The urge to develop invented and imaginary categories of discourse rather than drawing upon the categories of real history is one of the most troublesome aspects of the criticism of our time; it puts a premium upon ingenuity and esoteric fireworks rather than upon a striving for correctness and demonstrable results that would be transmittable intact from one mind to another. When one insists upon talking about "myths" of concern and freedom rather than about classes, politics, specific historical circumstances, flesh-and-blood authors, actual audiences, oppressive or emancipatory implications, the suspicion arises, whether justly or not, that there is an intention to block our understanding of these matters.*

---

* Needless to say, I am not unmindful that what I persist in calling "real history" has its own ambivalence and that any historiography may be seen as an imposition of plot and interpretation on the raw material of the historical record. From Hayden White, who is partly dependent on Frye, I have learned with interest that my own view of history is satirical in emplotment, contextualist in mode of explanation, and liberal in mode of ideological application, and with salutary surprise that romantic-ideographic-anarchist, comic-organicist-conservative, or tragic-mechanistic-radical types can be regarded as just as good—although I naturally don't accept this ("Interpretation in History," *New Literary History* 4 [1972/73]:307). First of all, there is in all history an irreducible realm that is not

It seems to me, however, that the main task of literary sociology should not be to refute intrinsic positions—this is becoming a monotonous industry—just as it is not wholly helpful for literary critics to keep pointing to the not infrequent blindness and brutality of extrinsic claims. It would seem more useful to seek out areas of potential agreement that would allow a new beginning in criticism without losing the benefit of the intellectual treasure stored up in all camps. We find, I think, that the immanent critics are more extrinsic than they or others have wanted to believe; and that the best extrinsic and even Marxist criticism does not seek to legislate the specificity of the literary work out of existence with concepts of determinism. Even Ingarden admits that a literary work can have external referents, although he does not think them very important. Even Jameson gives a variegated list of ways in which we can conceive the relationship of literature and society, at least one of which acknowledges the imaginative or symbolic character of the fictional work.[60] As soon as literary sociology calls attention to the *negative* correlation of art and society, a very considerable concession is made in favor of the freedom of the imagination. Jameson says that for Adorno, "the work of art 'reflects' society and is historical to the degree that it *refuses* the social, and represents the last refuge of individual subjectivity from the historical forces that threaten to crush it. . . . Thus the socio-economic is inscribed in the work, but as concave to convex, as negative to positive."[61] This quite precise observation exposes the wholly metaphorical character of the concept of reflection. A negative correlation of this kind could hardly be a wholly determined one, for the negations generated will be of widely different character and themselves suggest a substantial degree of freedom of the imagination in protest, or at least in an unwillingness to reflect dumbly and uncritically the light cast on it by social convention and reality. But in order to attempt rational criticism, we must know something about that reality and acknowledge it as a foil against which the creative imagination works.

---

subject to "mythic" transformation; no *historiographical* "plot" can be devised in which Napoleon conquered Russia or the South fought the Civil War to a stalemate, though a fictional one certainly could. I should think it would be the striving of learning to make this unmanipulable realm as large as possible. More important, I believe that excessive recourse to the concept of myth is threatening to undermine and trivialize intellectual pursuits. It generates a cynicism about the pursuit of truth of fact and correctness of interpretation, which revenges itself in anti-intellectualism and assaults upon learning and its institutions. In addition, it shares with certain aspects of our subject an unwillingness to believe that there can be a reciprocal pressure from reality upon consciousness, understanding, and a preordered mind set. The notion that all intellectual ordering is the imposition of fictional pattern and myth threatens to lead to monologism and indifference.

Lionel Trilling remarks succinctly that, although the connection between literature and politics is denied by some critics, it is easily understood by both governments and writers;[62] while Lukács, threading his way between esoteric aesthetics and vulgar claims that art "directly facilitates the pursuit of specific concrete social tasks," points out that the mainstream of aesthetics from Classical antiquity was concerned with art's influence on human and social life.[63] In discussing the gap between the politics of the best modern writers and those of the liberal educated class, Trilling worries that there is "no connection between the political ideas of our educated class and the deep places of the imagination," and warns that "unless we insist that politics is imagination and mind, we will learn that imagination and mind are politics, and of a kind that we will not like."[64] There is plenty of past precedent and present evidence to encourage us to take this warning seriously. "It is not possible," he asserts, "to conceive of a person standing beyond his culture. . . . Even when a person rejects his culture (as the phrase goes) and rebels against it, he does so in a culturally determined way."[65] This insight runs parallel to that of the negative correlation and calls our attention to extrinsic determinants without obliging us to believe that their effect is one of strict causality. Finally, Trilling makes a cautious observation on the obligations of what we are doing: "the world will not be saved by teaching English at universities, nor, indeed, by any other literary activity. It is very hard to say what will save the world. But we can be perfectly certain that denying the actualities of the world will not work its salvation."[66]

This consideration seems to me of more importance than technical inquiries into the nature and limits of determination or the quantity of our interest in the space of freedom within the literary work relative to that in its given extrinsic circumstances. These matters are important and need to be sorted out carefully. But the overriding issue for our intellectual activity is what students, admittedly sometimes trapped in their own inarticulateness or in a conservative refusal to reach beyond their own horizons, are pointing to when they speak of "relevance." Either literature is relevant to matters outside it or it is not. If we insist that it is not, we cannot complain of the lack of interest by the majority of even educated people in what we are presenting as a hobby of refined spirits or an introverted relevance that seeks to salvage poetry as a universal, internally unified but externally walled human activity. If we believe that it is relevant, we ought not to invent evasive and obscure categories for dealing with its extrinsic referentiality, but should try to find a realistic mode of discourse that will respect the freedom of the imagination without acquiescing in its every vagary.

VIII

Some Conclusions

All mapmakers should place the Mississippi in the
same location, and avoid originality.
    —SAUL BELLOW, *Mr. Sammler's Planet*

THE FOREGOING will have shown that inquiring into literary sociology for
answers to the crisis of interpretation and criticism will not yield easy
answers or a methodology in which one can comfortably rest. The
discipline hardly exists as a coherent body of thought; it is sharply
divided by differences between empirical and speculative approaches;
there will be found widely differing conceptions of the nature of the
work of art, its status, value, and utility, and the most appropriate,
relevant way of taking it in hand; and the massive presence of Marxism
involves the inquiry with every aspect of reality and consciousness. "It is
one thing for us to understand" that there is an intimate relation between
literature and society, writes Malcolm Bradbury, "and another for us to
be good at talking about it."[1] While considerable progress is being made
on several peninsulas of scholarship, a unified theory is not yet in view.
The first step toward the possibility of such progress would be an attempt
to solve some communication difficulties. These are of two kinds. In the
first place, either literary critics are going to have to make an effort to
master the neo-Hegelian pidgin in which German, some French, and,
increasingly, English-language contributions to this subject are written,
or scholars pursuing sociological criticism must be encouraged to express themselves in some language spoken by human beings. I have a
personal preference for the latter solution—that it can be done has been
demonstrated by the Marxist George Thomson—but I think it the less
likely one, especially as Germans and German traditions are centrally
involved; therefore both sympathetic and critical translators are needed.
In English, Fredric Jameson has made a beginning, but it would be good

to have similar studies from observers less afflicted with true faith. Secondly, there is a need for the critics on all sides of the issue to listen to one another more carefully and desist from stock responses and the misrepresentation of opposing positions. Certain words—like "autonomy" or "coherence" on the one side, or "determination" and "reflection" on the other—arouse allergic reactions that not infrequently hinder a willingness to penetrate into the logic of the opposing argument. The issues involved are difficult and cannot be argued out of existence by polemic, apodictic assertions, or sovereign gestures.

Despite the present state of the discipline, there seems to me a powerful potential in it for the renovation of literary studies, although certain concomitant problems require exceptional alertness. First of all, if an inquiry into literary sociology does nothing else, its challenge ought to impel the critic to reflect upon the foundations of his own standpoint and become more alert to the ideological components of other critical positions. Looking at the history of interpretation from the long view, there seems to be no literary theory or practice of literary understanding without some order of commitment, regardless of claims to the contrary; therefore not only conscious reflection on our own order of commitment but also bringing it into a more defensible and self-aware ethical stance would seem to be a desirable beginning for improving the state of literary criticism. Such self-questioning would, of course, be futile if the freedom of inquiry were as wholly impossible as Roland Barthes makes it out to be,[2] for then we should not be able to improve our intellectual standpoint except, perhaps, by the amazing grace of Marxist conversion. Intellectual discourse has no point without a conviction that opinions can be changed or expanded in their range by the force of argument. The denial of at least this much freedom leads the critic to a posture of supercilious arrogance, exchanging knowing snickers with the like-minded, a posture that has become not uncommon among oppositional intellectuals and that is assumed by, among others, Roland Barthes, at least in the *Mythologies*. But the notion that the critic is a kind of pure and empty vessel into which the literary experience pours itself will not stand up to any kind of scrutiny. "Our convictions even about the most purely intellectual matters cannot help fundamentally affecting our literary responses," says Wayne Booth,[3] in notably close agreement with Lukács, who says of the receiver of a work of art generally that he is "never a blank page on which anything can be encoded."[4] This would appear to imply an obligation for reflection upon one's convictions, and especially that part of them that seems the most instinctual or self-evident, for they are the most likely to have been socially determined, and thus to involve allegiances of which we may at first only be dimly aware.

That such reflective self-awareness may not in itself be sufficient is a point that has been made by Erwin Leibfried: "in reflection . . . a dependence cannot be eliminated. It can and must be exposed and made conscious, we must see through its function; but why should this unveiling reflection have an emancipatory effect? . . . . The one thing (reflection) belongs to epistemology, the other (decision) to ethics."[5] I have said earlier that I do not believe reflection must lead to a total abandonment of one's convictions, although it is likely to put them on a more cautious footing. The ethical commitment that literary sociology seems to imply with regard to both literature and criticism is troubling to some people; "they smell moralism or something of the kind," as Müller-Seidel put it.[6] But it may be that the legislation of the moral consciousness out of criticism and a denial of its interest in literature itself have partly contributed to our confusions. The danger lies not in the ethical appeal itself, but in the tendency, especially of Marxism, to demand that one set of commitments be replaced by another. The idea that thinking can only take place within one fixed ideological order or another is flatly wrong; it is a self-serving argument of Marxists and leads, as I tried to show elsewhere, to the anguished acceptance of nonsense or atrocities. Caudwell's argument that there is only a choice between determination by unreflected instinct and determination by rationally perceived necessity, for all the light it throws upon the careless use of the idea of freedom, is self-contradictory, for if it were true, there would be no choice. Imagination is the enemy of determinism, and in this lies the possiblity of literature as well as of criticism. Literary sociology can help the critic to understand that he carries much socially determined faith around with him,[7] just as there is much carried by literary texts to which he may be inclined to respond affirmatively rather than skeptically; its proper purpose, in my view, is not to substitute one faith for another, but to get all matters of faith under rational control. Nor need this result in the legislation of the artistic imagination out of existence, as some may fear; here the neo-Marxist axiom that the imagination is rational, for all that it has been applied to silly purposes, has force and value. It is a curious indication of the way the threads of these problems run that the East German—and therefore to some extent official—Marxist Robert Weimann, in mounting a critique of the rigidity of Goldmann's concept of homology, seeks to balance a view of the individual, concrete work of literature as *parole* with its embracing and interpenetrating real, general, historical context as *langue* from which the work is selectively actualized and in so doing adverts to none other than E. D. Hirsch.[8]

However, as soon as literary sociology appears in any sense to point to an ethical dimension of criticism, the danger emerges of overrunning the text with considerations that obscure its own particularity and complexity. The most extreme example of this is the employment of literary texts as political weapons—marching against capitalism with Shakespeare and Goethe. Even the sober, urbane Weimann asserts that American New Criticism should be combatted with Lessing and Goethe, whose heritage only Marxist literary study preserves.[9] Any objections to this form of politicization of literature is likely to be denounced as a reactionary resistance. This is not, or should not be, the source of the objection. Doubtless all literature occurs in a political environment, even when it denies politics, and, insofar as the imagination is critical and oppositional, it is political. But when a total and single-minded political endeavor is allowed to absorb the whole critical enterprise, the result is a loss of respect for the text, its nuances and internal stresses, its intentionality, and its historical actuality. Signs of this are a mania for allegorization, the tendency to quote selectively from a body of literature as though it were a corpus of statements, and in-group interpretation not subject to reciprocal validation by the text and its circumstances as a whole. A signal of the concomitant loss of any empirical restraint in interpretation is often the use of the word "objectively," which introduces an argument that a thing is not what it appears to be at all but something quite different. "Objectively," we are told, the two sets of parents in Gottfried Keller's story *A Village Romeo and Juliet*, whose economic and moral decline looks to the untutored eye to be the result of failings of character, "come to ruin as a result of the loss of class status of the individual peasant determined by developments in production techniques";[10] "objectively," the sleazy Queen Elizabeth of Schiller's *Maria Stuart* is in reality its heroine because she represented the progressive principle historically and Schiller is by definition a progressive writer.[11]

It is easy to make fun of such foolishness, although it might be more appropriate to be dismayed at its frequent occurrence and to feel some fear of the sort of political purposes that impel it. The trouble is that there is a problem all across the critical spectrum concerning the binding force of the literal implications of a text. Geoffrey Hartman asserts in his critique of formalism that "great exegetes . . . have always, at some point, swerved from the literal sense of the text. This text, like the world, was a prison for Rabbinic, Patristic, or Neoplatonic interpreters, yet by their hermeneutic act the prison opened into a palace and the extremes of man's dependence and of his capacity for vision came simultaneously into view."[12] Once again we note the ever recurring tendency to draw parallels from religion. For the Rabbis the text was law; for the Fathers, truth; for Neoplatonists, an intimation of a higher mystical unity. A literary text is none of these things. Law stands in a tension between its literal meaning and both the spirit of justice and the practical exigencies of life, and Rabbinical hermeneutics is a technique to keep the Law both intact and functioning. If a text as contradictory and often incredible as the Christian scriptures is to be regarded as divinely inspired truth, then certainly great feats of ingenuity will have to be performed upon it to defend its inspired status. Neoplatonist mysticism is one of the burdens that German Romanticism loaded upon criticism, along with many blessings, and it is hardly a model we can tolerate today. Why is it so difficult in the twentieth century to accept the idea that the poet is neither a lawgiver nor a prophet nor an inspired visionary, but a particular and often peculiar imagination possessed of a partial vision of specially focused intensity?

Contemporary radical criticism appears to me often to have a paradoxical view of the status of literary art. On the one hand radicals are by nature iconoclastic, contemptuous of the canon, and of claims of special privilege for the literary object, taking a presentist, moral line away from disinterested contemplation and toward political utility. On the other hand, frequently when they take a particular literary phenomenon in hand, they will themselves make claims for prodigies of cognition, of irresistible appellativeness, of representativeness and inclusiveness, all of which contribute to excruciating apologetics. Sometimes when reading the contemporary discussion I find myself saying: No, no, the literary work in its own character is more important than this; while in other places I will say: No literary work can be this important, can be expected to encompass so much truth or bear the responsibility for unimpeachable solutions to the distress of its times and of the human condition. Marxists in particular seem to me to require more of the great works especially than they can perform, and consequently I wonder whether Marxist literary criticism, in the largest historical sense, is not part of the whole effort of the Western intelligentsia in the first half of this century to seek salvation from the apparent disintegration of traditional civilization in literary culture. Naturally I believe that literature is important to the well-being of the race, specifically in respect of its fictionality, for it supplies subjunctive, optative, sometimes hortatory, often negating possibilities that make more precise the vision into the human condition and give body and substance to our meditation upon it; consequently I think literary criticism important as a mediation of this significant kind of human behavior. But I would plead in all directions for a more modest sense of literature's weight and importance in human affairs—a modesty forced upon us by the results of empirical literary sociology—and for resisting any mode of criticism that would lose interest in literature's partial, relative, tentative, experimental, and idiosyncratic values by insisting that it embrace the whole realm of human value. When the failure of it to do this emerges, a violent reaction can set in, an embittered feeling of betrayal of an investment that ought not to have been made in the first place.

We have become accustomed to believe that conscious intentionality is not binding on criticism and that the text can release energies of which the author was unaware. Doubtless there is truth in this; doubtless it is one of the secrets of endurance; doubtless the concept of the "intentional fallacy" put into circulation by Wimsatt and Beardsley was, in its time, an emancipatory event for criticism. Some literary sociologists have associated themselves with a version of this view. Lucien Goldmann consistently takes the position that the individual writer's consciousness is not wholly determinative of his work's meaning, and remarks that "literary history is full of examples of writers whose ideas completely contradict the meaning and structure of their work (Balzac and Goethe, for example)";[13] and Escarpit's idea of "creative treason" and his argument that the reader has no choice but to make a myth if there is a historical gap of understanding between him and the work belong here as well.[14] But of late there has been a growing suspicion that our age has gone too far in abandoning fidelity to the original meaning of a text. Wayne Booth is one of those who came to be worried about this: "When Cervantes labors to place his woeful knight as a blind (though lovable) fool, we simply ignore him: the Don is really a Christian Saint, a great Ironic Hero whom Cervantes himself does not fully understand."[15] Perhaps this is right; it is very hard to say; or, more likely it would be better to say that Cervantes' vision became more complex than his initial intention, so that we do not ignore the intention but recognize that the process of creation has reached well beyond it. Something of this sort happened to Schiller's early dramas, which turned out to be more complex and ironic than his fairly rigorous intention would suggest, because the process of creation brought to the surface so much more of his fierce intelligence than his philosophical and moral reasoning was able to do; and no one

has been able to accept Brecht's insistence that Mother Courage is a
horrible example—though in neither case would it be right to argue that
the work has simply separated itself from its author, for it is the author's
partly unacknowledged complexities that are at work. But we have
perhaps lost our sense of caution in talking about such things. Booth
continues: "Once we decide that against their conscious aims authors
work their wonders, no criticial hypothesis, however far from the author's provable intentions inside the work or out can be refuted; this in
turn means that nothing can be proved, since no evidence is more
relevant than any other." [16]

Booth's strictures apply to Marxist literary criticism as well, which is, if
anything, even more insouciant about validity in interpretation. It does
not matter that Goethe was a firmly anti-democratic counterrevolutio-
nary, that Balzac was a royalist, that Heine strove to keep an elitist
conception of the poetic dignity intact, for "objectively" they were all
progressive or even revolutionary writers. On the other hand, it does
matter that Eliot was a "royalist"—whatever that was supposed to mean in
the twentieth century—and Yeats was susceptible to Fascism, for "objectively"—and so on. Operating with concepts like "false consciousness"
and negative dialectical correlation can do as much violence to the
original sense of a text as concepts of intentional fallacy or autonomy.
Here the major call to order has not come from literary sociology, as one
logically might expect, but from the hermeneuticist E. D. Hirsch, for
whom the "preference for original meaning over anachronistic meaning" is "ultimately an ethical choice." Hirsch ingeniously turns the question against anti-intentional critics themselves: "The question I always
want to ask critics who dismiss authorial intention as their norm is one
that could be transposed into the categorical imperative or simply into
the golden rule. I want to ask them this: 'When you write a piece of
criticism, do you want me to disregard *your* intention and original meaning? Why do you say to me 'That is not what I meant at all; that is not it at
all'? Why do you ask me to honor the ethics of language for your writings
when you do not honor them for the writings of others?'" [17] * Some might

---

*Recently Kenneth Burke has unwittingly supplied us with a splendid illustration of
Hirsch's point. Burke has been a regular defender of "anagogic" meaning—a synthetic
ingenuity that gives the interpreter every privilege over the intentionality of the text and is
scornful of interpreting a literary object by endeavoring to see what is there. But when
Wayne Booth attempted a generally sympathetic and admiring explication of Burke's
views, Burke burst out in exasperation at what seemed to him to be misrepresentations.
Burke, I am afraid, had the worst of this exchange. Apart from the consideration that
Burke, like the rest of us, is not immune from criticism, despite his acknowledged genius,

reply that the artistic work is simply incommensurable with an expository utterance in this regard, a point on which Hirsch is skeptical, while the Marxist would no doubt reply that what you think your private meaning to be is of no importance anyway. Hirsch leaves room for a decision to go beyond intentional meaning; he is merely calling for moderation. It appears to me that literary sociology would reach results that could command more general assent if it associated itself more with the position of Hirsch than with the Marxist technique of extrapolating a "use value" from a partially apprehended original text.

There can be no doubt that literary sociology opens up valuable new paths of scholarship. Its stress upon seeing literary phenomena as components in a real process surrounding them holds the promise of liberating us from the constraints modern criticism imposed upon itself, no doubt usefully at one time. Its construction of a literary equation that includes authors and readers, its synchronic expansion of our purview to include subliterature and bestsellers, its refocus of attention on the political environment of literature, and its introduction of solid techniques such as those of statistics all contain the potential for renovating literary studies. The danger, of course, is that these efforts, too, will become a *perpetuum mobile* of "research" pursued as an end in itself, as some current literary study has become, without a link to the pursuit of intelligent and humane criticism. There is nothing to be said against statistics, and its proper application can help preserve literary history from certain kinds of complacency. But a point can be reached where statistical data become too easy to accumulate and keep pointing over and over to the same conclusions. A literary sociology that does not operate inside the text as well as outside it, runs the risk, as Goldmann clearly saw, of losing any interest as a mode of literary study. Some of Kenneth Burke's synthetic spirit is required here. "Every document bequeathed us by history," he writes, "must be treated as a *strategy for encompassing a situation* . . . as the *answer* or *rejoinder* to assertions current in the situation in which it arose."[18] This genuinely dialectical concept of the relationship of a text with its surrounding reality, in the words of the sociologist of art Jean Duvignaud, "authorizes criticism to speak of a work of art as an effort that attempts to surmount an obstacle, an obstacle

---

on his own premises he has no grounds for objecting to any use made of his texts whatever. See Wayne C. Booth, "Kenneth Burke's Way of Knowing," and Burke, "In Response to Booth: Dancing with Tears in My Eyes," *Critical Inquiry* 1 (1974/75):1–31. For one example of Burke's advocacy of anagogic interpretation, see *A Rhetoric of Motives* (Berkeley: University of California Press, 1969), pp.219–221.

of receptivity failing to receive a message unattended to or poorly comprehended, an obstacle of the distance and dispersion or irreducible separation into castes, classes, groups, an obstacle of the changing meaning of signs."[19] There is probably an underlying sense in which most kinds of criticism pursue this end in one way or another; literary sociology can help us become more concretely aware of it and remind us in particular that some firm knowledge of the reality to which literature offers an answer is required.

There is at present no generally acceptable systematic theory of the nature of the correlation of literary events and complexities to core patterns of society. In fact, as far as I can see, there are only two comprehensive pretenders to such a theory: Lukács' uncompleted aesthetics and Goldmann's concept of globality. I have already indicated why the latter appears to me unacceptable as a general theory, although Goldmann's specific applications of it may be illuminating of their objects. It is not within the scope of my interest to mount a systematic critique of Lukács' aesthetics; such a task would probably exceed my powers. I believe I am not alone in this limitation and, frankly, I worry about the usefulness for practical critical tasks of a philosophical system of such technical abstruseness that its mastery becomes a full-time occupation. The task draws us away from the subject of literature, as, so it appears to me, Lukács' aesthetics does as well; it is not only abstract but also exceedingly normative, so that it cannot fully account for the variety and detail of literary creation and experience. Furthermore, a theory that sees practically every mental act as a reflection of reality runs the risk, despite its philosophical sophistication, of falling into banality and tautology, for a concept so broad lacks the specificity needed for precise apprehension of artistic objects.

I am by no means convinced that such a general theory is even possible. While I do not doubt the existence of correlations between literature and society, it seems improbable that they are of the same nature in all cases. Whether we are concerned with content, with form, with the persistence of works or the continuity of genres, with the moral quality of consciousness and values, with the interrelationship of passive or affirmative and active or critical ideology, with the location of authors or received works in social groups—the kinds of possible relationships and contrasts are of great variety and it is hard to conceive of a kind of theory that could accommodate all of them in a formal scheme. Any theory that is unable to cope, not only with contingency, but with the constant emergence of eccentricity and idiosyncrasy in significant literary developments is doomed to impotence. It may be, as L. C. Knights observed a good many years ago, "that the subject, as usually formulated, is too large and general. It can only be discussed at all in relation to a particular place and time, and then it is seen to split into a multitude of smaller problems, a bewildering complexity supervening upon the simplicity of the dialectical formulation."[20] The pursuit of detail, whether critical or factual, is a notorious enemy of speculative literary-sociological patterns. Even so apparently obvious a connection between the development of the realistic novel and the increasing self-awareness of the middle class can be subjected to a wide variety of detailed objections, as Diana Spearman's *The Novel and Society* has shown.

Spearman's book, however, is in turn no very satisfactory model for dealing with these matters. Nowhere does she seriously contend with any literary-sociological position, except in an unsystematic way with the views of Ian Watt. This permits her the unfortunately all too common practice of setting up straw men on the ground of determinism and reflection and then refuting claims that no modern exponent of the subject has entertained. She would have us believe, for example, that "to prove that any book is the creation of a particular class," it would be necessary to show that the author was of the class, the book was intended for that class, and that it displays an explicit attitude of that class, requirements that would indeed inhibit the literary-sociological pursuit. Her most evident weakness, however, is her attempt to oppose to sociological explanations determinants arising internally from literary tradition. This is worth mentioning because the notion that literature is the final or sufficient cause of literature has a remarkable currency in contemporary scholarship, although it is a good deal more implausible than any species of sociological argument. Spearman's examples are so poorly taken that it is perhaps unfair to use them to attack the position, but, since they loom so large in her argument, something may be said about them. She makes a great deal of the persistence of Arthurian themes from the Middle Ages through Malory to the present, and seems to think that this alleged continuity refutes reflection theories, as though *Stoff* (in the German distinction from *Gehalt* and *Gestalt*) were the single controlling aspect of a literary phenomenon. She argues in the same place that the appearance of romance in troubled times refutes determinism, which is really a most obtuse and elementary example of an undialectical argument. She asks: "How could Marlowe and Goethe in such different societies have both written plays based on a German medieval legend?"[21] The fact that the Faust legend is not medieval, but is associated with the early modern world, as the legendary connection of Faust with Gutenberg and the invention of printing illustrates, may be mentioned as a detail. But more important is the emptiness of the point she thinks she is making. No one could seriously compare Marlowe and Goethe, or any of the other *Fausts* from the chapbook to Thomas Mann, on the grounds of continuing elements in an internal, autonomous literary tradition. The extraordinary inherent radiance of the Faust legend is, of course, an interesting phenomenon of "modern," i.e., post-medieval literature. But who would set the *Fausts* of Marlowe and Goethe side by side without being attentive to the fundamentally different use made of the legend? Who could begin to talk about Goethe's *Faust* in the most elementary way without being aware that Goethe profoundly altered and complicated the social and moral significance of the Faust figure? It could be said that Goethe found Marlowe's Faust standing on his head and set him on his feet, if such operations were as simple in literature as they are alleged to be in philosophy. Doubtless it is true that Thomas Mann, out of his ambition to be the representative German writer, wrote *Doktor Faustus* because of the existence of Goethe's *Faust*; but this, like all his other parodistic echoes and transformations of literary tradition, is not internally literary but occurs out of a concern for the location and function of cultural traditions in the modern social situation. *Doktor Faustus*, though we may not assent to it in every respect, is one of the few truly great literary responses to German Fascism; what can this possibly have to do with Marlowe? The case shows the most fundamental need for subordinating literary history to general history, or at least for an insistence upon historical irreversibility. I hold with Marx in the *German Ideology* that there is only one history,[22] and one does not have to yield to Marxist eschatology to believe that any segmentation of history is a matter of methodological focus only. Some versions of the argument for metahistorical literary autonomy would seem to suggest that literary phenomena are mutually comprehensible irrespective of historical time. It is the peculiar misconception that Edmund Wilson, more than forty years ago, detected in the view of Eliot and Valéry, who "confuse certain questions by talking as if the whole of literature existed simultaneously in a vacuum, as if Homer's and Shakespeare's situations had been the same as Mallarmé's and Laforgue's, as if the latter had been attempting to play the same sort of rôles as the former and could be judged on the same basis."[23] While Mann had a very considerable grasp of Goethe, if Goethe, by some magical contrivance, could have been given *Doktor Faustus* to read in his lifetime, he could not have had the remotest understanding of what it is about.

So much mystification has been generated with the notion of internal literary history that it probably would be well, for the time being at least, to look upon the literary tradition as merely one segment of the raw material of reality that the artist's consciousness confronts. Internal literary history is an example of a self-verifying argument; because sequences of literary influences are present, they are therefore determined to be causative. Certainly there is an inertia of artistic style and technique, as there is a conservative back pressure in all aspects of civilization. But, at any historical moment, the writer is confronted with a vast and varied literary tradition, and the kinds of choices he makes cannot be accounted for by an impetus emerging from this tradition alone. Stendhal perceived this a century and a half ago.[24] No young person reading Homer and Vergil today would be inspired with the ambition to write a heroic national epic in Classical meter, though such a response was common in nineteenth-century Germany. Brecht had a very strong feeling for literary traditions of all kinds, but he selected those most useful to him, on principles too well known to be repeated, in opposition to the forms and conventions to which he was most directly the heir. It would be far more absurd to say that the street ballad and the Chinese theater are the "causes" of Brecht's forms than to find their causes in social and political purposes. As for the novel, its death is proclaimed daily, and, while the announcement continues to appear premature, the fuss about the question shows an awareness that the novel is situated in a particular kind of historical constellation, and what it has come to be certainly would have looked very peculiar to novelists of the past. Spearman's effort to refute the theory of the middle-class origins of the European realistic novel by pointing to one eleventh-century Japanese novel, Chinese popular narrations, the Spanish Picaresque, *Don Quixote*, and aristocratic French novels of manners—while they may have some value in encouraging us to make our arguments more precise—are irrelevant in the face of the massive quantitative and qualitative novelty of the genre since the eighteenth century. This is not to say that the literary heritage is not a portion of reality of the intensest interest to the writer; that apprenticeship on or opposition to models, imitation, and literary inspiration do not inform his own creative practice in the most concrete way. James Baldwin once said somewhere that the Black writer does not come out of the ghetto, but out of the library; just as Malraux says somewhere that it is not sheep that inspire a Giotto, but the first sight of paintings of them.[25] Although these are hyperboles, they are no doubt useful ones at a time when cultural illiteracy is sometimes offered as a positive value. We shall want to keep in view Harry Levin's argument that no art is free from conventions and that "realism" is the application of new forms of illusion as a rectification of other illusions;[26] but the question is to which aspect of this process our attention ought to be directed. The history of literary influence, that most abused and disdained of critical pursuits, is one of transformations, not of retentions, and the determinants of these transformations have to be sought outside the literary tradition itself.

One of the most difficult unsolved problems is to know how to keep literary sociology and interpretation in proper balance with one another. The relative lack of examples of fine literary-sociological criticism is a symptom of this, and proponents of a genuine *literary* sociology are becoming concerned about its characteristic avoidance of texts.[27] Some modes of literary sociology allow a hatred of "bourgeois" society to spill over into an indifference to or actual dislike of art itself. On the other hand, much literary criticism has brought upon itself the anger it has drawn from some quarters. Its denial of history, its manipulation of dubious concepts like "timelessness," its efforts to sever the contemplation of literature from the most pressing concerns of mankind, its irrational esotericism and ideological orthodoxy have all contributed to a sometimes embittered sense of its irrelevance. Despite these burdens, we can surely be confident that interpretation has a real object and is necessary if we are to retain true possession of literary works. It is not hard to point to examples of literary-sociological criticism that distort, reduce, or falsify texts by failing to attend to formal considerations, to internal tensions, nuances, and cohesions, and, very frequently, to the exigencies of fictionality. After a half-century of critical effort, it is depressing how often fictional speakers are confused with narrators and narrators with authors, how often poems are taken to be assertions and novels as tracts, how often the experimental, provisional nature of fictional assertions is transmuted into philosophy. These failings can be so crude that they arouse impatience in the reader and may therefore block his reception of other, truer insights in the same criticism. It is doubtful that conceptions that make one of the endeavors subordinate or ancillary to the other ought to be encouraged. Learning to distinguish effectively between pluralism and eclecticism is one of the hard problems now facing us; it is true, as R. S. Crane has pointed out, that there are questions concerning how things hang together and concerning how they are different,[28] and both kinds of inquiry are legitimate. But the need in the present fragmented state of affairs is to try to maintain a simultaneous vision on both kinds of question and make literary sociology and interpretation as complementary as possible.

Pluralism of method, or at least of vision, must be kept open because of the high cost of seeing the literary object as a single, welded unity or as a unitary element inseparable from its context. Sometimes the longing for an unambiguous, unalienated existence leads to a pressure to unify the experience of present and past reality by force. But this cannot be done without impoverishment, and the excessively maligned pluralism of perspectives in the West is an effort to make cultural experience additive rather than reductive. I find that, in the working out of these essays, I have had recourse several times to a simultaneous double vision. I have stressed, for example, the need to keep different and competing systems of value intact in judging the literary phenomenon, and this duality or multiplicity of vision I find to be an attitude that has risen to the surface in the course of this inquiry; it was not an articulated initial position with which I began.

Without wishing to be too schematic about it, this leads me to suggest that our subject encourages a perception of the literary object as duple, rather than a yielding to intrinsic or extrinsic pressures toward union and harmony. In this view, the work is a compound of two portions, which for the sake of the argument I shall call the conventional and the critical. It is important to understand that I do not mean these to be evaluative distinctions. The conventional portion draws upon and refines tradition, formal and otherwise, and is shaped as well by the socially ordered affirmative consciousness and by the expectations of a real or projected audience. It is this portion that, insofar as it can be distinguished from the other, is in the tightest reciprocal relationship with context and therefore not only yields information to sociological questioning, but in the course of its reception is most likely to bear symbols, doubtless in ideological and reified form, into the future. Our attentiveness to this aspect of the work need not, however, diminish aesthetic judgment. It has become a cliché of oppositional literary criticism to observe that the most coherent and harmonious work may be the most epigonal. But the epigonal is one of those categories that requires cautious and tender application. The *Spätlese* of a tradition may be as fine as the wine gathered in the dying of the autumn season.

Nevertheless it appears to me that if we in our time are to be willing to keep hold of the work in our attention, the critical portion suffused with its conventional portion must be of some weight and substance. It is that questioning, probing, experimental, inventive aspect that sets the work apart from what has been delivered into it. This is not just another way of speaking of originality, although originality is an important quality in the empirical process of artistic success and endurance. But a large part of the critical portion may well be an inflow into the work of new collective, class, historical forces that dislodge the conventional vision. Whether the critical portion is private or social in its main genesis again does not impinge on aesthetic judgment, although it will usually be found that it is both at once, that no artist is majestically alone, but that none of any interest is nothing but a blotter or a conduit. The conventional and critical portions may vary greatly in their proportion to one another. But it appears to me that works in which the conventional portion over-whelmingly preponderates become objects of antiquarian interest at best, while those in which the critical portion violently overwhelms any aspect that appeals to a horizon of expectation may be events of the moment but arouse little enduring interest once their path-breaking function is accomplished. They are actions, not creations. Who now would go across the street to see the Mona Lisa decorated with a mous-tache?

In terms of value, of defensibly placing the artistic phenomenon in our whole experience of the world, a parallel may with every justification be drawn with the duplicity of the historical phenomenon. In the United States of the 1970s we contemplate Thomas Jefferson. We see the ex-traordinary allegiance to the emancipatory thrust of the Enlighten-ment, the conviction that, no matter what, the only rational form of government depends on the judgment of the people, a great, eloquent democrat and insistent advocate of peace; and we see also a slave-holder, a man who for private emotional and no doubt also economic reasons, as well as social conventions, was unable to think clearly or consistently on the question of race, a man who made hypocritical personal decisions and quite ominous public ones from whose long-term effects black and white Americans suffer daily. What do we do? Do we abolish from our purview the slave-holding practice and the racist pattern of mind, extol-ling the great patriot and statesman, weighing his virtues and ignoring the rest as insignificant, time-bound, or non-tangential to his greater vision? This would be an analogy to the practice, not only of the New Criticism, but also to some of the current literary hagiography on the Left. Or do we find ourselves so focused on the racial disasters of our society that this aspect overwhelms our vision of Jefferson, colors his philosophy and politics and thus consigns the whole work of the founding of the American nation and the carpentering of its Constitution to the realm of evil? Some radical literary criticism is undertaken in this manner. But neither approach would be acceptable history, and neither yields adequate criticism. To speak of a "double optic" is of course a simplification of the complexity of our process of understanding and judging; but the concept is meant to resist a tendency toward a "single optic" that would fail to hold apart the components we must weigh in our present judgment. In the literary work, the conventional portion, though refined, is likely to be conservative, that is, accepting of all the suffering and barbarism of the world around; the critical aspect may be idiosyncratic or utopian, that is, inclined to embody easy, short, irrelevant ways to human relief. But it might be the other way about: the conventional portion might be a reaffirmation of values by which a society or some segment of it aspires to live; the critical portion may set new values and visions against old ones, attempt to raise into consciousness inadequacies, contradictions between reality and ideology, evils.

None of this is determinable without extrinsic categories. "Convention" is itself a social category, for it implies the sharing of language, of form, of a common construction of reality. The critical portion as well is unlikely to be wholly private and idiosyncratic, but a reflex of some kind of movement or breach in society, and ordinarily it means as well to speak to someone, to change consciousness. At the same time the art work is singular, in every sense of the word, even in its conventional portion. It is not exactly like any other, though under very strict conventions there may be a very narrow range of variations within which the aesthetic play can occur. But it is also singular in the sense that it is not comprehensive; it is a possible vision, a more or less possible account of the world. For all the hue and cry that now goes up for a unitary, "scientific" grasp of the genesis, context, and reception of the work, it is not excessively liberal eclecticism to form statements about the work of the type "both . . . and" or even "yes, but." It is not eclecticism to see the work as composite by its nature, or to prefer a perception of it and judgment upon it that is consciously composite as a matter of principle. If literary sociology is to have anything plausible to do with practical criticism, it must abandon the search for massive, congruent correlations with abstracted social structures, and give up as well the curious notion frequently encountered in Germany that it is useful to "demask" the work of art. This is of no more use than would be a claim to "demask" Thomas Jefferson; it is

one thing to reveal contradictions and complicities and be honest about
them; but when an exclusive stress on ideology and false consciousness
leads to a conspiracy theory of culture, works and events slip through
our fingers. At the same time, a duple or multiple view of the work of art
would of necessity see it in its involvement with the social, political, ethical
life of its own time as well as of ours, and only the integration of the social
sciences with criticism can accomplish this.

One of the consequences of this approach, as I have suggested before,
would be a widening of our evaluative base. Let us take as an example
Rainer Maria Rilke, a poet of such truly exquisite refinement that in his
presence we can have that experience described by Ingarden as being
"overwhelmed by a certain amazement that such a thing is at all possible."[29] This response can be a shared enrichment and excitement, just
as the very existence of Beethoven increases the dignity of us all insofar
as he and we are members of the same human race. But Rilke's head was
full of foolishness and carefully nurtured neurosis, as well as that susceptibility to Fascism that he shared with many of the Symbolists and
Futurists of his time and that must have something to do with the mode
and purpose of the poetry; and the character of the audience that most
enthusiastically received him teaches us that decadence is a real social
category in cultural history. These considerations do not invalidate his
aesthetic achievement, but neither may the latter serve to obliterate the
dubious side of the Rilke phenomenon; a rational overall judgment
would be one of interrelated admiration and skepticism that would
neither deprive us of the treasure of his poetry nor make us indifferent
to its cost. Hemingway is another useful example. As the pathos of his
American ideology of eternal youth and vigor recedes into perspective
and as contemporary history makes us less patient with his heroes' stance
of intransitive courage and belligerence as an aesthetic form, a certain
general weariness with Hemingway is making itself apparent. I believe
that this restraint is right, but I do not believe it should be allowed to cost
us Hemingway altogether. It takes a historically tuned sensibility to grasp
his achievement, to enable us to share Ford Madox Ford's excited reaction upon first encountering a sentence of Hemingway's of having met a
writer of impeccable freshness of language and stylistic discipline.[30] An
example of the opposite kind would be Lessing, who thought of himself
that he lacked natural wellsprings of creativity and had to squeeze out his
literary works by the force of will power. There is some truth in this; his
literary language, which he to some extent had to create for himself, is
sometimes graceless, his verse humpy, his plays occasionally lacking in

dramatic technique. It would be easy and perhaps not even wrong to demote him on aesthetic principles. But few will be found who know anything of Lessing and would not agree that the exclusion of *Minna von Barnhelm* and *Nathan the Wise* from the literary canon would be an unbearable loss to our humane patrimony.

"A real literary interest," wrote F. R. Leavis, "is an interest in man, society and civilization."[31] Leavis himself is a good example of the kind of trouble that this sort of proposition gets us into. He has been at the center of controversies that have not infrequently been fought on moral and social grounds. Many may think Leavis a particularly effective warning example against involving extrinsic principles in criticism. Certainly he is exasperating, and his style of argument perhaps ought not to be emulated. But he has the advantage that all his convictions, allegiances, and prejudices lie explicitly on the surface, so that one has the impression of confronting a whole, living person. We can, therefore, see more clearly what is wrong with his criticism, for the link between anti-progressive ideology and certain criteria of criticism is more plainly evident in him than in most major critics of our time. Debating such issues is stressful, but the fact that an intellectual pursuit is troublesome is the last reason for evading it. It is difficult to see what is gained by a retreat into the wholly immanent contemplation of literature other than the falsification of literary reality and the erection of a dwelling place in a dangerously fragile and illusory idyll of peace. Literary criticism has lately been too unwilling to debate openly on moral and political grounds. The corresponding implications of literature have, by and large, been left in our own country to charlatans, who have generally better success than rational critics with students and sometimes with the public or the chic part of it, and in Europe to "revolutionaries" seeking to politicize literary studies; it is not, however, the politicization itself that is offensive, but the kind of politics they propagate. These challenges can be met only by standing on the same ground, and for this reason alone the tool of literary sociology should not be left only in the hands of those who would employ it against liberalism or against art and literature itself. It is not unreasonable simply to argue, as Jost Hermand does, that because the study of literature is such a major enterprise (and a costly one), it should have some responsibility to society.[32]

Out of the contemporary brouhaha is arising an intensified sense of the oppositional and critical function of the imagination. While it is not true, as radicals often suggest, that an aesthetic criterion of coherence or even of harmony necessarily implies a harmonizing and affirmative character of literature, it is true that some modern criticism has suggested such a link or has argued that all literature in some vague Neoplatonic sense is One and wholly distinct from the disparateness of the lower emanations of reality. But there are also certain kinds of sociological arguments that see literature and art as wholly, "globally" affirmative and expressive of a social situation or a group ideology, and much of what is unconvincing in literary sociology derives from this monolithic identification. Altogether more promising is Jean Duvignaud's proposition that the "most profound creative attitude" is "ethical opposition to the traditional cultural experience of a society and to the established values it has given itself." [33] In this regard, Lukács' admittedly defeatingly abstract argument that art "de-fetishizes" reified social relations and restores to them their original human content may be one of the more usable contributions of his aesthetics. [34] Even in literature that has a strong affirmative component this can be seen to be so. C. M. Bowra observed that, although Kipling "thought that the British had a divinely appointed mission to rule large parts of the world, he devoted much energy and eloquence to deploring how unfitted they were to do so." [35] Lionel Trilling speaks of William Faulkner's "awareness of the inadequacy and wrongness of the very tradition he loves." [36] Anyone who would disqualify Faulkner's fiction as "racist" is an ignoramus who needs to be instructed. But Faulkner provides an excellent example of Ernst Fischer's dictum that literature can often supply "a victory of reality over ideology." [37] Here is a case where social awareness and literary interpretation would have to work hand in hand if the meaning of the text were not to be falsified. Even escapism, when it is a literary motive, can have a critical component and articulate a refusal to affirm things as they are. Romance, a subject now of such wide critical interest, is perhaps the most pervasive example of the imagination offering alternatives to things as they are. At the same time, binding works entirely to their critical portion will not yield accurate reading, and at its worst tends to turn criticism into progressive iconography.

The newly developing concern with reader response gives these considerations an added dimension. For one thing, much modern and contemporary literature simply cannot generate the forms of aesthetic response that have been traditionally recommended, and we are faced with the choice of legislating it out of the critical purview, as Emil Staiger has tried to do, or altering our critical principles to accommodate it. If we pursue the latter course, we may come to recognize that the effect of much traditional literature also can be disruptive of fixed expectations and unreflected convictions. Walter J. Slatoff has expanded this point into an extended argument:

> We rarely question the value of our pervasive attention to the patterns and unifying aspects of literary works—to recurrences, symmetries, contrasts, correspondences, and tyings together—and do not wonder much about their disorderly, disruptive, and explosive aspects. Little of our work contemplates the extent to which much of the greatest literature involves a disordering as well as an ordering of experience and the extent to which the life and power and even form of a work may come from that disordering or from the very struggle or even failure of the artist to provide order.[38]

Slatoff also points out, I think fairly and importantly, that we need "a sharp awareness of the fact that distance, detachment, impersonality, and objectivity have affinities not only with certain kinds of truth and beauty but with indifference, complacency, callousness, and finally inhumanity."[39] At the same time we can continue to insist that art is a humane victory, even, and especially, in its opposition, negation, and disruptiveness; what keeps art alive, says Ernst Fischer, is the pressure of chaos, and art is a dialogue with chaos.[40]

The practical critic making an inquiry into literary sociology may come away with disappointments. He may feel that what he finds there that is convincing is not interesting, and what is interesting is not convincing. If he is weary of the quantity of platitudinous routine and outright nonsense that academic criticism can·generate, he will not find less of it among the speculative literary sociologists and Marxists. He may feel with some justice that he *knows* something about literary works that some literary sociologists and Marxists bullheadedly refuse to acknowledge. He may find even some of the most ambitious edifices of sociological criticism to be tendentious Potemkin villages. It is hard to find a habitable middle ground between propositions that the literary imagination is a vessel of prophetic truth and denunciations of both literature and criticism as elitist irrelevance. In the issues I have tried to delineate in these pages there are sufficient internal contradictions and cause for disbelief that one may well despair of the whole venture. The working critic may feel a temptation to chuck the whole business and return to a private communion with congenial works in order, with great care and conscientious intellectual effort, to produce articles and books that will generate other articles and books that will renuance the same subject.

But the hour has grown late for this. As we indulge in such pursuits, every day's newspapers tell us that we are losing the battle for civilization and human freedom. It would be outrageous to claim that literary sociology will turn the tide, and I do not wish to be misunderstood in this sense. But it is not clear where the tide can be turned if not in learning and education. Literary criticism has in its hands one of the most universal of all human undertakings: the making of fictions. The obligation to seek truth, rationality, and liberation in the pursuit of this study is therefore very strong, and there is hardly another field of learning that has gone farther toward abdicating it. Literary sociology can tell us much about how and why we did this and has much potential for bringing literary study back into the service of human needs. Insofar as it reminds us that literature is a product of human beings in their relations with one another and speaks to human beings in their relations with one another, it can help literary criticism retain its claim to being a humanistic discipline. Perhaps the whole range of things I have come to touch upon in this inquiry, with their sometimes disturbingly universalistic pretensions and ambitions of intellectual imperialism, suggest that "literary sociology" has become a name, perhaps a not wholly fortunate one, for a complex and contentious effort to integrate the fact and the experience of literature into the whole diachronic and synchronic fabric of human reality, proceeding from the elementary principle that consciousness is a derivative of social relations, so that the dialectical distance and deviance of consciousness that we call the faculty of imagination, or, alternatively, of creative freedom, is the object of a rational, practical criticism.

REFERENCE NOTES

For each essay, first references are given in full, thereafter by short titles.

I. INTRODUCTION

1. E.g., James H. Barnett, "The Sociology of Art," *Sociology Today*, ed. Robert K. Merton et al. (New York: Basic Books, 1959), pp.198–199; Lewis A. Coser in the introduction to *Sociology Through Literature: An Introductory Reader*, ed. Coser (Englewood Cliffs, New Jersey: Prentice-Hall, 1963), p.4.

2. E.g., Robert Escarpit, *Das Buch und der Leser: Entwurf einer Literatursoziologie* (Cologne: Westdeutscher Verlag, 1961), p.17; Hans Norbert Fügen, ed., *Wege der Literatursoziologie* (Neuwied: Luchterhand, 1968), p.19; Fügen, *Die Hauptrichtungen der Literatursoziologie und ihre Methoden*, 5th ed. (Bonn: Bouvier, 1971), p.2.

3. See, for example, the interesting and persuasive researches on the economic history of American literature by William Charvat, *The Profession of Authorship in America, 1800–1870*, ed. Matthew J. Bruccoli (Columbus: Ohio State University Press, 1968).

4. Richard Foster, *The New Romantics: A Reappraisal of the New Criticism* (Bloomington: Indiana University Press, 1962), p.178.

5. T. S. Eliot, *Selected Essays 1917–1932* (New York: Harcourt, Brace, 1932), p.19.

6. Alvin B. Kernan, "The Idea of Literature," *New Literary History* 5 (1973/74):39.

7. Paul Merker in 1921 and Karl Viëtor in 1934. See Erwin Leibfried, *Kritische Wissenschaft vom Text: Manipulation, Reflexion, transparente Poetologie* (Stuttgart: Metzler, 1970), pp.5,171.

8. Albert Guérard, *Literature and Society* (Boston: Lothrop, Lee and Shepard, 1935), pp.3–4.

9. Stanley Edgar Hyman, *The Armed Vision: A Study in the Methods of Modern Literary Criticism* (New York: Knopf, 1948), p.3.

10. See M. H. Abrams and Nathan A. Scott, Jr., in *Literature and Belief: English Institute Essays 1957*, ed. Abrams (New York: Columbia University Press, 1958), pp.1–30,106–138.

11. E.g., Stefan Morawski, *Inquiries into the Fundamentals of Aesthetics* (Cambridge, Mass.: MIT Press, 1974), pp.295–298: Bente Hansen, *Den marxistiske litteraturkritik* (Copenhagen: Hans Reitzel, 1967), pp.9–10.

12. Florian Vassen, *Methoden der Literaturwissenschaft II: Marxistische Literatur-*

theorie und Literatursoziologie (Düsseldorf: Bertelsmann Universitätsverlag, 1972), p.54.

13. Fügen, *Hauptrichtungen*, p.58.

14. Lenin, "The Three Sources and the Three Component Parts of Marxism," *Reader in Marxist Philosophy from the Writings of Marx, Engels, and Lenin*, ed. Howard Selsam and Harry Martel (New York: International Publishers, 1963), p.37.

15. Eberhard Lämmert, "Das Ende der Germanistik und ihre Zukunft," *Ansichten einer künftigen Germanistik*, ed. Jürgen Kolbe (Munich: Hanser, 1969), pp.96–97.

16. See the instructive discussion by Walter Hinderer, "Die regressive Universalideologie. Zum Klassikbild der marxistischen Literaturkritik von Franz Mehring bis zu den *Weimarer Beiträgen*," *Die Klassik-Legende*, ed. Reinhold Grimm and Jost Hermand (Frankfurt am Main: Athenäum, 1971), pp.141–175.

17. Ernest H. Templin, *The Social Approach to Literature*, University of California Publications in Modern Philology, XXVIII, No. 1 (Berkeley: University of California Press, 1944), p.14.

18. Peter Demetz, "Wandlungen der marxistischen Literaturkritik: Hans Mayer, Ernst Fischer, Lucien Goldmann," *Der Dichter und seine Zeit—Politik im Spiegel der Literatur: Drittes Amherster Kolloquium zur modernen deutschen Literatur 1969*, ed. Wolfgang Paulsen (Heidelberg: Lothar Stiehm, 1970), p.14; Martin Jay, *The Dialectical Imagination: A History of the Frankfurt School and the Institute of Social Research 1923–1950* (Boston: Little, Brown, and Company, 1972). p.173.

19. For examples of these formulations from different points of view, see Fügen, *Hauptrichtungen*, pp.14,27; Alphons Silbermann, "Literaturphilosophie, soziologische Literaturästhetik oder Literatursoziologie," *Kölner Zeitschrift für Soziologie und Sozialpsychologie* 18 (1966):140–144; Leibfried, *Kritische Wissenschaft vom Text*, pp.172–175; Lucien Goldmann, Michel Bernard, and Roger Lallemand, eds., *Littérature et Société: Problèmes de méthodologie en sociologie de la littérature* (Brussels: Editions de l'Institut de Sociologie de l'Université Libre de Bruxelles, 1967), p.21; a plain statement of the difference under Goldmann's influence by Erich Köhler, "Einige Thesen zur Literatursoziologie," *Germanisch-romanische Monatsschrift* n.s. 24 (1974):257; Diana Laurenson and Alan Swingewood, *The Sociology of Literature* (London: MacGibbon & Kee, 1972), pp.16,22,78. Silbermann's formulation is taken almost verbatim, though without acknowledgment, from an essay of a generation ago, Herbert A. Bloch, "Towards the Development of a Sociology of Literary and Art-Forms," *American Sociological Review* 8 (1953):313–314.

20. Michel Zéraffa, *Roman et société* (Paris: Presses Universitaires de France, 1971), p.90.

21. Manon Maren-Grisebach, *Methoden der Literaturwissenschaft* (Berne: Francke Verlag, 1970), pp.81–82.

22. Jochen Schulte-Sasse, "Aspekte einer kontextbezogenen Literatursemantik," *Historizität in Sprach- und Literaturwissenschaft: Vorträge und Berichte der*

Stuttgarter Germanistentagung 1972, ed. Walter Müller-Seidel et al. (Munich: Fink, 1974), p.259n.

23. Jay, *The Dialectical Imagination*, pp.175–176.

24. Lucien Goldmann, *The Hidden God: A Study of Tragic Vision in the* Pensées *of* Pascal *and the Tragedies of* Racine (New York: Humanities Press, 1964), p.7.

25. Ernst Bloch, *Das Prinzip Hoffnung* (Frankfurt am Main: Suhrkamp, 1959), pp.106–107. The phrase is borrowed from Engels.

26. Fredric Jameson, *Marxism and Form: Twentieth-Century Dialectical Theories of Literature* (Princeton: Princeton University Press, 1971), p.xiii.

27. Jürgen Habermas, "Gegen einen positivistisch halbierten Rationalismus," *Der Positivismusstreit in der deutschen Soziologie*, ed. Theodor W. Adorno et al. (Neuwied: Luchterhand, 1969), p.265.

28. Roland Barthes, *Mythologies* (New York: Hill and Wang, 1972), p.35.

29. Dietrich Harth, "Begriffsbildung in der Literaturwissenschaft, Beobachtungen zum Wandel der 'semantischen Orientierung,'" *Deutsche Vierteljahrsschrift für Literaturwissenschaft und Geistesgeschichte* 45 (1971):397, 431–433.

30. Leibfried, *Kritische Wissenschaft vom Text*, p.2.

31. Goldmann, *The Hidden God*, p.x.

32. Jameson, *Marxism and Form*, pp.24,307–308.

33. In *Das Kapital*, Book III, Section 7, Ch. 48. Karl Marx, Friedrich Engels, *Werke*, ed. Institut für Marxismus-Leninismus beim ZK der SED, XXV (Berlin: Dietz Verlag, 1964), 825.

34. George Lichtheim, *George Lukács* (New York: Viking Press, 1970), pp.12–13.

II. ANALOGY, HOMOLOGY, EQUIVOCATION

1. Arnold Hauser, *The Social History of Art* (New York: Knopf, 1952), I,39.

2. M. H. Abrams, *The Mirror and the Lamp: Romantic Theory and the Critical Tradition* (New York: Oxford University Press, 1953), pp.viii,31,158,34–35.

3. Robert Musil, *Gesammelte Werke in Einzelausgaben*, ed. Adolf Frisé, II, *Tagebücher, Aphorismen, Essays und Reden* (Hamburg: Rowohlt 1955),652,651.

4. Erich Koehler, "Les possibilités de l'interprétation sociologique illustrées par l'analyse de textes littéraires français de différentes époques," *Littérature et Société: Problèmes de méthodologie en sociologie de la littérature*, ed. Lucien Goldmann, Michel Bernard, and Roger Lallemand (Brussels: Editions de l'Institut de Sociologie de l'Université Libre de Bruxelles, 1967), p.53.

5. David Daiches, *Literature and Society* (London: Gollancz, 1938), pp.39–46.

6. Ernst Bloch, *Das Prinzip Hoffnung* (Frankfurt am Main: Suhrkamp, 1959), p.147.

7. Edoardo Sanguinetti, "Sociologie de l'avant-garde," *Littérature et Société*, ed. Goldmann et al., p.17.

8. Neil Harris, "The Pattern of Artistic Community," *The Sociology of Art and Literature: A Reader*, ed. Milton C. Albrecht, James H. Barnett, and Mason Griff (New York: Praeger, 1970), p.300.

9. Christopher Caudwell, *Illusion and Reality: A Study of the Sources of Poetry* (London: Macmillan, 1937), pp.53–54,136.

10. Ernst Fischer, *Kunst und Koexistenz: Beitrag zu einer modernen marxistischen Ästhetik* (Reinbek: Rowohlt, 1966), pp.156–157.

11. Roland Barthes, *Essais critiques* (Paris: Editions du Seuil, 1964), p.250.

12. Northrop Frye, *The Critical Path: An Essay on the Social Context of Literary Criticism* (Bloomington: Indiana University Press, 1971), p.99.

13. Fredric Jameson, *Marxism and Form: Twentieth-Century Dialectical Theories of Literature* (Princeton: Princeton University Press, 1971), pp.3–59.

14. Ibid., p.15.

15. Bloch, *Das Prinzip Hoffnung*, p.457.

16. Theodor W. Adorno, "Die Wunde Heine," *Noten zur Literatur*, I (Frankfurt am Main: Suhrkamp, 1958),147–149,151,152.

17. On this point, see Nigel Reeves, *Heinrich Heine: Poetry and Politics* (Oxford: University Press, 1974), pp.37–53.

18. Heinrich Heine, *Sämtliche Werke*, ed. Ernst Elster (Leipzig: Bibliographisches Institut, [1887–90]), III,304.

19. Cf. my elaboration of this view in *Heinrich Heine: The Elusive Poet* (New Haven: Yale University Press, 1969), pp.26–87.

20. David Caute, *The Illusion: An Essay on Politics, Theatre and the Novel* (New York: Harper & Row, 1971), p. 156.

21. Lucien Goldmann, *Pour une sociologie du roman* (Paris: Gallimard, 1964), p.24.

22. Ibid., pp.27–28.

23. Lucien Goldmann, *The Hidden God: A Study of Tragic Vision in the* Pensées *of* Pascal *and the* Tragedies *of* Racine (New York: Humanities Press, 1964), p.ix.

24. Goldmann, *Pour une sociologie du roman*, p.28.

25. Urs Jaeggi, *Literatur und Politik: Ein Essay* (Frankfurt am Main: Suhrkamp, 1972), p.51.

26. Lucien Goldmann, "Le Structuralisme génétique en sociologie de la littérature," *Littératur et Société*, ed. Goldmann et al., p.200.

27. Goldmann, *The Hidden God*, pp.ix,210,205–207.

28. Goldmann, "Le Structuralisme génétique," p.195.

29. Georg Lukács, *Ästhetik* (Neuwied: Luchterhand, 1972), I,219.

30. T. B. Bottomore, *Sociology: A Guide to Problems and Literature*, 2nd ed. (New York: Pantheon, 1971), p.28. On the difficulties this raises, see ibid., p.80.

31. Geoffrey H. Hartman, *Beyond Formalism: Literary Essays 1958–1970* (New Haven: Yale University Press, 1970), p.7.

32. John O'Neill, *Sociology as a Skin Trade: Essays Towards a Reflexive Sociology* (New York: Harper & Row, 1972), p.23, n. 1. See the review by D. I. Davies in *The Canadian Forum* 52, No. 12 (Dec., 1972):21–23, which admiringly points out the link to conservatism in O'Neill's extreme radicalism.

33. Kenneth Burke, "The Rhetoric of Hitler's 'Battle,'" *Terms for Order*, ed.

Stanley Edgar Hyman with the assistance of Barbara Karmiller (Bloomington: Indiana University Press, 1964), pp.107,117. The essay originally appeared in *The Southern Review* in 1939. It is also to be found in Burke, *The Philosophy of Literary Form: Studies in Symbolic Action*, 3rd ed. (Berkeley: University of California Press, 1973), pp.191–220.

34. Q. D. Leavis, *Fiction and the Reading Public* (London: Chatto & Windus, 1932), p.98.

35. Lukács, *Ästhetik*, I,25–32.

36. Jameson, *Marxism and Form*, p.xvi.

37. Peter Gay, *Weimar Culture: The Outsider as Insider* (New York: Harper & Row, 1968), pp.70–101.

38. See E. H. Gombrich, *In Search of Cultural History* (Oxford: Clarendon Press, 1969).

39. Bloch, *Das Prinzip Hoffnung*, pp.13,256–257.

40. Ernst Fischer, *Von der Notwendigkeit der Kunst* (Hamburg: Claassen, 1967), pp.47–49, 53–54.

41. Jameson, *Marxism and Form*, pp.116–118.

42. Goldmann, *The Hidden God*, pp.90, 172, 92–93.

43. Ibid., pp.188,264.

44. Fischer, *Von der Notwendigkeit der Kunst*, p.10.

45. István Mészáros, "Lukács' Concept of Dialectic," *George Lukács: The Man, His Work, and His Ideas*, ed. G. H. R. Parkinson (New York: Vintage Books, 1970), p.65.

46. Gerald Graff, *Poetic Statement and Critical Dogma* (Evanston: Northwestern University Press, 1970), pp.81–82.

47. William Empson, *Some Versions of Pastoral* (Norfolk, Conn.: New Directions, [1950]), p.22.

48. Jean Duvignaud, *Sociologie de l'Art* (Paris: Presses Universitaires de France, 1967), p.55.

49. Ernst Bloch, *Die Kunst, Schiller zu sprechen* (Frankfurt am Main: Suhrkamp, 1969), p.91.

50. See the examples given by Monroe C. Beardsley, *Aethetics: Problems in the Philosophy of Criticism* (New York: Harcourt, Brace, 1958), p.205. Cf. Stefan Morawski, *Inquiries into the Fundamentals of Aesthetics* (Cambridge, Mass.: MIT Press, 1974), pp.130–131.

51. Robert Escarpit, *Das Buch und der Leser: Entwurf einer Literatursoziologie* (Cologne: Westdeutscher Verlag, 1961), p.110.

52. Marc Gaboriau, "Structural Anthropology and History," *Introduction to Structuralism*, ed. Michael Lane (New York: Basic Books, 1970), p.159.

53. R. S. Crane, *Critical and Historical Principles of Literary History* (Chicago: University of Chicago Press, 1971), pp.53–55.

54. See Morris Ginsberg, "Social Change," *British Journal of Sociology* 9 (1958):205–229.

55. René Wellek, "The Fall of Literary History," *Geschichte—Ereignis und Erzählung*, ed. Reinhard Koselleck and Wolf-Dieter Stempel (Munich: Wilhelm Fink Verlag, 1973), p.434.

56. Harry Levin, *Refractions: Essays in Comparative Literature* (New York: Oxford University Press, 1966), p.246.

57. Goldmann, *The Hidden God*, p.97.

58. Hans Norbert Fügen, ed., *Wege der Literatursoziologie* (Neuwied: Luchterhand, 1968), p.16.

59. Olaf Hansen, "Hermeneutik und Literatursoziologie. Zwei Modelle: Marxistische Literaturtheorie in Amerika/Zum Problem der 'American Studies,'" *Literaturwissenschaft und Sozialwissenschaft: Grundlagen und Modellanalysen*, ed. by a collective (Stuttgart: Metzler, 1971), 359,362.

60. Jameson, *Marxism and Form*, pp.5–8.

61. George A. Huaco, "Ideology and Literature," *New Literary History* 4 (1972/73):422,423. My emphasis.

62. Pierre Macherey, *Pour une théorie de la production littéraire* (Paris: Maspero, 1966), p.159.

63. Cf. Vytautas Kavolis, *Artistic Expression: A Sociological Analysis* (Ithaca: Cornell University Press, 1968), p.192.

64. Alan Lomax, "Song Structure and Social Structure," *The Sociology of Art and Literature*, ed. Albrecht et al., pp.55–71.

65. Nathan A. Scott, Jr., "The Collaboration of Vision in the Poetic Act: The Religious Dimension," *Literature and Belief: English Institute Essays 1957* (New York: Columbia University Press, 1958), p.119.

66. Fernando Ferrara, "Theory and Model for the Structural Analysis of Fiction," *New Literary History* 5 (1973/74):268.

III. TRUTH AND TIME

1. See John Dewey, "The Live Creature," *The Sociology of Art and Literature*, ed., Milton C. Albrecht, James H. Barnett, and Mason Griff (New York: Praeger, 1970), pp.651–659.

2. E. D. Hirsch, Jr., "Three Dimensions of Hermeneutics," *New Literary History* 3 (1971/72):248–249.

3. Erwin Leibfried, *Kritische Wissenschaft vom Text: Manipulation, Reflexion, transparente Poetologie* (Stuttgart: Metzler, 1970), p.27.

4. Tzvetan Todorov, "The Notion of Literature," *New Literary History* 5 (1973/74):7–8.

5. See the excellent discussion in Gerald Graff, *Poetic Statement and Critical Dogma* (Evanston: Northwestern University Press, 1970), esp. Ch. I and II.

6. Roman Ingarden, *Vom Erkennen des literarischen Kunstwerks* (Tübingen: Niemeyer, 1968), pp.151–152.

7. Howard S. Becker and Irving Louis Horowitz, "Radical Politics and

Sociological Research: Observations on Methodology and Ideology," *Varieties of Political Expression in Sociology*, ed. C. Arnold Anderson et al. (Chicago: University of Chicago Press, 1972), p.50.

8. Northrop Frye, *The Critical Path: An Essay on the Social Context of Literary Criticism* (Bloomington: Indiana University Press, 1971), p.83.

9. M. H. Abrams, *The Mirror and the Lamp: Romantic Theory and the Critical Tradition* (New York: Oxford University Press, 1953), p.307.

10. Geoffrey H. Hartman, *Beyond Formalism: Literary Essays 1958–1970* (New Haven: Yale University Press, 1970), p.25.

11. Richard E. Palmer, *Hermeneutics: Interpretation Theory in Schleiermacher, Dilthey, Heidegger, and Gadamer* (Evanston: Northwestern University Press, 1969), pp.167–168.

12. In the famous French preface to *Lutezia*: Heine, *Sämtliche Werke*, ed. Ernst Elster (Leipzig: Bibliographisches Institut, [1887–90]), VI,571–573.

13. O.K. Werckmeister, "Marx on Ideology and Art," *New Literary History* 4 (1972/73):509–510.

14. René Wellek, *A History of Modern Criticism 1750–1950* (New Haven: Yale University Press, 1955-), IV,40.

15. Walter Abell, *The Collective Dream in Art: A Psycho-Historical Theory of Culture Based on Relations Between the Arts, Psychology, and the Social Sciences* (Cambridge, Mass.: Harvard University Press, 1957), p.359.

16. Ernst Fischer, *Von der Notwendigkeit der Kunst* (Hamburg: Claasscn, 1967), p.54. The phrase may be an echo of Lukács' *nostra causa agitur*. See Peter Demetz, *Marx, Engels, and the Poets* (Chicago: University of Chicago Press, 1967), p.221.

17. Ernst Bloch, *Das Prinzip Hoffnung* (Frankfurt am Main: Suhrkamp, 1959), p.140.

18. Georg Lukács, *Ästhetik* (Neuwied: Luchterhand, 1972), II,133.

19. See Abrams, *The Mirror and the Lamp*, p.225.

20. Lukács, *Ästhetik*, III,33.

21. See Hartmut Rosshoff, "Die ästhetische Theorie des späten Lukács. Ihre allgemeine Wahrheit und ihre Nichtanwendbarkeit im einzelnen," *Erweiterung der materialistischen Literaturtheorie durch Bestimmung ihrer Grenzen*, ed. Heinz Schlaffer (Stuttgart: Metzler, 1974), pp.213–250, esp. pp.220,227–228. For a helpful explication of this difficult concept, see Béla Királyfalvi, *The Aesthetics of György Lukács* (Princeton: Princeton University Press, 1975), pp.71–87.

22. Erich Koehler, "Les possibilités de l'interprétation sociologique illustrées par l'analyse de textes littéraires français de différentes époques," *Littérature et Société: Problèmes de méthodologie en sociologie de la littérature*, ed. Lucien Goldmann, Michel Bernard, and Roger Lallemand (Brussels: Editions de l'Institut de Sociologie de l'Université Libre de Bruxelles, 1967), p.48.

23. Hans Holländer, "Kitsch, Anmerkungen zum Begriff und zur Sache," *Das Triviale in der Literatur, Musik und bildender Kunst*, ed. Helga de la Motte-Haber (Frankfurt am Main: Vittorio Klostermann, 1972), pp.184–209.

24. See Zdenko Škreb, "Littérature engagée," *Yearbook of Comparative Criticism* 5 (1973):203.

25. Cf. L. C. Knights, *Drama & Society in the Age of Jonson* (London: Chatto & Windus, 1937), p.173.

26. Lucien Goldmann, *The Hidden God: A Study of Tragic Vision in the* Pensées *of* Pascal *and the Tragedies of Racine* (New York: Humanities Press, 1964), pp.12–13,17,18,315.

27. Lucien Goldmann, *Recherches dialectiques* (Paris: Gallimard, 1959), pp.47,60.

28. Albert Guérard, *Literature and Society* (Boston: Lathrop, Lee and Shepard, 1935), p.135.

29. See Rolf Sannwald, *Marx und die Antike* (Einsiedeln: Benziger & Co., 1956), esp. p.171.

30. Introduction to Henri Arvon, *Marxist Esthetics* (Ithaca: Cornell University Press, 1973), p.xviii.

31. Lucien Goldmann, *Pour une sociologie du roman* (Paris: Gallimard, 1964), pp.30–33.

32. Diana Laurenson and Alan Swingewood, *The Sociology of Literature* (London: MacGibbon & Kee, 1972), pp.94–95.

33. George A. Huaco, "Ideology and Literature," New Literary History 4 (1972/73):435.

34. See, for example, the similar views of Leon Trotsky, *Literature and Revolution* (New York: International Publishers, 1925), p.20, and Jost Hermand, *Synthetisches Interpretieren: Zur Methodik der Literaturwissenschaft* (Munich: Nymphenburger, 1968), p.216.

35. Pierre Orecchioni, "Pour une histoire sociologique de la littérature," *Le Littéraire et le social*, ed. Robert Escarpit (Paris: Flammarion, 1970), p.50.

36. Jean Duvignaud, *Sociologie de l'Art* (Paris: Presses Universitaires de France, 1967), p.26.

37. Helga Gallas, *Marxistische Literaturtheorie: Kontroversen im Bund proletarisch-revolutionärer Schriftsteller* (Neuwied: Luchterhand, 1971), p.169.

38. William Empson, *Some Versions of Pastoral* (Norfolk, Conn.: New Directions, [1950]), p.199.

39. For a contrary view, grounded in the communicative truthfulness of emotional response, see Richard Hoggart, "Literature and Society," *A Guide to the Social Sciences*, ed. Norman MacKenzie (London: Weidenfeld & Nicolson, 1966), pp.228–238.

40. Knights, *Drama & Society*, p.246.

41. Georg Lukács, *Schicksalswende: Beiträge zu einer neuen deutschen Ideologie* (Berlin: Aufbau-Verlag, 1948), p.137.

42. See Abrams, *The Mirror and the Lamp*, p.35.

43. Lukács, *Ästhetik*, IV,218.

44. Lukács, *Die Seele und die Formen* (Neuwied: Luchterhand, 1971), p.61.

45. Norbert Mecklenburg, *Kritisches Interpretieren: Untersuchungen zur Theorie der Literaturkritik* (Munich: Nymphenburger, 1972), p.118.

46. Richard Brinkmann, "Zum Begriff des Realismus für die erzählende Dichtung des neunzehnten Jahrhunderts," *Begriffsbestimmung des literarischen Realismus*, ed. Brinkmann (Darmstadt: Wissenschaftliche Buchgesellschaft, 1969), p.222.

47. Cf. Lukács, *Ästhetik*, III,58–61.

48. For the problem of German realism in this light, see Hermann Kinder, *Poesie als Synthese: Ausbreitung eines deutschen Realismus-Verständnisses in der Mitte des 19. Jahrhunderts* (Frankfurt am Main: Athenäum, 1973).

49. Thomas W. H. Metscher, "Hegel und die philosophische Grundlegung der Kunstsoziologie," *Literaturwissenschaft und Sozialwissenschaft: Grundlagen und Modellanalysen*, ed. by a collective (Stuttgart: Metzler, 1971), pp.19,20–21,22.

50. Emile Durkheim, *Montesquieu and Rousseau*, quoted Robert Nisbet, *The Sociology of Emile Durkheim* (New York: Oxford University Press, 1974), p.46. Cf. Nisbet, pp.249–256.

51. Christopher Caudwell, *Illusion and Reality: A Study of the Sources of Poetry* (London: Macmillan, 1937), pp.21–22.

52. Ernst Bloch, *Das Prinzip Hoffnung*, p.178.

53. Ibid.

54. Cf. M. H. Abrams, *Natural Supernaturalism: Tradition and Revolution in Romantic Literature* (New York: W. W. Norton, 1971), pp.313–316.

55. Lukács, *Ästhetik*, I,118.

56. Goethe, *Dichtung und Wahrheit*, Pt. IV, Book 17, *Werke*, ed. Erich Trunz et al., X (Hamburg: Wegner, 1959),114–120.

57. Harry Elmer Barnes, ed., *An Introduction to the History of Sociology*, abridged ed. (Chicago: University of Chicago Press, 1966), pp.12–13.

58. Christopher Caudwell, *Romance and Realism: A Study of English Bourgeois Literature*, ed. Samuel Hynes (Princeton: Princeton University Press, 1970), p.64.

59. Ernst Fischer, *Kunst und Koexistenz: Beitrag zu einer modernen marxistischen Ästhetik* (Reinbek: Rowohlt, 1966), p.220.

60. Paul Gerhard Völker, "Skizze einer marxistischen Literaturwissenschaft," *Methodenkritik der Germanistik*, ed. Marie Luise Gansberg and Völker (Stuttgart: Metzler, 1970), p.120.

61. Urs Jaeggi, *Ordnung und Chaos: Der Strukturalismus als Methode und Mode* (Frankfort am Main: Suhrkamp, 1968), p.18.

62. See my *Six Essays on the Young German Novel* (Chapel Hill: University of North Carolina Press, 1972), p.13, and Kinder, *Poesie als Synthese*, pp.50–58.

63. Walter Müller-Seidel, *Probleme der literarischen Wertung: Über die Wissenschaftlichkeit eines unwissenschaftlichen Themas* (Stuttgart: Metzler, 1969), p.142.

64. Wolfgang Binder, *Literatur als Denkschule: Eine Vorlesung mit zwei Kapiteln*

von Klaus Weimar (Zuric: Artemis Verlag, 1972), p.107.

65. Friedrich Nietzsche, *Werke in drei Bänden*, ed. Karl Schlechta (Munich: Hanser, 1966), II,705–706.

66. Novalis, *Schriften*, ed. Paul Kluckhohn and Richard Samuel, II (Stuttgart: Kohlhammer, 1960),461.

67. José Ortega y Gasset, *The Dehumanization of Art and Other Essays on Art, Culture, and Literature* (Princeton: Princeton University Press, 1968), p.45.

68. Bloch, *Das Prinzip Hoffnung*, pp.442–449.

69. Ernst Bloch, *Politische Messungen, Pestzeit, Vormärz* (Frankfurt am Main: Suhrkamp, 1970), p.367.

70. Fredric Jameson, *Marxism and Form: Twentieth-Century Dialectical Theories of Literature* (Princeton: Princeton University Press, 1971), pp.129–130,140.

71. Ernst Fischer, *Von der Notwendigkeit der Kunst*, p.66.

72. Jameson, *Marxism and Form*, pp.361–362.

73. Fredric Jameson, "The Vanishing Mediator: Narrative Structure in Max Weber," *New German Critique* 1, No. 1 (Winter, 1973):61.

74. Monroe C. Beardsley, *Aesthetics: Problems in the Philosophy of Criticism* (New York: Harcourt, Brace, 1958), pp.369–372,422–423,373,376.

75. M. H. Abrams, "Belief and Suspension of Disbelief," *Literature and Belief: English Institute Essays 1957* (New York: Columbia University Press, 1958), pp.16–21.

76. Lionel Trilling, *Beyond Culture: Essays on Literature and Learning* (New York: Viking Press, 1965), pp.166–167.

77. Ibid.,p.168. Admirable examples of similar efforts are Eugene Goodheart, *Culture and the Radical Conscience* (Cambridge, Mass.: Harvard University Press, 1973), pp.146–147, and Frank Kermode, *The Sense of an Ending: Studies in the Theory of Fiction* (New York: Oxford University Press, 1967), pp.93–124.

78. See Hans-Dietrich Sander, *Marxistische Ideologie und allgemeine Kunsttheorie* (Basel and Tübingen: Kyklos-Verlag and J. C. B. Mohr, 1970), pp.127–128.

79. Sander, ibid., pp.240–241, associates himself with this solution.

80. See Trilling, *Beyond Culture*, pp.xvi–xvii; Harry Levin, *The Gates of Horn: A Study of Five French Realists* (New York: Oxford, 1963), p.17.

81. Malcolm Bradbury, *The Social Context of Modern English Literature* (New York: Schocken Books, 1971), pp.101–102.

82. César Graña, *Fact and Symbol: Essays in the Sociology of Art and Literature* (New York: Oxford University Press, 1971), p.66.

83. See David Craig, *The Real Foundations: Literature and Social Change* (New York: Oxford University Press, 1974), p.112.

84. See Raymond Williams, *Culture and Society 1780–1950* (New York: Columbia University Press, 1958), p.97.

85. Howard Lee Nostrand, "Literature in the Describing of a Literate Culture," *The Sociology of Art and Literature*, ed. Albrecht et al., pp.564–565.

86. Lukács, *Ästhetik*, II,53–54.

87. Caudwell, *Illusion and Reality*, p.27.

88. Ibid., p.29.

89. See the editor's introduction to Caudwell, *Romance and Realism*, pp.20–22.

IV. VALUE

1. Heinrich Heine, *Sämtliche Werke*, ed. Ernst Elster (Leipzig: Bibliographisches Institut, [1887–90], IV,232.

2. Stefan Morawski, *Inquiries into the Fundamentals of Aesthetics* (Cambridge, Mass.: MIT Press, 1974), p.67.

3. Richard Foster, *The New Romantics: A Reappraisal of the New Criticism* (Bloomington: Indiana University Press, 1962), p.29. Cf. Robert Langbaum, "The Function of Criticism Once More," *Yale Review* 54 (1964/65):207.

4. Walter Müller-Seidel, *Probleme der literarischen Wertung: Über die Wissenschaftlichkeit eines unwissenschaftlichen Themas*, 2nd ed. (Stuttgart: Metzler, 1969), p.35.

5. Emil Staiger, "The Questionable Nature of Value Problems," *Yearbook of Comparative Criticism* 2 (1969):198.

6. Northrop Frye, *The Critical Path: An Essay on the Social Context of Literary Criticism* (Bloomington: Indiana University Press, 1971), p.99.

7. R. Peacock, *Criticism and Personal Taste* (Oxford: Clarendon Press, 1972), p.8.

8. Northrop Frye, "Contexts of Literary Evaluation," *Yearbook of Comparative Criticism* 2 (1969):16.

9. Richard E. Palmer, *Hermeneutics: Interpretation Theory in Schleiermacher, Dilthey, Heidegger, and Gadamer* (Evanston: Northwestern University Press, 1969), p.147.

10. Quoted Norbert Mecklenburg, *Kritisches Interpretieren: Untersuchungen zur Theorie der Literaturkritik* (Munich: Nymphenburger, 1972), p.53.

11. Cf. on Frye's stance of non-evaluation W. K. Wimsatt, *Hateful Contraries: Studies in Literature and Criticism* (Lexington: University of Kentucky Press, 1966), p.18.

12. Erwin Leibfried, *Kritische Wissenschaft vom Text: Manipulation, Reflexion, transparente Poetologie* (Stuttgart: Metzler, 1970), p.109.

13. Hans Norbert Fügen, ed., *Wege der Literatursoziologie* (Neuwied: Luchterhand, 1968), p.16; Fügen, *Die Hauptrichtungen der Literatursoziologie und ihre Methoden*, 5th ed. (Bonn: Bouvier, 1971), p.41.

14. Hans-Egon Hass, *Das Problem der literarischen Wertung* (Darmstadt: Wissenschaftliche Buchgesellschaft, 1970), p.4.

15. Mecklenburg, *Kritisches Interpretieren*, p.167.

16. Ernst Bloch, *Das Prinzip Hoffnung* (Frankfurt am Main: Suhrkamp, 1959), p.252.

17. Robert Escarpit, *Das Buch und der Leser: Entwurf einer Literatursoziologie*

(Cologne: Westdeutscher Verlag, 1961), p.116.

18. Ibid. Cf. Escarpit's more moderate statement in "Le Littéraire et le social," Escarpit, ed., *Le Littéraire et le social* (Paris: Flammarion, 1970), p.27.

19. See Georg Lukács, *Ästhetik* (Neuwied: Luchterhand, 1972), II,117.

20. Escarpit, *Das Buch und der Leser*, p.120.

21. Walter Benjamin, *Angelus Novus* (Frankfurt am Main: Suhrkamp, 1966), p.103.

22. Bloch, *Das Prinzip Hoffnung*, p.236.

23. See a strong statement of the behaviorist view in Morse Peckham, *Rage for Chaos: Biology, Behavior, and the Arts* (Philadelphia: Chilton Books, 1965), pp.210–212.

24. Walter Benjamin, *Versuche über Brecht* (Frankfurt am Main: Suhrkamp, 1966), p.109.

25. Christopher Caudwell, *Romance and Realism: A Study in English Bourgeois Literature*, ed. Samuel Hynes (Princeton: Princeton University Press, 1970), p.132.

26. Iring Fetscher, ed., Karl Marx, Friedrich Engels, *Pressefreiheit und Zensur* (Frankfurt am Main and Vienna: Europäische Verlagsanstalt and Europa Verlag, 1969).

27. Quoted Hans-Dietrich Sander, *Marxistische Ideologie und allgemeine Kunsttheorie* (Basel and Tübingen: Kyklos-Verlag and J. C. B. Mohr, 1970), p.25.

28. Louis Kampf, "The Trouble with Literature," *Change in Higher Education*, 2, No. 3 (May–June, 1970):32.

29. Richard R. Lingeman, *Don't You Know There's a War On? The American Home Front 1941–1945* (New York: Putnam, 1970), pp.168–233.

30. Cf. J. S. R. Goodlad, *A Sociology of Popular Drama* (Totowa, New Jersey: Rowman and Littlefield, 1972), pp.4–7.

31. Lingeman, *Don't You Know There's a War On?* p.201.

32. See the review in Goodlad, *A Sociology of Popular Drama*, pp.61–93.

33. For a lengthy and technical review of the subject, see Ernst H. Liebhart, "Ergebnisse, Probleme und Methoden der Wirkungsforschung," *Lesen—Ein Handbuch*, ed. Alfred Clemens Baumgärtner (Hamburg: Verlag für Buchmarkt-Forschung, 1973), pp.231–312.

34. See Malte Dahrendorf, "Literarische Wirkung und Literaturdidaktik," ibid., pp.313–352. While not able to accept all of Dahrendorf's premises, I am indebted to him for the points in the remainder of this paragraph.

35. See Goodlad, *A Sociology of Popular Drama*, pp.94–139. Cf. the criticism of this method by Herbert J. Gans, *Popular Culture and High Culture: An Analysis and Evaluation of Taste* (New York: Basic Books, 1974), p.35.

36. In *Die Weltbühne*, December 1, 1931, quoted by Jürgen Rühle, *Literature and Revolution: A Critical Study of the Writer and Communism in the Twentieth Century* (New York: Praeger, 1969), p.167.

37. Wayne C. Booth, *The Rhetoric of Fiction* (Chicago: University of Chicago Press, 1961), p.144.

38. Ibid., p.383.
39. On the question of Céline, cf. George Steiner, "Cry Havoc," *Extraterritorial: Papers on Literature and the Language Revolution* (New York: Atheneum, 1971), pp.35–46.
40. Karl Otto Conrady, *Einführung in die Neuere deutsche Literaturwissenschaft* (Reinbek: Rowohlt, 1966), p.71.
41. Jean-Paul Sartre, *What is Literature?* (New York: Philosophical Library, 1949), pp.63–64.
42. Horst Althaus, *Georg Lukács oder Bürgerlichkeit als Vorschule einer marxistischen Ästhetik* (Berne: Francke Verlag, 1962), p.70.
43. E.g., Urs Jaeggi, *Literatur und Politik: Ein Essay* (Frankfurt am Main: Suhrkamp, 1972), pp.75–76.
44. Georg Lukács, *Schicksalswende: Beiträge zu einer neuen deutschen Ideologie* (Berlin: Aufbau-Verlag, 1948), pp.135–137.
45. Benjamin, *Versuche über Brecht*, pp.96,98–99.
46. Lucien Goldmann, *The Hidden God: A Study of Tragic Vision in the Pensées of Pascal and the Tragedies of Racine* (New York: Humanities Press, 1964), p.106.
47. *Littérature et Société: Problèmes de méthodologie en sociologie de la littérature*, ed. Lucien Goldmann, Michel Bernard, and Roger Lallemand (Brussels: Editions de l'Institut de Sociologie de l'Université Libre de Bruxelles, 1967), p.44.
48. Benjamin, *Angelus Novus*, p.291.
49. Ernst Bloch, *Die Kunst, Schiller zu sprechen* (Frankfurt am Main: Suhrkamp, 1969), p.92.
50. Cf. Müller-Seidel, *Probleme der literarischen Wertung*, pp.36–37.
51. A prominent example is Jost Hermand, *Synthetisches Interpretieren: Zur Methodik der Literaturwissenschaft* (Munich: Nymphenburger, 1968), pp.168–169.
52. Mecklenburg, *Kritisches Interpretieren*, p.36.
53. Cf. Peacock, *Criticism and Personal Taste*, pp.107–109.
54. See Mecklenburg, *Kritisches Interpretieren*, pp.78–88.
55. Robert Weimann, *"New Criticism" und die Entwicklung bürgerlicher Literaturwissenschaft: Geschichte und Kritik neuer Interpretationsmethoden* (Halle: VEB Max Niemeyer Verlag, 1962), p.211,n.32.
56. See Friedrich Sengle, *Biedermeierzeit: Deutsche Literatur im Spannungsfeld zwischen Restauration und Revolution 1815–1848*, Vol. II, *Die Formenwelt* (Stuttgart: Metzler, 1972), p.991.
57. For a relatively blunt assertion of this priority, see Sartre, *What is Literature?* p.26. A more cautious Marxist view is given by Morawski, *Inquiries into the Fundamentals of Aesthetics*, pp.137–138. For a thoughtful reconsideration of the form-content difference, see Gerald Graff, *Poetic Statement and Critical Dogma* (Evanston: Northwestern University Press, 1970), pp.138–148.
58. David Daiches, *Critical Approaches to Literature* (Englewood Cliffs, New Jersey: Prentice-Hall, 1956), p.362.
59. Monroe C. Beardsley, *Aesthetics: Problems in the Philosophy of Criticism* (New York: Harcourt, Brace, 1958), p.565.

60. Stephen C. Pepper, *The Basis of Criticism in the Arts* (Cambridge, Mass.: Harvard University Press, 1946), p.55.

61. Hermand, *Synthetisches Interpretieren*, p.149.

62. James S. Ackerman, "Toward a New Social Theory of Art," *New Literary History* 4 (1972/73):323.

63. Cf. Müller-Seidel, *Probleme der literarischen Wertung*, p.9.

64. See Mecklenburg, *Kritisches Interpretieren*, p.108.

65. See Sander, *Marxistische Ideologie und allgemeine Kunsttheorie*, p.153.

66. Theodor W. Adorno, *Noten zur Literatur*, III (Frankfurt am Main: Suhrkamp, 1965), p.125.

67. Cf. Müller-Seidel, *Probleme der literarischen Wertung*, p.180.

68. Theodor W. Adorno, *Prismen: Kulturkritik und Gesellschaft* (Frankfurt am Main: Suhrkamp, 1955), p.31.

69. See Fellows in American Letters of the Library of Congress, *The Case Against the* Saturday Review of Literature (Chicago: Modern Poetry Association, 1949).

70. *New York Review of Books*, February 8, 1973, p.7. For an example of one of these broadcasts, see the appendix to William M. Chace, *The Political Identities of Ezra Pound & T. S. Eliot* (Stanford: Stanford University Press, 1973).

71. Wood, p.10. See the bitter exchange on the subject, *New York Review of Books*, June 14, 1973, pp.36–37. Some valuable remarks on the connection between the obsession with beauty and order and totalitarianism are made by George L. Mosse, "The Poet and the Exercise of Political Power: Gabriele D'Annunzio," *Yearbook of Comparative and General Literature* 22 (1973):32–41.

72. See Chace, *The Political Identities of Ezra Pound & T. S. Eliot*, p.48.

73. *Hermann Hesse—Thomas Mann Briefwechsel*, ed. Anni Carlsson (Frankfurt am Main: Suhrkamp, 1968), p.35.

74. Beardsley, *Aesthetics*, pp.574–576.

V. ENDURANCE

1. Ernst Fischer, *Von der Notwendigkeit der Kunst* (Hamburg: Claassen, 1967), pp.15–16. Cf. on this point Kenneth Burke, "Literature as Equipment for Living," *The Philosophy of Literary Form: Studies in Symbolic Action*, 3rd ed. (Berkeley: University of California Press, 1973), p.301.

2. Peter Brang, "Sociological Methods in Twentieth-Century Russian Literary Criticism," *Yearbook of Comparative Criticism* 5 (1973):220–221.

3. Paul Gerhard Völker, "Skizze einer marxistischen Literaturwissenschaft," *Methodenkritik der Germanistik*, ed. Marie Luise Gansberg and Völker (Stuttgart: Metzler, 1970), p.120.

4. See Mikhail Lifshitz, *The Philosophy of Art of Karl Marx* (New York: Critics Group, 1938), pp.70–72.

5. Ibid., pp.88–90.

6. Georg Lukács, *Ästhetik* (Neuwied: Luchterhand, 1972), I,56–57.

7. Cambridge, Eng.: The University Press, 1935.

8. Engels, *Anti-Dühring*, Karl Marx, Friedrich Engels, *Über Kunst und Literatur*, ed. Manfred Kliem (Berlin: Dietz Verlag, 1967–68), I,417.

9. See Peter Demetz, *Marx, Engels, and the Poets: Origins of Marxist Literary Criticism* (Chicago: University of Chicago Press, 1967).

10. See the analysis by Rolf Sannwald, *Marx und die Antike* (Einsiedeln: Benziger & Co., 1956), p.195.

11. O. K. Werckmeister, "Marx on Ideology and Art," *New Literary History* 4 (1972/73):501–519.

12. René Wellek, *A History of Modern Criticism 1750–1950* (New Haven: Yale University Press, 1955-), I,126.

13. David Daiches, "Literary Evaluation," *Yearbook of Comparative Criticism* 2 (1969):171.

14. *The Yale Edition of the Works of Samuel Johnson*, Vol. VII, ed. Arthur Sherbo (New Haven: Yale University Press, 1968),59–60.

15. Jean Starobinski, "On the Fundamental Gestures of Criticism," *New Literary History* 5 (1973/74):494–495.

16. Vytautas Kavolis, *History on Art's Side: Social Dynamism in Artistic Efflorescences* (Ithaca: Cornell University Press, 1972), p.2.

17. Louis Kampf, "The Trouble with Literature," *Change in Higher Education* 2, No. 3 (May–June, 1970):30.

18. Ibid., p.27.

19. For a typical German view of this contentious matter, see Malte Dahrendorf, "Literarische Wirkung und Literaturdidaktik," *Lesen—Ein Handbuch*, ed. Alfred Clemens Baumgärtner (Hamburg: Verlag für Buchmarkt-Forschung, 1973), pp.346–347.

20. Robert Escarpit, "The Sociology of Literature," *International Encyclopedia of the Social Sciences*, IX ([New York]: The Macmillan Company and The Free Press, 1968), 420. For the complete statistics, see Escarpit, *The Book Revolution* (London: Harrap and Paris: UNESCO, 1966), pp.115–120.

21. Robert Escarpit, *Das Buch und der Leser: Entwurf einer Literatursoziologie* (Cologne: Westdeutscher Verlag, 1961), p.117.

22. Ibid., n.81.

23. Karl Erik Rosengren, *Sociological Aspects of the Literary System* (Stockholm: Natur och Kultur, 1968), pp.85,83. Cf. in a similar vein Jean-Paul Sartre, *What is Literature?* (New York: Philosophical Library, 1949), pp.28–35.

24. By Lars Lönnroth, *Scandinavian Studies* 41 (1969):79–81.

25. A somewhat primitive but nevertheless differentiated treatment of this matter is Kurt Lang, "Mass, Class, and the Reviewer," *The Sociology of Art and Literature*, ed. Milton C. Albrecht, James H. Barnett, and Mason Griff (New York: Praeger, 1970), pp.455–468.

26. Robert Escarpit, "L'image historique de la littérature chez les jeunes.

Problèmes de tri et de classement," *Littérature et Société: Problèmes de méthodologie en sociologie de la littérature*, ed. Lucien Goldmann, Michel Bernard, and Roger Lallemand (Brussels: Editions de l'Institut de Sociologie de l'Université Libre de Bruxelles, 1967), p.160.

27. See Joseph Strelka, *Die gelenkten Musen: Dichtung und Gesellschaft* (Vienna: Europa Verlag, 1971), p.294.

28. Hans Robert Jauss, "Literary History as a Challenge to Literary Theory," *New Literary History* 2 (1970/71):16.

29. Rosengren, "Litterära attityder och litterärt beteende," *Litteratursociologi*, ed. Karl Erik Rosengren and Jan Thavenius (Stockholm: Natur och Kultur, 1970), p.174.

30. Escarpit, "L'image historique de la littérature chez les jeunes," p.153.

31. A chart, broken down by educational level, is given in Escarpit, ed., *Le Littéraire et le social* (Paris: Flammarion, 1970), p.297.

32. Escarpit, "L'image historique de la littérature chez les jeunes," p.154.

33. Geoffrey H. Hartman, *Beyond Formalism: Literary Essays 1958–1970* (New Haven: Yale University Press, 1970), p.358.

34. David Daiches, *Critical Approaches to Literature* (Englewood Cliffs, New Jersey: Prentice-Hall, 1956), p.54.

35. Harry Levin, *Grounds for Comparison* (Cambridge, Mass.: Harvard University Press, 1972), p.165; Hans-Egon Hass, *Das Problem der literarischen Wertung* (Darmstadt: Wissenschaftliche Buchgesellschaft, 1970), p.83.

36. Diana Laurenson and Alan Swingewood, *The Sociology of Literature* (London: MacGibbon & Kee, 1972), p.22. A more historicist, moderate Marxist version of the argument from antiquity is implied by Stefan Morawski, *Inquiries into the Fundamentals of Aesthetics* (Cambridge, Mass.: MIT Press, 1974), esp. pp.5 and 36.

37. Escarpit, *Das Buch und der Leser*, pp.33,104,118ff.

38. Murray Krieger, "The Critic as Person and Persona," *Yearbook of Comparative Criticism* 6 (1974):84.

39. Escarpit, "The Sociology of Literature," p.424.

40. Escarpit, *Das Buch und der Leser*, p.121.

41. Jauss, "Literary History as a Challenge to Literary Theory," p.11.

42. See Ernest K. Bramsted, *Aristocracy and the Middle-Classes in Germany: Social Types in German Literature 1830–1900*, rev. ed. (Chicago: University of Chicago Press, 1964), passim; T. E. Carter, "Freytag's *Soll und Haben*; a Liberal National Manifesto as a Best-Seller," *German Life & Letters*, n.s. 21 (1967/68):320–329; Jeffrey L. Sammons, "The Evaluation of Freytag's *Soll und Haben*," ibid. n.s. 22 (1968/69):315–324.

43. See Wolfgang Leppmann, *The German Image of Goethe* (Oxford: Oxford University Press, 1961): Norbert Oellers, *Schiller: Geschichte seiner Wirkung bis zu Goethes Tod 1805–1832* (Bonn: Bouvier, 1967).

44. See Götz Wienold, *Semiotik der Literatur* (Frankfurt am Main: Athenäum, 1972).

45. Oellers, *Schiller*, p.12.

46. Ernst Bloch, *Das Prinzip Hoffnung* (Frankfurt am Main: Suhrkamp, 1959), p.176.

47. Walter Benjamin, *Illuminations*, ed. Hannah Arendt (New York: Harcourt, Brace & World, 1968), p.258.

48. See, for example, Lukács, *Ästhetik*, II,145–149.

49. Völker, "Skizze einer marxistischen Literaturwissenschaft," pp.116–117.

50. Robert Weimann, *Literaturgeschichte und Mythologie: Methodologische und historische Studien* (Berlin: Aufbau-Verlag, 1971), pp.44,42–43,68–69,95–96.

51. Erich Koehler, "Les possibilités de l'interprétation sociologique illustrées par l'analyse de textes littéraires français de différentes époques," *Littérature et Société*, ed. Goldmann et al., p.54.

52. On this point, cf. Michel Zéraffa, *Roman et société* (Paris: Presses Universitaires de France, 1971), pp.36–54.

53. David Caute, *The Illusion: An Essay on Politics, Theatre, and the Novel* (New York: Harper & Row, 1972), p.55.

54. George Thomson, *Aeschylus and Athens: A Study in the Social Origins of Drama*, 3rd ed. (New York: Grosset & Dunlap, 1968), p.341.

55. Cited by Marie-Béatrice Mesnet, "Graham Greene," *The Politics of Twentieth-Century Novelists*, ed. George A. Panichas (New York: Crowell, 1974), p.100.

56. Helmut Kreuzer, "Trivialliteratur als Forschungsproblem. Zur Kritik des deutschen Trivialromans seit der Aufklärung," *Methodenfragen der Germanistik*, ed. Reinhold Grimm and Jost Hermand (Darmstadt: Wissenschaftliche Buchgesellschaft, 1973), p.482.

57. Miroslav Červenka, "Die Grundkategorien des Prager literaturwissenschaftlichen Strukturalismus," *Zur Kritik literaturwissenschaftlicher Methode*, ed. Viktor Žmegač and Zdenko Škreb (Frankfurt am Main: Athenäum, 1973), pp.145–146.

58. Hans Robert Jauss, "Levels of Identification of Hero and Audience," *New Literary History* 5 (1974):283–317, esp. p.298.

59. T. W. Adorno, "Theses upon Art and Religion Today," *Kenyon Review* 7 (1945):678.

60. Erwin Leibfried, *Kritische Wissenschaft vom Text: Manipulation, Reflexion, transparente Poetologie* (Stuttgart: Metzler, 1970), p.8.

VI. ELITISM

1. José Ortega y Gasset, *The Dehumanization of Art and Other Essays on Art, Culture, and Literature* (Princeton: Princeton University Press), pp.5–6.

2. H. A. Hodges, "Lukács on Irrationalism," *Georg Lukács: The Man, His Work, and His Ideas*, ed. G. H. R. Parkinson (New York: Vintage Books, 1970), p.89.

3. Norbert Mecklenburg, *Kritisches Interpretieren: Untersuchungen zur Theorie der Literaturkritik* (Munich: Nymphenburger, 1972), p.33. The objection is aimed at Ingarden.

4. Wayne C. Booth, *The Rhetoric of Fiction* (Chicago: University of Chicago Press, 1961), pp.391–392.

5. *Menschliches, Allzumenschliches*, II, section 169, Friedrich Nietzsche, *Werke in drei Bänden*, ed. Karl Schlechta (Munich: Hanser, 1966), I, 798–799.

6. Edmund Wilson, *Axel's Castle: A Study in the Imaginative Literature of 1870–1930* (New York: Scribner's, 1931), p.286.

7. T. B. Bottomore, *Elites and Society* (New York: Basic Books, 1964), p.141.

8. See J. S. R. Goodlad, *A Sociology of Popular Drama* (Totowa, New Jersey: Rowman and Littlefield, 1972), pp. 115–120 and passim.

9. See Max L. Bäumer, "Der Begriff 'klassisch' bei Goethe und Schiller," *Die Klassik-Legende*, ed. Reinhold Grimm and Jost Hermand (Frankfurt am Main: Athenäum, 1971), pp.17–19.

10. M. H. Abrams, *The Mirror and the Lamp: Romantic Theory and the Critical Tradition* (New York: Oxford University Press, 1953), p.301–302.

11. Jean-Paul Sartre, *What is Literature?* (New York: Philosophical Library, 1949), pp.86–97.

12. Q. D. Leavis, *Fiction and the Reading Public* (London: Chatto & Windus, 1932), pp.51,73–74,85.

13. See the discussion by Lennox Grey, "Literary Audience," *Contemporary Literary Scholarship: A Critical Review*, ed. Lewis Leary (New York: Appleton-Century-Crofts, 1958), pp.412–420.

14. Richard Hoggart, "Literature and Society," *A Guide to the Social Sciences*, ed. Norman MacKenzie (London: Weidenfeld & Nicolson, 1966), p.242. Cf. the critique of Mrs. Leavis' random and superficial apprehension of the body of popular literature by Margaret Dalziel, *Popular Fiction 100 Years Ago: An Unexplored Tract of Literary History* (Philadelphia: Dufour Editions, 1958), pp.175–176.

15. Richard Hoggart, *The Uses of Literacy: Changing Patterns in English Mass Culture* (Fair Lawn, N.J.: Essential Books, 1957).

16. Marion Beaujean, Hans Norbert Fügen, Wolfgang R. Langenbecher, and Wolfgang Strauss, *Der Leser als Teil des literarischen Lebens* (Bonn: Bouvier, 1971), p.70.

17. See J. W. Appell, *Die Ritter-, Räuber- und Schauerromantik: Zur Geschichte der deutschen Unterhaltungs-Literatur* (Leipzig: Wilhelm Engelmann, 1859).

18. See Jochen Schulte-Sasse, *Die Kritik an der Trivialliteratur seit der Aufklärung* (Munich: Fink, 1971), pp.116–117.

19. Goethe, *Werke*, ed. Erich Trunz et al., V (Hamburg: Wegner, 1952), 403.

20. Abrams, *The Mirror and the Lamp*, p.109.

21. Walter H. Bruford, "Literary Criticism and Sociology," *Yearbook of Comparative Criticism* 5 (1973):17.

22. *Popular Culture and High Culture: An Analysis and Evaluation of Taste* (New York: Basic Books, 1974).

23. Ibid., pp.7–8; cf. pp.55–57; p.32 and passim.

24. Ibid., pp.128–132,31.

25. Richard D. Altick, *The English Common Reader: A Social History of the Mass Reading Public 1800–1900* (Chicago: University of Chicago Press, 1957), p.1.

26. Rudolf Schenda, *Volk ohne Buch: Studien zur Sozialgeschichte der populären Lesestoffe 1770–1910* (Frankfurt am Main: Vittorio Klostermann, 1970), pp.41–50,141,153.

27. Harry Elmer Barnes, ed., *An Introduction to the History of Sociology*, abridged ed. (Chicago: University of Chicago Press, 1966), pp.156–157.

28. Sartre, *What is Literature?* p.162.

29. John F. Danby, *Poets on Fortune's Hill: Studies in Sidney, Shakespeare, Beaumont & Fletcher* (London: Faber and Faber, 1952), pp.25–26.

30. Eugene Goodheart, *Culture and the Radical Conscience* (Cambridge, Mass.: Harvard University Press, 1973), p.39.

31. Raymond Williams, *Communications*, 2nd ed. (London: Chatto & Windus, 1966), pp.102–103.

32. Walter Benjamin, *Das Kunstwerk im Zeitalter seiner technischen Reproduzierbarkeit* (Frankfurt am Main: Suhrkamp, 1968), p.112.

33. Ernst Fischer, "Ein Geisterseher in der Bürgerwelt," Theodor W. Adorno, et al., *Über Walter Benjamin* (Frankfurt am Main: Suhrkamp, 1968), pp.111–112,120.

34. Klaus-Peter Philippi, "Methodologische Probleme der Literatursoziologie. Kritische Bemerkungen zu einer fragwürdigen Situation," *Wirkendes Wort* 20 (1970);229–230.

35. Louis Kampf, "The Trouble with Literature," *Change in Higher Education* 2, No. 3 (May–June, 1970):29.

36. Michael Pehlke, "Aufstieg und Fall der Germanistik—von der Agonie einer bürgerlichen Wissenschaft," *Ansichten einer künftigen Germanistik*, ed. Jürgen Kolbe (Munich: Hanser, 1969), p.44.

37. Bottomore, *Elites and Society*, pp.25,64,68–69; cf. p.38.

38. Michael Scharang, *Zur Emanzipation der Kunst* (Neuwied: Luchterhand, 1971), p.16.

39. Levin L. Schücking, *Soziologie der literarischen Geschmacksbildung* (Berne: Francke Verlag, 1961), p.105.

40. Daniel M. Fox, "Artists in the Modern State: The Nineteenth-Century Background," *The Sociology of Art and Literature*, ed. Milton C. Albrecht, James H. Barnett, and Mason Griff (New York: Praeger, 1970), p.376.

41. See Jürgen Habermas, *Strukturwandel der Öffentlichkeit: Untersuchungen zu einer Kategorie der bürgerlichen Gesellschaft*, 2nd ed. (Neuwied: Luchterhand, 1965), pp.181–182,183,187–188.

42. See Gans, *Popular Culture and High Culture*, p.36.

43. Schenda, *Volk ohne Buch*, pp.33–34.

44. E.g., Jost Hermand, "Probleme der heutigen Gattungsgeschichte," *Jahrbuch für Internationale Germanistik* 2, No. 1 (1970):85–94.

45. Conor Cruise O'Brien, "Passion and Cunning: The Politics of W. B. Yeats," *TriQuarterly*, Nos. 23/24 (Winter/Spring, 1972):156.

46. Ehrhard Bahr, *Georg Lukács* (Berlin: Colloquium Verlag, 1970), p.63.

47. E.g., in the preface to *Atta Troll*, Heinrich Heine, *Sämtliche Werke*, ed. Ernst Elster (Leipzig: Bibliographisches Institut, [1887–90]), II,352–353.

48. Raymond Williams, *Culture and Society 1780–1950* (New York: Columbia University Press, 1958), p.xviii.

49. Christopher Caudwell, *Illusion and Reality: A Study of the Sources of Poetry* (London: Macmillan, 1937), pp.36–37.

50. Leon Trotsky, *Literature and Revolution* (New York: International Publishers, 1925), p.10, and Georg Lukács, *Ästhetik* (Neuwied: Luchterhand, 1972), IV,52.

51. Kenneth Clark, "Art and Society," *The Sociology of Art and Literature*, ed. Albrecht et al., p.650.

52. Caudwell, *Illusion and Reality*, p.38.

53. S. T. Coleridge, *Biographia Literaria*, ed. J. Shawcross (Oxford: Oxford University Press, 1973), II,39–40.

54. Geoffrey H. Hartman, *Beyond Formalism: Literary Essays 1958–1970* (New Haven: Yale University Press, 1970), p.359.

55. Harry Levin, *Refractions: Essays in Comparative Literature* (New York: Oxford University Press, 1966), p.11.

56. Leonard Forster, "Literary History as an Academic Discipline: Is it Respectable?" *Western Canadian Studies in Modern Languages and Literature* 1 (1969):21.

57. Walter Hinderer, "Literary Value Judgments and Value Cognition," *Yearbook of Comparative Criticism* 2 (1969):58.

VII. EXTRINSICALITY

1. Robert Escarpit, "The Sociology of Literature," *International Encyclopedia of the Social Sciences*, IX ([New York]: The Macmillan Company and The Free Press, 1968),419.

2. Roland Barthes, *Writing Degree Zero* (Boston: Beacon Press, 1970), p.9.

3. W. K. Wimsatt, *Hateful Contraries: Studies in Literature and Criticism* (Lexington: University of Kentucky Press, 1966), p.218.

4. For a review of the discussion, beginning with Ingarden's recognition of the difficulty, see Zoran Konstantinović, *Phänomenologie und Literaturwissenschaft: Skizzen zu einer wissenschaftstheoretischen Begründung* (Munich: List Verlag, 1973), pp.112–119. See also the treatment by Paul Hernadi, *Beyond Genre: New Directions in Literary Classification* (Ithaca: Cornell University Press, 1972), pp.38,84.

5. John R. Searle, "The Logical Status of Fictional Discourse," *New Literary History* 6 (1974/75): 330–332.

6. See Walter J. Slatoff's plea for good sense in this matter, *With Respect to Readers: Dimensions of Literary Response* (Ithaca: Cornell University Press, 1970).

7. Monroe C. Beardsley, *Aesthetics: Problems in the Philosophy of Criticism* (New York: Harcourt, Brace, 1958), p.9; cf. Edgar Lohner, "The Intrinsic Method: Some Reconsiderations," *The Disciplines of Criticism*, ed. Peter Demetz, Thomas

Greene, and Lowry Nelson, Jr. (New Haven: Yale University Press, 1968), p.170.

8. Roman Ingarden, *Vom Erkennen des literarischen Kunstwerks* (Tübingen: Niemeyer, 1968), p.35.

9. See John Fizer, "The Concept of Strata and Phases in Roman Ingarden's Theory of Literary Structure," *Yearbook of Comparative Criticism* 6 (1973): 17–18.

10. Harry Levin, "Comparing the Literature," *Grounds for Comparison* (Cambridge, Mass.: Harvard University Press, 1972), p.85.

11. T. S. Eliot, *The Use of Poetry and the Use of Criticism: Studies in the Relation of Criticism to Poetry in England* (London: Faber and Faber, 1948), pp.75, 22.

12. See Murray Krieger, *The Play and Place of Criticism* (Baltimore: Johns Hopkins University Press, 1967), p.159, and cf. the acknowledgment and critique by Gerald Graff, *Poetic Statement and Critical Dogma* (Evanston: Northwestern University Press, 1970), p.171.

13. R. S. Crane, *Critical and Historical Principles of Literary History* (Chicago: University of Chicago Press, 1971), p.1.

14. Richard Foster, *The New Romantics: A Reappraisal of the New Criticism* (Bloomington: Indiana University Press, 1962), p.123.

15. Richard Wollheim, "Sociological Explanation of the Arts: Some Distinctions," *The Sociology of Art and Literature*, ed. Milton C. Albrecht, James H. Barnett, and Mason Griff (New York: Praeger, 1970). p.575.

16. Hans L. Zetterberg, *On Theory and Verification in Sociology*, 3rd ed. (Totowa, New Jersey: Bedminster Press, 1965), p.70.

17. T. M. Bottomore, *Sociology: A Guide to Problems and Literature*, 2nd ed. (New York: Pantheon, 1971), p.42.

18. Crane, *Critical and Historical Principles of Literary History*, p.53.

19. Hans Norbert Fügen, *Die Hauptrichtungen der Literatursoziologie und ihre Methoden*, 5th ed. (Bonn: Bouvier, 1971), pp.30,116.

20. Georg Lukács, *Ästhetik* (Neuwied: Luchterhand, 1972), II, 143–144.

21. Jean Duvignaud, *Sociologie de l'Art* (Paris: Presses Universitaires de France, 1967), p.113.

22. Ian Watt, *The Rise of the Novel: Studies in Defoe, Richardson and Fielding* (Berkeley: University of California Press, 1967), p.60.

23. Thus Ernst Fischer, *Von der Notwendigkeit der Kunst* (Hamburg: Claassen, 1967), p.8.

24. E.g., Erich Koehler, "Les possibilités de l'interprétation sociologique illustrées par l'analyse de textes littéraires français de différentes époques," *Littérature et Société: Problèmes de méthodologie en sociologie de la littérature*, ed. Lucien Goldmann, Michael Bernard, and Roger Lallemand (Brussels: Editions de l'Institut de Sociologie de l'Université Libre de Bruxelles, 1967), p.63; Bente Hansen, *Den marxistiske litteraturkritik* (Copenhagen: Hans Reitzel, 1967), p.9.

25. Lukács, *Ästhetik*, I, 165–167.

26. See the often quoted late letters of Engels to Joseph Bloch, Sept. 21, 1890; to Conrad Schmidt, Oct. 27, 1890; to W. Borgius, Jan. 25, 1894, in Karl Marx, Friedrich Engels, *Werke*, ed. Institut für Marxismus-Leninismus beim ZK der

SED, XXXVII (Berlin: Dietz Verlag, 1967),462–465, 488–495; XXXIX (Berlin: Dietz Verlag, 1968),205–207. The recipient of the third letter was previously thought to be Hans Starkenburg and it used to be so cited.

27. Peter Demetz, *Marx, Engels, and the Poets: Origins of Marxist Literary Criticism* (Chicago: Chicago University Press, 1967), pp.138–151.

28. Béla Királyfalvi, *The Aesthetics of György Lukács* (Princeton: Princeton University Press, 1975), p.29.

29. Kenneth Burke, *A Grammar of Motives* (Berkeley: University of California Press, 1969), pp.200–202.

30. Fredric Jameson, *Marxism and Form: Twentieth-Century Theories of Literature* (Princeton: Princeton University Press, 1971), p.345.

31. Michael Lane, ed., *Introduction to Structuralism* (New York: Basic Books, 1970), p.17.

32. Diana Laurenson and Alan Swingewood, *The Sociology of Literature* (London: MacGibbon & Kee, 1972), pp.170,243.

33. Erwin Leibfried, *Kritische Wissenschaft vom Text: Manipulation, Reflexion, transparente Poetologie* (Stuttgart: Metzler, 1970), pp.204–205; Walter Müller-Seidel, *Probleme der literarischen Wertung: Über die Wissenschaftlichkeit eines unwissenschaftlichen Themas*, 2nd ed. (Stuttgart: Metzler, 1969), pp.158–159.

34. Eric Donald Hirsch, Jr., "Privileged Criteria in Literary Evaluation," *Yearbook of Comparative Criticism* 2 (1969):29,31.

35. *The Poetical Works of William Wordsworth*, ed. E. de Selincourt, II (Oxford: Clarendon Press, 1944), p.385.

36. Ernst Fischer, *Kunst und Koexistenz: Beitrag zu einer modernen marxistischen Ästhetik* (Reinbek: Rowohlt, 1966), p.62.

37. Roy Pascal, "Georg Lukács: the Concept of Totality," *Georg Lukács: The Man, His Work and His Ideas*, ed. G. H. R. Parkinson (New York: Vintage Books, 1970), p.148.

38. Királyfalvi, *The Aesthetics of György Lukács*, pp.54–58.

39. Christopher Caudwell, *Illusion and Reality: A Study of the Sources of Poetry* (London: Macmillan, 1937), p.xiv.

40. Viktor Žmegač, "Probleme der Literatursoziologie," *Zur Kritik literaturwissenschaftlicher Methodologie*, ed. Žmegač and Zdenko Škreb (Frankfurt am Main: Athenäum, 1973), pp.265–266.

41. See Margaret Dalziel, *Popular Fiction 100 Years Ago: An Unexplored Tract of Literary History* (Philadelphia: Dufour Editions, 1958), pp.4–12.

42. Robert Escarpit, *The Book Revolution* (London: Harrap, and Paris: UNESCO, 1966), p.152. The statistic is taken over without acknowledgment and applied to Germany by Urs Jaeggi, *Literatur und Politik: Ein Essay* (Frankfurt am Main: Suhrkamp, 1972), p.22.

43. Malcolm Bradbury, *The Social Context of Modern English Literature* (New York: Schocken Books, 1971), pp.215–216, n.4.

44. Escarpit, *The Book Revolution*, p.151.

45. Fügen, *Die Hauptrichtungen der Literatursoziologie und ihre Methoden*, p.187.

46. Jürgen Habermas, *Strukturwandel der Öffentlichkeit: Untersuchungen zu einer Kategorie der bürgerlichen Gesellschaft*, 2nd ed. (Neuwied: Luchterhand, 1965), p.48.

47. Hans Olof Johansson, "Utgivningen av svensk lyrik 1931–1960," *Litteratursociologi*, ed. Karl Erik Rosengren and Jan Thavenius (Stockholm: Natur och Kultur, 1970), pp.93–109.

48. The following points are taken from Dan Lacy, "The Economics of Publishing, or Adam Smith and Literature," *The Sociology of Art and Literature*, ed. Albrecht et al., pp.407–425. Cf. the more systematic and hard-headed summary of this set of problems by Robert Escarpit, "Succès et survie littéraires," *Le Littéraire et le social*, ed. Escarpit (Paris: Flammarion, 1970), pp.129–148.

49. *International Herald Tribune*, January 12, 1973, p.5.

50. Hannelore Schlaffer, "Kritik eines Klischees," *Erweiterung der materialistischen Literaturtheorie durch Bestimmung ihrer Grenzen*, ed. Heinz Schlaffer (Stuttgart: Metzler, 1974), pp.265–287.

51. Jameson, *Marxism and Form*, p.329.

52. See Albert Memmi, "Cinq propositions pour une sociologie de la littérature," *Cahiers Internationaux de Sociologie* 26 (1959):155.

53. Michel Zéraffa, *Roman et société* (Paris: Presses Universitaires de France, 1971), p.80.

54. W. K. Wimsatt, Jr., *The Verbal Icon: Studies in the Meaning of Poetry* (Lexington: University of Kentucky Press, 1954), p.10.

55. Beardsley, *Aesthetics*, pp.534–535.

56. Ingarden, *Vom Erkennen des literarischen Kunstwerks*, p.323. I find myself supported by Graff, *Poetic Statement and Critical Dogma*, p.152.

57. David Daiches, *Critical Approaches to Literature* (Englewood Cliffs, New Jersey: Prentice-Hall, 1956), p.324.

58. R. Peacock, *Criticism and Personal Taste* (Oxford: Clarendon Press, 1972), p.29.

59. Northrop Frye, *The Critical Path: An Essay on the Social Context of Literary Criticism* (Bloomington: Indiana University Press, 1971), p.19.

60. Jameson, *Marxism and Form*, pp.4–5.

61. Ibid., p.35.

62. Lionel Trilling, *The Liberal Imagination: Essays on Literature and Society* (New York: Viking Press, 1951), p.xii.

63. Lukács, *Ästhetik*, III,13–14.

64. Trilling, *The Liberal Imagination*, p.100.

65. Lionel Trilling, *Beyond Culture: Essays on Literature and Learning* (New York: Viking Press, 1965), p.xii.

66. Ibid., p.163.

VIII. SOME CONCLUSIONS

1. Malcolm Bradbury, *The Social Context of Modern English Literature* (New York: Schocken Books, 1971), p.xiv.

2. Roland Barthes, *Mythologies* (New York: Hill and Wang, 1972), p.82.

3. Wayne C. Booth, *The Rhetoric of Fiction* (Chicago: University of Chicago Press, 1961), p.140.

4. Georg Lukács, *Ästhetik* (Neuwied: Luchterhand, 1972), III,11.

5. Erwin Leibfried, *Kritische Wissenschaft vom Text: Manipulation, Reflexion, transparente Poetologie* (Stuttgart: Metzler, 1970), p.63.

6. Walter Müller-Seidel, *Probleme der literarischen Wertung: Über die Wissenschaftlichkeit eines unwissenschaftlichen Themas*, 2nd ed. (Stuttgart: Metzler, 1969), p.159.

7. Everyone concerned with these matters will have great benefit from Peter L. Berger and Thomas Luckmann, *The Social Construction of Reality: A Treatise in the Sociology of Knowledge* (Garden City, New York: Anchor Books, 1967).

8. Robert Weimann, "French Structuralism and Literary History," *New Literary History* 4 (1972/73):462–463.

9. Robert Weimann, *"New Criticism" und die Entwicklung bürgerlicher Literaturwissenschaft: Geschichte und Kritik neuer Interpretationsmethoden* (Halle: VEB Max Niemeyer Verlag, 1962), p.277.

10. Michael Scharang, *Zur Emanzipation der Kunst* (Neuwied: Luchterhand, 1971), p.57.

11. Hans-Günther Thalheim, *Zur Literatur der Goethezeit* (Berlin: Rütten & Loening, 1969), p.137.

12. Geoffrey H. Hartman, *Beyond Formalism: Literary Essays 1958–1970* (New Haven: Yale University Press, 1970), p.xiii.

13. Lucien Goldmann, *The Hidden God: A Study of Tragic Vision in the* Pensées *of* Pascal *and the Tragedies of* Racine (New York: Humanities Press, 1964), p.328; cf.p.7.

14. Robert Escarpit, *Das Buch und der Leser: Entwurf einer Literatursoziologie* (Cologne: Westdeutscher Verlag, 1961), p.116.

15. Booth, *The Rhetoric of Fiction*, p.369.

16. Ibid., p.370.

17. E. D. Hirsch, Jr., "Three Dimensions of Hermeneutics," *New Literary History* 3 (1971/72):259,260.

18. Kenneth Burke, *Terms for Order*, ed. Stanley Edgar Hyman with the assistance of Barbara Karmiller (Bloomington: Indiana University Press, 1964), pp.124–125.

19. Jean Duvignaud, *Sociologie de l'Art* (Paris: Presses Universitaires de France, 1967),p.37.

20. L. C. Knights, *Drama & Society in the Age of Jonson* (London: Chatto & Windus, 1937), p.5.

21. Diana Spearman, *The Novel and Society* (London: Routledge and Kegan Paul, 1966), pp.29,5.

22. Karl Marx, Friedrich Engels, *Werke*, ed. Institut für Marxismus-Leninismus beim ZK der SED, III (Berlin: Dietz Verlag, 1962),18,27.

23. Edmund Wilson, *Axel's Castle: A Study in the Imaginative Literature of 1870–1930* (New York: Scribner's, 1931), p.121.

24. Cf. the discussion by Hans Robert Jauss, "Das Ende der Kunstperiode—Aspekte der literarischen Revolution bei Heine, Hugo und Stendhal," *Beiträge zur französischen Aufklärung und zur spanischen Literatur: Festgabe für Werner Krauss zum 70. Geburtstag,* ed. Werner Bahner (Berlin: Akademie-Verlag, 1971), pp.141–167, esp. p.164.

25. See A. L. Kroeber, "Style in the Fine Arts," *The Sociology of Art and Literature,* ed. Milton C. Albrecht, James H. Barnett, and Mason Griff (New York: Praeger, 1970), p.123.

26. Harry Levin, *The Gates of Horn: A Study of Five French Realists* (New York: Oxford University Press, 1963), pp.48–56.

27. E.g., Erich Köhler, "Einige Thesen zur Literatursoziologie," *Germanisch-romanische Monatsschrift* n.s. 24 (1974):257.

28. R. S. Crane, *Critical and Historical Principles of Literary History* (Chicago: University of Chicago Press, 1971), p.107.

29. Roman Ingarden, *Vom Erkennen des literarischen Kunstwerks* (Tübingen: Niemeyer, 1968), p.224.

30. See Ford's introduction to *A Farewell to Arms* in the Modern Liberary Edition (New York: Random House, 1932).

31. F. R. Leavis, *The Common Pursuit* (London: Chatto & Windus, 1952), p.200.

32. Jost Hermand, *Synthetisches Interpretieren: Zur Methodik der Literaturwissenschaft* (Munich: Nymphenburger, 1968), p.11.

33. Duvignaud, *Sociologie de l'Art,* p.74.

34. Lukács, *Ästhetik,* II,234–281.

35. C. M. Bowra, *Poetry & Politics 1900–1960* (Cambridge, Eng.: University Press, 1966), p.13.

36. Lionel Trilling, *The Liberal Imagination: Essays on Literature and Society* (New York: Viking Press, 1951), p.298.

37. Ernst Fischer, *Kunst und Koexistenz: Beitrag zu einer modernen marxistischen Ästhetik* (Reinbek: Rowohlt, 1966), p.58.

38. Walter J. Slatoff, *With Respect to Readers: Dimensions of Literary Response* (Ithaca: Cornell University Press, 1970), p.14.

39. Ibid., pp.168–169.

40. Ernst Fischer, *Auf den Spuren der Wirklichkeit* (Reinbek: Rowohlt, 1968), p.64.

BIBLIOGRAPHY

The bibliography does not pretend to be comprehensive. The construction of a full bibliography of literary sociology would be, given the character of literary study today, especially in Europe, a task of dispiriting magnitude. What is offered here is primarily a list of works I have encountered in my inquiry. A few others have been added at certain points for the sake of local completeness. The selection is canted toward current work. Volumes that contain several pertinent papers are listed once. For convenience the bibliography is organized as follows:

I. THE PREHISTORY

Not listed, but basic to the prehistory of literary sociology are Plato, especially the *Ion* and Books II, III, and X of the *Republic*; Aristotle's *Poetics*, and G. W. F. Hegel's *Aesthetics* as well as his system as a whole.

Mehring, Franz. *Die Lessing-Legende*, ed. Hans Mayer. Basel: Mundus-Verlag, 1946.

Plekhanov, Georgiĭ Valentinovich. *Art and Social Life*, ed. Andrew Rothstein. London: Lawrence & Wishart, 1953.

Staël, Germaine Necker de. *De la littérature considerée dans ses rapports avec les institutions sociales.* 2nd ed. Paris: Crapelet, [1801].

Taine, Hippolyte. *History of English Literature.* Tr. H. Van Laun. Reprinted from the 1883 edition. 4 vols. New York: Ungar, 1965.

II. BIBLIOGRAPHIES

Birnbaum, Norman. "The Sociological Study of Ideology (1940–1960): A Trend Report and Bibliography." *Current Sociology* 9 (1960):91–172.

Duncan, Hugh D. *Language and Literature in Society.* Chicago: University of Chicago Press, 1953. Pp.143–214.

International Bibliography of Sociology, published by UNESCO. 1951 ff.

International Social Science Journal 20 (1968):681–687.

Marshall, Thomas F., et al., eds. *Literature and Society, 1950–1955: A Selective Bibliography*; Marshall, Thomas F., and George K. Smart, eds., *Literature and Society, 1956–1960: A Selective Bibliography*; Carter, Paul J., and George K. Smart, eds., *Literature and Society, 1961–1965: A Selective Bibliography.* Coral Gables: University of Miami Press, 1956, 1962, 1967.

III. SOCIOLOGY

Anderson, C. Arnold, et al., eds. *Varieties of Political Expression in Sociology.* Chicago: University of Chicago Press, 1972.

Barnes, Harry Elmer, ed. *An Introduction to the History of Sociology.* Abridged ed. Chicago: University of Chicago Press, 1966.

Berger, Peter L., and Thomas Luckmann. *The Social Construction of Reality: A Treatise in the Sociology of Knowledge.* Garden City, New York: Anchor Books, 1967.

Bottomore, T. B. *Sociology: A Guide to Problems and Literature.* 2nd ed. New York: Pantheon, 1971.

Freund, Julien. *The Sociology of Max Weber.* Tr. Mary Ilford. New York: Pantheon, 1968.

Ginsberg, Morris. "Social Change." *British Journal of Sociology* 9 (1958):205–229.

Jameson, Fredric. "The Vanishing Mediator: Narrative Structure in Max Weber." *New German Critique* 1, No. 1 (Winter, 1974):52–89.

MacKenzie, Norman, ed. *A Guide to the Social Sciences.* London: Weidenfeld & Nicolson, 1966.

Nisbet, Robert. *The Sociology of Emile Durkheim.* New York: Oxford University Press, 1974.

Oberschall, Anthony. *Empirical Social Research in Germany 1848–1914.* New York: Basic Books; The Hague: Mouton, 1965.

O'Neill, John. *Sociology as a Skin Trade: Essays Towards a Reflexive Sociology.* Harper & Row, 1972.

Zetterberg, Hans L. *On Theory and Verification in Sociology.* 3rd enlarged ed. Totowa, New Jersey: Bedminster Press, 1965.

IV. GENERAL STUDIES AND ESSAYS

Abell, Walter. *The Collective Dream in Art: A Psycho-Historical Theory of Culture Based on Relations Between the Arts, Psychology, and the Social Sciences.* Cambridge, Mass.: Harvard University Press, 1957.

Ackerman, James S. "Toward a New Social Theory of Art." *New Literary History* 4 (1972/73):315–330.

Albrecht, Milton C. "Does Literature Reflect Common Values?" *American Sociological Review* 21 (1956):722–729.

——. "The Relationship of Literature and Society." *American Journal of Sociology* 59 (1953/54):425–436.

——, James H. Barnett, and Mason Griff, eds. *The Sociology of Art and Literature.* New York: Praeger, 1970.

Althaus, Horst. *Ästhetik, Ökonomie und Gesellschaft.* Berne: Francke Verlag, 1971.

Bark, Joachim, ed. *Literatursoziologie. I. Begriff und Methodik. II. Beiträge zur Praxis.* Stuttgart: Kohlhammer, 1974.

Barnett, James H. "The Sociology of Art." *Sociology Today,* ed. Robert K. Merton, Leonard Broom, and Leonard S. Cottrell, Jr. New York: Basic Books, 1959. Pp.197–214.

Baxandall, Lee, ed. *Radical Perspectives in the Arts.* Harmondsworth: Penguin Books, 1972.

Bloch, Herbert A. "Towards the Development of a Sociology of Literary and Art-Forms." *American Sociological Review* 8 (1943):313–320.

Bouazis, Charles. "L'Implication du texte idéologique." *Mosaic* 5, No. 2 (Winter, 1971/72):125–137.

Bourdieu, Pierre. "Outline of a Sociological Theory of Art Perception." *International Social Science Journal* 20 (1961):589–612.

Bradbury, Malcolm. *The Social Context of Modern English Literature.* New York: Schocken Books, 1971.

Brang, Peter. "Sociological Methods in Twentieth-Century Russian Criticism." *Yearbook of Comparative Criticism* 5 (1973):209–251.

Bruford, Walter H. "Literary Criticism and Sociology." *Yearbook of Comparative Criticism* 5 (1973):3–20.

Burns, Elizabeth, and Tom Burns, eds. *Sociology of Literature and Drama.* Harmondsworth: Penguin Books, 1973.

Caute, David. *The Illusion: An Essay on Politics, Theatre and the Novel.* New York: Harper & Row, 1972.

Clark, Priscilla P. "The Comparative Method: Sociology and the Study of Literature." *Yearbook of Comparative and General Literature* 23 (1974):5–13.

——, and Terry N. Clark. "Writers, Literature and Student Movements in France." *Sociology of Education* 42, No. 4 (Fall, 1969):293–314.

Coser, Lewis. *Men of Ideas—A Sociologist's View.* New York: The Free Press, 1965.

———, ed. *Sociology Through Literature: An Introductory Reader*. Englewood Cliffs, N.J.: Prentice-Hall, 1963.

Craig, David. *The Real Foundations: Literature and Social Change*. New York: Oxford University Press, 1974.

———. "Towards Laws of Literary Development." *Mosaic* 5, No. 2 (Winter, 1971/72):11–30.

Creedy, Jean, ed. *The Social Context of Art*. London: Tavistock Publications, 1970.

Culler, Jonathan. "Structure of Ideology and Ideology of Structure." *New Literary History* 4 (1972/73):471–482.

Daiches, David. *Literature and Society*. London: Gollancz, 1938.

Darnton, Robert. "Reading, Writing, and Publishing in Eighteenth-Century France: A Case Study in the Sociology of Literature." *Daedalus* 100 (1971):214–256.

Dickie, George. *Art and the Aesthetic: An Institutional Analysis*. Ithaca: Cornell University Press, 1974.

Duncan, Hugh D. *Communication and Social Order*. New York: Bedminster Press, 1962.

———. *Language and Literature in Society*. Chicago: University of Chicago Press, 1953.

Duvignaud, Jean. *Sociologie de l'Art*. Paris: Presses Universitaires de France, 1972. *The Sociology of Art*. Tr. Timothy Wilson. New York: Harper & Row, 1972.

Escarpit, Robert, ed. *La Littéraire et le social*. Paris: Flammarion, 1970.

———. *La Révolution du livre*. Paris: UNESCO, Presses Universitaires de France, 1965. *The Book Revolution*. London: Harrap, and Paris: UNESCO, 1966.

———. *Sociologie de la littérature*. Que sais-je? No. 777. Paris: Presses Universitaires de France, 1958. Expanded and revised as *Das Buch und der Leser: Entwurf einer Literatursoziologie*. Cologne: Westdeutscher Verlag, 1961.

———. "The Sociology of Literature." *International Encyclopedia of the Social Sciences*, IX. [New York]: The Macmillan Company and The Free Press, 1968. Pp.417–425.

Fügen, Hans Norbert. *Dichtung in der bürgerlichen Gesellschaft*. Bonn: Bouvier, 1972.

———. *Die Hauptrichtungen der Literatursoziologie und ihre Methoden*. 5th ed. Bonn: Bouvier, 1971.

———. "Literary Criticism and Sociology in Germany." *Yearbook of Comparative Criticism* 5 (1973):252–269.

———, ed. *Wege der Literatursoziologie*. Soziologische Texte, 46. Neuwied: Luchterhand, 1968.

Graña, César. *Fact and Symbol: Essays in the Sociology of Art and Literature*. New York: Oxford University Press, 1971.

Guérard, Albert. *Literature and Society*. Boston: Lothrop, Lee and Shepard, 1935.

Hamburger, Michael. *Vernunft und Rebellion: Aufsätze zur Gesellschaftskritik in der deutschen Literatur*. Munich: Hanser, 1969.

Hård af Segerstad, Peder. *Litteratursociologi: Ett bidrag till ämnets teoriutveckling*. Uppsala: Almqvist & Wiksell, 1974.

Hauser, Arnold. *The Social History of Art*. 2 vols. Tr. Hauser and Stanley Godman. New York: Knopf, 1952. The original as *Sozialgeschichte der Kunst und Literatur*. Munich: Beck, 1953.

Hoggart, Richard. "Literature and Society." *A Guide to the Social Sciences*, ed. Norman MacKenzie. London: Weidenfeld & Nicolson, 1966. Pp.225–248.

Howe, Irving. *Politics and the Novel*. New York: Horizon Press, 1957.

Jaeggi, Urs. *Literatur und Politik: Ein Essay*. edition suhrkamp, No. 522. Frankfurt am Main: Suhrkamp, 1972.

Jens, Walter. *Literatur und Politik*. opuscula, No. 18. Pfullingen: Neske, 1963.

Karbusicky, Vladimír. "The Interaction Between 'Reality–Work of Art–Society.'" *International Social Science Journal* 20 (1968):644–655.

Kavolis, Vytautas. *Artistic Expression: A Sociological Analysis*. Ithaca: Cornell University Press, 1968.

——. *History on Art's Side: Social Dynamism in Artistic Efflorescences*. Ithaca: Cornell University Press, 1972.

Kinder, Hermann. *Poesie als Synthese: Ausbreitung eines deutschen Realismus-Verständnisses in der Mitte des 19. Jahrhunderts*. Frankfurt am Main: Athenäum, 1973.

Knights, L. C. *Drama & Society in the Age of Jonson*. London: Chatto & Windus, 1937.

Köhler, Erich. "Einige Thesen zur Literatursoziologie." *Germanisch-romanische Monatsschrift* N.S. 24 (1974):257–264.

Kreuzer, Helmut. *Die Boheme: Beiträge zu ihrer Beschreibung*. Stuttgart: Metzler, 1968.

——, ed., with Käte Hamburger. *Gestaltungsgeschichte und Gesellschaftsgeschichte: Literatur-, Kunst- und Musikwissenschaftliche Studien*. Stuttgart: Metzler, 1969.

Lange, Victor, and Hans-Gert Roloff, eds. *Dichtung, Sprache, Gesellschaft: Akten des IV. Internationalen Germanisten-Kongresses 1970 in Princeton*. Frankfurt am Main: Athenäum, 1971.

Laurenson, Diana T., and Alan Swingewood. *The Sociology of Literature*. London: MacGibbon & Kee, 1972.

Leenhardt, Jacques. "Introduction à la sociologie de la littérature." *Mosaic* 5, No. 2 (Winter, 1971/72):1–10.

——. "The Sociology of Literature. Some Stages in its History." *International Social Science Journal* 19 (1967):517–533.

Literaturwissenschaft und Sozialwissenschaften: Grundlagen und Modellanalysen. Ed. by a collective. Stuttgart: Metzler, 1971.

Lowenthal, Leo. *Literature and the Image of Man: Sociological Studies of the European Drama and Novel, 1600–1900*. Boston: The Beacon Press, 1957.

————. "Literature and Sociology." *Relations of Literary Study: Essays on Interdisciplinary Contributions*, ed. James Thorpe. New York: Modern Language Association of America, 1967. Pp.89–110.

Macherey, Pierre. *Pour une théorie de la production littéraire*. Paris: Maspero, 1966.

Mannheim, Karl. "Ideologische und soziologische Interpretation der geistigen Gebilde." *Jahrbuch für Soziologie* 2 (1926):424–440.

Memmi, Albert. "Cinq propositions pour une sociologie de la littérature." *Cahiers Internationaux de Sociologie* 26 (1959):149–163.

Miles, David H. "Literary Sociology: Some Introductory Notes." *German Quarterly* 48 (1975):1–35.

Minder, Robert. *Dichter in der Gesellschaft: Erfahrungen mit deutscher und französischer Literatur*. Frankfurt am Main: Insel Verlag, 1966.

Müller-Seidel, Walter, et al., eds. *Historizität in Sprach- und Literaturwissenschaft: Vorträge und Berichte der Stuttgarter Germanistentagung 1972*. Munich: Fink, 1974.

Neumann, Thomas. *Der Künstler in der bürgerlichen Gesellschaft: Entwurf einer Kunstsoziologie am Beispiel der Künstlerästhetik Friedrich Schillers*. Stuttgart: Enke, 1968.

Otto, Ulla. *Die literarische Zensur als Problem der Soziologie der Politik*. Stuttgart: Enke, 1968.

Poggioli, Renato. *The Theory of the Avant-Garde*. Cambridge, Mass.: Harvard-Belknap, 1968.

Ramsey, Paul. "Literary Criticism and Sociology." *Yearbook of Comparative Criticism* 5 (1973):21–29.

————. "Society and Poetry." *Princeton Encyclopedia of Poetry and Poetics*, ed. Alex Preminger. Princeton: Princeton University Press, 1965. Pp.775–779.

Reszler, André, and Thomas G. Sauer, eds. *Politics and Literature: Papers Presented at the Conference on Politics and Literature Held at Indiana University October 5–7, 1972*. Bloomington: Department of Comparative Literature, Indiana University, 1973. (Reprinted from the *Yearbook of Comparative and General Literature* 22 [1973]).

Rosengren, Karl Erik, and Jan Thavenius, eds. *Litteratursociologi*. Stockholm: Natur och Kultur, 1970.

Rosengren, Karl Erik. *Sociological Aspects of the Literary System*. Stockholm: Natur och Kultur, 1968.

Rothe, Wolfgang. "Schriftsteller und Gesellschaft im 20. Jahrhundert." *Deutsche Literatur im 20. Jahrhundert: Strukturen und Gestalten*, ed. Otto Mann and Wolfgang Rothe. 5th ed. Berne: Francke Verlag, 1967. I,189–221.

Rudnick, Hans H. "Recent British and American Studies Concerning Sociology of Literature." *Yearbook of Comparative Criticism* 5 (1973):270–281.

Sammons, Jeffrey L. "The Threat of Literary Sociology and What to Do About It." *Yearbook of Comparative Criticism* 5 (1973):30–40.

Schücking, Levin L. *Soziologie der literarischen Geschmacksbildung*. 3rd ed. Berne: Francke Verlag, 1961.

Scott, Wilbur, ed. *Five Approaches of Literary Criticism.* New York: Collier-Macmillan, 1962.

Silbermann, Alphons. "Introduction: A Definition of the Sociology of Art." *International Social Science Journal* 20 (1968):567–588.

Škreb, Zdenko. "Littérature engagée." *Yearbook of Comparative Criticism* 5 (1973):195–206.

Slote, Bernice, ed. *Literature and Society.* Lincoln: University of Nebraska Press, 1964.

Swingewood, Alan. "Literature and *Praxis.* A Sociological Commentary." *New Literary History* 5 (1973/74):169–176.

Templin, Ernest H. *The Social Approach to Literature.* University of California Publications in Modern Philology, Vol. 28, No. 1. Berkeley: University of California Press, 1944.

Tober, Karl. "Poetry, History, and Society? Reflections on Method." *Yearbook of Comparative Criticism* 5 (1973):41–55.

Watt, Ian. *The Rise of the Novel: Studies in Defoe, Richardson and Fielding.* Berkeley: University of California Press, 1967.

Williams, Raymond. *Communications.* 2nd ed. London: Chatto & Windus, 1966.

――. *Culture and Society 1780–1950.* New York: Columbia University Press, 1958.

Wilson, Robert N., ed. *The Arts in Society.* Englewood Cliffs, New Jersey: Prentice-Hall, 1964.

Zéraffa, Michel. *Roman et société.* Paris: Presses Universitaires de France, 1971.

V. LITERATURE IN SOCIETY; EMPIRICAL STUDIES

Altick, Richard D. *The English Common Reader: A Social History of the Mass Reading Public 1800–1900.* Chicago: University of Chicago Press, 1957.

Bruford, W. H. *Culture and Society in Classical Weimar 1775–1806.* Cambridge, Eng.: University Press, 1962.

――. *Germany in the Eighteenth Century: The Social Background of the Literary Revival.* 5th ed. Cambridge, Eng.: University Press, 1965.

Charvat, William. "Literary Economics and Literary History." *English Institute Essays, 1949,* ed. Alan S. Downer. New York: Columbia University Press, 1950. Pp.73–91.

――. *The Profession of Authorship in America, 1800–1870: The Papers of William Charvat,* ed. Matthew J. Bruccoli. Columbus: Ohio State University Press, 1968.

Devert, Krystyna. "Hermann Hesse: Apostle of the Apolitical 'Revolution.'" *TriQuarterly* Nos. 23/24 (Winter/Spring, 1972):302–317.

Goodlad, J. S. R. *A Sociology of Popular Drama.* Totowa, New Jersey: Rowman and Littlefield, 1972.

Hoggart, Richard. *The Uses of Literacy: Changing Patterns in English Mass Culture.* Fair Lawn, N.J.: Essential Books, 1957.

Laurenson, D. T. "A Sociological Study of Authorship." *British Journal of Sociology.* 20 (1969):311–325.

Ohmann, Richard. "Speech, Literature, and the Space Between." *New Literary History* 4 (1972/73):47–63.

Richards, Donald Ray. *The German Bestseller in the 20th Century: A Complete Bibliography and Analysis 1915–1940.* Berne: Herbert Lang, 1968.

Roberts, Thomas J. "The Network of Literary Identification. A Sociological Preface." *New Literary History* 5 (1973/74):67–90.

Silbermann, Alphons. "On the Effects of Literature as a Means of Mass Communication." *Yearbook of Comparative Criticism* 5 (1973):174–194.

Ward, Albert. *Book Production, Fiction, and the German Reading Public 1740–1800.* Oxford: Clarendon Press, 1974.

VI. SOCIETY AND IDEOLOGY IN LITERATURE

Auerbach, Erich. *Mimesis: The Representation of Reality in Western Literature.* Princeton: Princeton University Press, 1953.

Barber, C. L. *Shakespeare's Festive Comedy: A Study of Dramatic Form and its Relation to Social Custom.* Princeton: Princeton University Press, 1959.

Bowra, C. M. *Poetry & Politics 1900–1960.* Cambridge, Eng.: University Press, 1966.

Bradbrook, M. C. *Literature in Action: Studies in Continental and Commonwealth Society.* London: Chatto & Windus, 1972.

Bramsted, Ernest K. *Aristocracy and the Middle-Classes in Germany: Social Types in German Literature 1830–1900.* Revised ed. Chicago: University of Chicago Press, 1964.

Chace, William M. *The Political Identities of Ezra Pound & T. S. Eliot.* Stanford: Stanford University Press, 1973.

Clark, Priscilla P. *The Battle of the Bourgeois: The Novel in France, 1789–1848.* Paris: Didier, 1973.

Danby, John F. *Poets on Fortune's Hill: Studies in Sidney, Shakespeare, Beaumont & Fletcher.* London: Faber and Faber, 1952.

Eco, Umberto. "Rhetoric and Ideology in Sue's *Les Mystères de Paris.*" *International Social Science Journal* 19 (1967):551–569.

Edwards, Thomas R. *Imagination and Power: A Study of Poetry on Public Themes.* New York: Oxford University Press, 1971.

Hohendahl, Peter Uwe. "Empfindsamkeit und gesellschaftliches Bewusstsein. Zur Soziologie des empfindsamen Romans am Beispiel von *La Vie de Marianne, Clarissa, Fräulein von Sternheim* und *Werther.*" *Jahrbuch der deutschen Schillergesellschaft* 16 (1972):176–207.

Holland, Henry M., Jr., ed. *Politics Through Literature.* Englewood Cliffs, New Jersey: Prentice-Hall, 1968.

Jäger, Hans-Wolf. *Politische Metaphorik im Jakobismus und im Vormärz.* Stuttgart: Metzler, 1971.

Kavolis, Vytautas. "Literature and the Dialectics of Modernization." *Yearbook of Comparative Criticism* 5 (1973):89–106.

Kreuzer, Helmut. "Die Jungfrau in Waffen. Hebbels 'Judith' und ihre Geschwister von Schiller bis Sartre." *Untersuchungen zur Literatur als Geschichte: Festschrift für Benno von Wiese*, ed. Vincent J. Günther et al. Berlin: Erich Schmidt Verlag, 1973. Pp.363–384.

Löwenthal, Leo. *Erzählkunst und Gesellschaft in der deutschen Literatur des 19. Jahrhunderts*. Neuwied: Luchterhand, 1971.

O'Brien, Conor Cruise. "Passion and Cunning: The Politics of W. B. Yeats." *TriQuarterly*, Nos. 23/24 (Winter/Spring, 1972):142–203.

Panichas, George A., ed. *The Politics of Twentieth-Century Novelists*. New York: Crowell, 1974.

Raskin, Jonah. *The Mythology of Imperialism: Rudyard Kipling, Joseph Conrad, E. M. Forster, D. H. Lawrence, and Joyce Cary*. New York: Random House, 1971.

Sagarra, Eda. *Tradition and Revolution: German Literature and Society 1830–1890*. London: Weidenfeld and Nicolson, 1971.

Schlaffer, Heinz. *Der Bürger als Held: Sozialgeschichtliche Auflösungen literarischer Widersprüche*. Frankfurt am Main: Suhrkamp, 1973.

Schöne, Albrecht. *Über politische Lyrik im 20. Jahrhundert*. 3rd ed. Göttingen: Vandenhoeck & Ruprecht, 1972.

Wesling, Donald. "The Dialectical Criticism of Poetry: An Instance from Keats." *Mosaic* 5, No. 2 (Winter, 1971/72):81–96.

White, George Abbott. "Ideology and Literature: *American Renaissance* and F. O. Matthiessen." *TriQuarterly*, Nos. 23/24 (Winter/Spring, 1972):430–500.

Woodring, Carl. *Politics in English Romantic Poetry*. Cambridge, Mass.: Harvard University Press, 1970.

VII. MARXISM; NEO-MARXISM; PARA-MARXISM; RADICAL CRITICISM

1. Bibliography
Baxandall, Lee. *Marxism and Aesthetics: A Selective Annotated Bibliography. Books and Articles in the English Language*. New York: Humanities Press, 1968.

2. Primary Texts
Baxandall, Lee, and Stefan Morawski, eds. *Marx & Engels on Literature & Art*. St. Louis: Telos Press, 1973.

Buch, Hans Christoph, ed. *Parteilichkeit der Literatur oder Parteiliteratur? Materialien zu einer undogmatischen marxistischen Ästhetik*. Reinbek: Rowohlt, 1972.

Fetscher, Iring, ed. Karl Marx, Friedrich Engels, *Pressefreiheit und Zensur*. Frankfurt am Main and Vienna: Europäische Verlagsanstalt and Europa Verlag, 1969.

Lang, Berel, and Forrest Williams, eds. *Marxism and Art: Writings in Aesthetics and Criticism*. New York: David McKay, 1972.

Marx, Karl, and Friedrich Engels. *Literature and Art*. New York: International Publishers, 1947.

——. *Über Kunst und Literatur*, ed. Manfred Kliem. 2 vols. Berlin: Dietz Verlag, 1967–68.

Raddatz, Fritz J., ed. *Marxismus und Literatur: Eine Dokumentation in drei Bänden.* Rowohlt Paperback Vols. 80, 81, 82. Reinbek: Rowohlt, 1969.

Solomon, Maynard, ed. *Marxism and Art: Essays Classic and Contemporary.* New York: Knopf, 1973.

Trotsky, Leon. *Literature and Revolution.* Tr. Rose Strunsky. New York: International Publishers, 1925.

Žmegač, Viktor, ed. *Marxistische Literaturkritik.*Bad Homburg: Athenäum, 1970.

3. **Expositions and Discussions**

Aptheker, Herbert, ed. *Marxism and Alienation.* New York: Humanities Press, 1965.

Aron, Raymond. *The Opium of the Intellectuals.* Tr. Terence Kilmartin. London: Secker & Warburg, 1957.

Arvon, Henri. *Marxist Esthetics.* Tr. Helen R. Lane, with an Introduction by Fredric Jameson. Ithaca: Cornell University Press, 1973.

Baxandall, Lee. "The Marxist Orientation to Art and Literature." *New German Critique* 1, No. 3 (Fall, 1974):163–180.

Bürger, Peter. "Für eine kritische Literaturwissenschaft." *Neue Rundschau* 85 (1974):410–419.

Curtis, Michael, ed. *Marxism.* New York: Atherton Press, 1970.

Demetz, Peter. *Marx, Engels, and the Poets: Origins of Marxist Literary Criticism.* Tr. Jeffrey L. Sammons. Chicago: University of Chicago Press, 1967.

——. "Marxist Literary Criticism Today." *Survey* 18 (1972):63–72.

Garber, Klaus. "Thirteen Theses on Literary Criticism." *New German Critique* 1, No. 1 (Winter, 1974):126–132.

Girnus, Wilhelm. "On the Problem of Ideology and Literature." *New Literary History* 4 (1972/73):483–500.

Hansen, Beate. *Den marxistiske litteraturkritik.* Copenhagen: Hans Reitzel, 1967.

Hinderer, Walter. "Die regressive Universalideologie. Zum Klassikbild der marxistischen Literaturkritik von Franz Mehring bis zu den *Weimarer Beiträgen.*" *Die Klassik-Legende*, ed. Reinhold Grimm and Jost Hermand. Frankfurt am Main: Athenäum Verlag, 1971. Pp.141–175.

Huaco, George A. "Ideology and Literature." *New Literary History* 4 (1972/73):421–436.

Jameson, Fredric. *Marxism and Form: Twentieth-Century Dialectical Theories of Literature.* Princeton: Princeton University Press, 1971.

——. "Metacommentary." *PMLA* 86 (1971):9–18.

——. "On Politics and Literature." *Salmagundi* 2, No. 3 (Spring/Summer, 1968):17–26.

Jay, Martin. *The Dialectical Imagination: A History of the Frankfurt School and the Institute of Social Research.* Boston: Little, Brown, 1973.

Karbusicky, Vladimir. *Widerspiegelungstheorie und Strukturalismus: Zur Ent-*

stehungsgeschichte und Kritik der marxistisch-leninistischen Ästhetik. Munich: Fink, 1973.

Keller, Werner. "Franz Mehring und die Anfänge der marxistischen Literaturkritik in Deutschland." *Zeiten und Formen in Sprache und Dichtung: Festschrift für Fritz Tschirch zum 70. Geburtstag,* ed. Karl Heinz Schirmer and Bernhard Sowinski. Cologne: Böhlau Verlag, 1972. Pp.307–331.

Kimpel, Dieter. "Die problematische Idealismuskritik von K. Marx und ihre Konsequenzen für die gegenwärtige Methodendiskussion in der Literaturwissenschaft." *Beiträge zur Theorie der Künste im 19. Jahrhundert,* Vol. II, ed. Helmut Koopmann and J. Adolf Schmoll gen. Eisenwerth. Frankfurt am Main: Vittorio Klostermann, 1972. Pp.1–28.

Köpeczi, Béla. "A Marxist View of Form in Literature." *New Literary History* 3 (1971/72):355–372.

LeRoy, Gaylord C. *Marxism and Modern Literature.* Occasional Papers of the American Institute of Marxist Studies, No. 5. New York: American Institute of Marxist Studies, 1967.

Ley-Piscator, Maria. *The Piscator Experiment: The Political Theatre.* 2nd ed. Carbondale: Southern Illinois University Press, 1970.

Lifshitz, Mikhail. *The Philosophy of Art of Karl Marx.* Tr. Ralph B. Winn. New York: Critics Group, 1938.

Markiewicz, Henryk. "The Limits of Literature." *New Literary History* 4 (1972/73):5–14.

Mayer, Hans. *Steppenwolf and Everyman.* Tr. and with an Introduction by Jack D. Zipes. New York: Crowell, 1971.

Morawski, Stefan. *Inquiries into the Fundamentals of Aesthetics.* Cambridge, Mass.: MIT Press, 1974.

Nikolyukin, A. N. "Past and Present Discussions of American National Literature." *New Literary History* 4 (1972/73):575–590.

Pforte, Dietger. "Franz Mehrings Literaturtheorie in ihrer Bedeutung für den Sozialistischen Realismus." *Beiträge zur Theorie der Künste im 19. Jahrhundert,* Vol. II, ed. Helmut Koopmann and J. Adolf Schmoll gen. Eisenwert. Frankfurt am Main: Vittorio Klostermann, 1972. Pp.106–131.

Rømhild, Lars Peter. "Marx/Engels' kunstteori." *Læsere: Artikler og foredrag.* Copenhagen: Munksgaard, 1971. Pp.118–143.

Sander, Hans-Dietrich. *Marxistische Ideologie und allgemeine Kunsttheorie.* Veröffentlichungen der List Gesellschaft e.V., Vol. 67. Basel and Tübingen: Kyklos-Verlag and J. C. B. Mohr, 1970.

Sannwald, Rolf. *Marx und die Antike.* Einsiedeln: Benziger & Co., 1956.

Sartre, Jean-Paul. *Qu'est-ce que la littérature?* Paris: Gallimard, 1970. *What Is Literature?* Tr. Bernard Frechtman. New York: Philosphical Library, 1949.

Scharang, Michael. *Zur Emanzipation der Kunst.* Neuwied: Luchterhand, 1971.

Schlaffer, Heinz, ed. *Erweiterung der materialistischen Literaturtheorie durch Bestimmung ihrer Grenzen.* Stuttgart: Metzler, 1974.

Steiner, George. "Marxism and the Literary Critic." *Language and Silence: Essays 1958–1966*. London: Faber and Faber, 1967. Pp.335–354.

Thomson, George. *Aeschylus and Athens: A Study in the Social Origins of Drama.* 3rd ed. New York: Grosset & Dunlap, 1968.

———. *Marxism and Poetry.* London: Lawrence and Wishart, 1945.

Vassen, Florian. *Methoden der Literaturwissenschaft II. Marxistische Literaturtheorie und Literatursoziologie.* Düsseldorf: Bertelsmann Universitätsverlag, 1972.

Werckmeister, O. K. "Marx on Ideology and Art." *New Literary History* 4 (1972/73):501–519.

4. Literature and Communist Politics

Bathrick, David. "The Dialectics of Legitimation: Brecht in the GDR." *New German Critique* 1, No. 2 (Spring, 1974):90–103.

Brettschneider, Werner. *Zwischen literarischer Autonomie und Staatsdienst: Die Literatur in der DDR.* 2nd ed. Berlin: Erich Schmidt Verlag, 1974.

Flores, John. *Poetry in East Germany: Adjustments, Visions, and Provocations 1945–1970.* New Haven: Yale University Press, 1971.

Fokkema, D. W. "The Forms and Values of Contemporary Chinese Literature." *New Literary History* 4 (1972/73):591–603.

Gallas, Helga. *Marxistische Literaturtheorie: Kontroversen im Bund proletarisch-revolutionärer Schriftsteller.* collection alternative, No. 1. Neuwied: Luchterhand, 1971.

Hayward, Max. "The Decline of Socialist Realism." *Survey* 18 (1972):73–97.

Hermand, Jost. "The 'Good New' and the 'Bad New': Metamorphoses in the Modernism Debate in the GDR since 1956." *New German Critique* 1, No. 3 (Fall, 1974):73–92.

Hohendahl, Peter Uwe. "Ästhetik und Sozialismus. Zur neueren Literaturtheorie der DDR." *Jahrbuch der deutschen Schillergesellschaft* 18 (1974):606–641.

Labedz, Leopold. "The Destiny of Writers in Revolutionary Movements." *Survey* 18 (1972):8–46.

Lenski, Branko. "Yugoslav Literature and Politics." *Survey* 18 (1972):158–171.

Maguire, Robert A. "Literary Conflicts in the 1920s." *Survey* 18 (1972):98–127.

Miklós, Pál. "Recent Disputes on Literary History Among Hungarian Critics." *New Literary History* 2 (1970/71):101–113.

Rühle, Jürgen. *Literature and Revolution: A Critical Study of the Writer and Communism in the Twentieth Century.* Tr. Jean Steinberg. New York: Praeger, 1969.

Stephen, Alexander. "Johannes R. Becker and the Cultural Development of the GDR." *New German Critique* 1, No. 2 (Spring, 1974):72–89.

Tertz, Abram [pseud. for Andrei Sinyavsky]. *The Trial Begins* and *On Socialist Realism.* Vintage Russian Library, V-750. New York: Vintage Books, [1965].

Williams, Raymond. "On Solzhenitsyn." *TriQuarterly*, Nos. 23/24 (Winter/Spring, 1972):318–334.

5. Leading Figures

Adorno, Theodor W. *Noten zur Literatur*. 4 vols. Bibliothek Suhrkamp, Nos. 47, 71, 146, 395. Frankfurt am Main: Suhrkamp, 1958–1974.

———, et al. *Der Positivismusstreit in der deutschen Soziologie*. Neuwied: Luchterhand, 1969.

———. *Prismen. Kulturkritik und Gesellschaft*. Frankfurt am Main: Suhrkamp, 1955. *Prisms: Cultural Criticism and Society*. Tr. Samuel and Shierry Weber. London: Neville Spearman, 1967.

———. "Theses Upon Art and Religion Today." *Kenyon Review* 7 (1945):677–682.

Benjamin, Walter. *Angelus Novus: Ausgewählte Schriften*, 2. Frankfurt am Main: Suhrkamp, 1966.

———. *Berliner Kindheit um Neunzehnhundert*. Frankfurt am Main: Suhrkamp, 1950.

———. *Illuminationen: Ausgewählte Schriften*. Frankfurt am Main: Suhrkamp, 1961. *Illuminations*. Tr. Harry Zohn. Ed. with an Introduction by Hannah Arendt. New York: Harcourt, Brace & World, 1968.

———. *Das Kunstwerk im Zeitalter seiner technischen Reproduzierbarkeit: Drei Studien zur Kunstsoziologie*. edition suhrkamp, No. 28. Frankfurt am Main: Suhrkamp, 1968.

———. *Versuche über Brecht*. edition suhrkamp, no. 172. Frankfurt am Main: Suhrkamp, 1966.

Adorno, Theodor W., et al. eds. *Über Walter Benjamin*. edition suhrkamp, No. 250. Frankfurt am Main: Suhrkamp, 1968.

Arendt, Hannah. "Walter Benjamin." *Merkur* 22 (1968):50–65,209–223,305–315.

Durzak, Manfred. "Walter Benjamin und die Literaturwissenschaft." *Monatshefte* 58 (1966):217–231.

Sahlberg, Oskar. "Die Widersprüche Walter Benjamins. Ein Vergleich der beiden Baudelaire-Arbeiten." *Neue Rundschau* 85 (1974):464–487.

Wellek, René. "The Early Literary Criticism of Walter Benjamin." *Studies in German in Memory of Robert L. Kahn*, ed. Hans Eichner and Lisa Kahn. Rice University Studies, Vol. 57, No. 4. Houston: Rice University, 1971. Pp.123–134.

———. "Walter Benjamin's Literary Criticism in his Marxist Phase." *Yearbook of Comparative Criticism* 6 (1973):168–178.

Witte, Bernd. "Benjamin and Lukács. Historical Notes

on the Relationship Between Their Political and Aesthetic Theories." *New German Critique* No. 5 (Spring 1975):3–26.
———. "Feststellung zu Walter Benjamin und Kafka." *Neue Rundschau* 84 (1973):480–494.

Bloch, Ernst. *Die Kunst, Schiller zu sprechen*. Frankfurt am Main: Suhrkamp, 1969.
———. *Politische Messungen, Pestzeit, Vormärz*. Frankfurt am Main: Suhrkamp, 1970.
———. *Das Prinzip Hoffnung*. Frankfurt am Main: Suhrkamp, 1959.
———. *Verfremdungen* I. Frankfurt am Main: Suhrkamp, 1962.
    Negt, Oskar. "Ernst Bloch—The German Philosopher of the October Revolution." *New German Critique* No. 4 (Winter, 1975):3–16.

Caudwell, Christopher. *Illusion and Reality: A Study of the Sources of Poetry*. London: Macmillan, 1937.
———. *Romance and Realism: A Study in English Bourgeois Literature*, ed. Samuel Hynes. Princeton: Princeton University Press, 1970.
    Margolies, David N. *The Function of Literature: A Study of Christopher Caudwell's Aesthetics*. New York: International Publishers, 1969.
    Rømhild, Lars Peter. "Den marxistiske litteraturkritik og Christopher Caudwell." *Laesere: Artikler og foredrag*. Copenhagen: Munksgaard, 1971. Pp.82–114.

Fischer, Ernst. *Auf den Spuren der Wirklichkeit: Sechs Essays*. Rowohlt Paperback No. 62. Reinbek: Rowohlt, 1968.
———. *Erinnerungen und Reflexionen*. Reinbek: Rowohlt, 1969.
———. *Kunst und Koexistenz: Beitrag zu einer modernen marxistischen Ästhetik*. Reinbek: Rowohlt, 1966. *Art Against Ideology*. Tr. Anna Bostock. New York: Braziller, 1969.
———. *The Necessity of Art*. Tr. Anna Bostock. London: Penguin Books, 1963. Retranslation by the author of the English version: *Von der Notwendigkeit der Kunst*. Hamburg: Claassen, 1967.
———. *Von Grillparzer zu Kafka: Sechs Essays*. Vienna: Globus Verlag, 1962.
    Rothschild, Thomas. "Ernst Fischer zum Gedenken." *Neue Rundschau* 84 (1973):767–771.

Goldmann, Lucien. *Le Dieu caché: Etude sur la vision tragique dans les* Pensées *de* Pascal *et dans le théâtre de Racine*. Paris: Gallimard, 1955. *The Hidden God: A Study of Tragic Vision in the* Pensées *of Pascal and the Tragedies of Racine*. Tr. Philip Thody. New York: Humanities Press, 1964.
———. *Pour une sociologie du roman*. Paris: Gallimard, 1964. *Soziologie des modernen*

Romans. Neuwied: Luchterhand, 1970. *Towards a Sociology of the Novel*. Tr. Alan Sheridan. London: Tavistock, 1975.

———. *Recherches dialectiques*. Paris: Gallimard, 1959. *Dialektische Untersuchungen*. Tr. Ingrid Peters and Gisela Schöning. Neuwied: Luchterhand, 1966.

———. "The Sociology of Literature: Status and Problems of Method." *International Social Science Journal* 19(1967):493–516.

———. "Le structuralisme génétique en sociologie de la littérature." *Littérature et Société: Problèmes de méthodologie en sociologie de la littérature*, ed. Goldmann, Michel Bernard, and Roger Lallemand. Brussels: Editions de l'Institut de Sociologie de l'Université Libre de Bruxelles, 1967. Pp.195–211.

Lukács, Georg. *Beiträge zur Geschichte der Ästhetik*. Berlin: Aufbau-Verlag, 1954.

———. *Deutsche Literatur im Zeitalter des Imperialismus: Eine Übersicht ihrer Hauptströmungen*. Berlin: Aufbau-Verlag, 1950.

———. *Deutsche Realisten des 19. Jahrhunderts*. Berlin: Aufbau-Verlag, 1952.

———. *Die Eigenart des Ästhetischen*. Vols. XI and XII of *Werke*. Neuwied: Luchterhand, 1963. Abridged by the author as *Ästhetik*. 4 vols. Sammlung Luchterhand, Nos. 63, 64, 70, 71. Neuwied: Luchterhand, 1972.

———. *Essays über Realismus*. Berlin: Aufbau-Verlag, 1948. *Studies in European Realism*. Introduction by Alfred Kazin. New York: Grosset & Dunlap, 1964.

———. *Fortschritt und Reaktion in der deutschen Literatur*. Berlin: Aufbau-Verlag, 1947.

———. *Geschichte und Klassenbewußtsein: Studien über marxistische Dialektik*. Neuwied: Luchterhand, 1970. *History and Class Conciousness: Studies in Marxist Dialectics*. Tr. Rodney Livingstone. Cambridge, Mass.: MIT Press, 1971.

———. *Goethe und seine Zeit*. Berlin: Aufbau-Verlag, 1953. *Goethe and His Age*. Tr. Robert Anchor. New York: Grosset and Dunlop, 1969.

———. *Gottfried Keller: Mit einer Einleitung*. Berlin: Aufbau-Verlag, 1946.

———. *Der historische Roman*. Berlin: Aufbau-Verlag, 1956. *The Historical Novel*. Tr. Hannah and Stanley Mitchell. London: Merlin Press, 1962.

———. *Karl Marx und Friedrich Engels als Literaturhistoriker*. Berlin: Aufbau-Verlag, 1948.

———. *Schicksalswende: Beiträge zu einer neuen deutschen Ideologie*. Berlin: Aufbau-Verlag, 1948.

———. *Schriften zur Literatursoziologie*, ed. Peter Ludz. 2nd ed. Neuwied: Luchterhand, 1963.

———. *Die Seele und die Formen*. Neuwied: Luchterhand, 1971. *Soul and Form*. Tr. Anna Bostock. Cambridge, Mass.: MIT Press, 1974.

———. *Die Theorie des Romans: Ein geschichtsphilosophischer Versuch über die Formen der großen Epik*. 2nd ed. Neuwied: Luchterhand, 1963. *The Theory of the Novel*. Tr. Anna Bostock. Cambridge, Mass.: MIT Press, 1971.

———. *Thomas Mann*. Berlin: Aufbau-Verlag, 1953. *Essays on Thomas Mann*. Tr. Stanley Mitchell. New York: Grosset & Dunlop, 1965.

———. *Über die Besonderheit als Kategorie der Ästhetik*. Neuwied: Luchterhand, 1967.

——. *Wider den mißverstandenen Realismus.* Hamburg: Claassen, 1958. *Realism in Our Time.* Tr. John and Necke Mander. Introduction by George Steiner. New York: Harper and Row, 1964.

——. *Writer and Critic.* Tr. Arthur Kahn. London: Merlin Press, 1970.

——. *Die Zerstörung der Vernunft.* Berlin: Aufbau-Verlag, 1954.

Althaus, Horst. *Georg Lukács oder Bürgerlichkeit als Vorschule einer marxistischen Ästhetik.* Berne: Francke Verlag, 1962.

Bahr, Ehrhard. *Georg Lukács.* Köpfe des XX. Jahrhunderts, Vol. 61. Berlin: Colloquium Verlag, 1970.

Goldmann, Lucien. "Introduction aux premiers écrits de Georges Lukacs [sic]." *Les Temps modernes* No. 195 (August, 1962). Reprinted in Lukács, *La Théorie du Roman* (Paris: Gonthier, 1963), pp.156–190.

Királyfalvi, Béla. *The Aesthetics of György Lukács.* Princeton: Princeton University Press, 1975.

Lichtheim, George. *George Lukács.* Modern Masters, ed. Frank Kermode. New York: Viking Press, 1970.

Lunn, Eugene. "Marxism and Art in the Era of Stalin and Hitler: A Comparison of Brecht and Lukács." *New German Critique.* 1, No. 3 (Fall, 1974):12–44.

Mittenzwei, Werner. "Die Brecht-Lukács-Debatte." *Sinn und Form* 19 (1967):235–269.

Parkinson, G. H. R., ed. *Georg Lukács: The Man, His Work, and His Ideas.* New York: Vintage Books, 1970.

Raddatz, Fritz J. *Georg Lukács in Selbstzeugnissen und Bilddokumenten.* Rowohlts Monographien, No. 193. Reinbek: Rowohlt, 1972.

Rømhild, Lars Peter. "Lidt om Lukács." *Laesere: Artikler og foredrag.* Copenhagen: Munksgaard, 1971. Pp.114–117.

VIII. CRITIQUES OF LITERARY CRITICISM, HISTORY, AND PEDAGOGY

Crews, Frederick. "Do Literary Studies Have an Ideology?" *PMLA* 85 (1970):423–428. Cf. the objections of Rima Drell Reck, cited below, section XI, and Crews's letter, "Objectivity in Scholarship," *PMLA* 86 (1971):280–281.

Demetz, Peter. "Zur Situation der Germanistik: Tradition und aktuelle Probleme." *Die deutsche Literatur der Gegenwart: Aspekte und Tendenzen,* ed. Manfred Durzak. Stuttgart: Reclam, 1971. Pp.322–336.

Foster, Richard. *The New Romantics: A Reappraisal of the New Criticism.* Bloomington: Indiana University Press, 1962.

Gansberg, Marie Luise, and Paul Gerhard Völker. *Methodenkritik der Germanistik.* Texte Metzler, No. 16. Stuttgart: Metzler, 1970.

Graff, Gerald. *Poetic Statetment and Critical Dogma.* Evanston: Northwestern University Press, 1970.

Grimm, Reinhold, and Jost Hermand, eds. *Die Klassik-Legende*. Frankfurt am Main: Athenäum, 1971.

Hädecke, Wolfgang. "Strukturalismus—Ideologie des Status quo?" *Neue Rundschau* 82 (1971):45–59.

Hamm, Peter, ed. *Kritik—von wem / für wen / wie: Eine Selbstdarstellung deutscher Kritiker*. Munich: Hanser, 1968.

Hebel, Franz. "Literatursoziologie und Deutschunterricht." *Der Berliner Germanistentag 1968*, ed. Karl Heinz Borck and Rudolf Henss. Heidelberg: Carl Winter, 1970. Pp.207–221.

Hermand, Jost. *Literaturwissenschaft und Kunstwissenschaft*. Sammlung Metzler, M 41. Stuttgart: Metzler, 1965.

——. *Stänker und Weismacher: Zur Dialektik eines Affekts*. Texte Metzler, No. 18. Stuttgart: Metzler, 1971.

Hyman, Stanley Edgar. *The Armed Vision: A Study in the Methods of Modern Literary Criticism*. New York: Alfred A. Knopf, 1948.

Jaeggi, Urs. *Ordnung und Chaos. Strukturalismus als Methode und Mode*. Frankfurt am Main: Suhrkamp, 1968.

Jauss, Hans Robert. "Literaturgeschichte als Provokation der Literaturwissenschaft." *Jahrbuch für Internationale Germanistik* 2, No. 1 (1970):25–28. Tr. and expanded as "Literary History as a Challenge to Literary Theory," *New Literary History* 2 (1970/71):7–37.

Kampf, Louis. "Real Students in Real Classrooms." *New Literary History* 5 (1973/74):595–604.

——. "The Trouble with Literature." *Change in Higher Education* 2, No. 3 (May–June, 1970):27–34.

Keil, Gundolf. "Literaturbegriff und Fachprosaforschung." *Jahrbuch für Internationale Germanistik* 2, No. 1 (1970):95–102.

Killy, Walther. *Bildungsfragen*. Munich: C. H. Beck, 1971.

Kolbe, Jürgen, ed. *Ansichten einer künftigen Germanistik*. Munich: Hanser, 1969.

Leavis, F. R. *English Literature in Our Time and the University: The Clark Lectures, 1967*. London: Chatto & Windus, 1969.

Mayer, Hans. "Deutsche Literaturwissenschaft heute." *Germanic Review* 45 (1970):163–178.

Ohmann, Richard. "English Departments and the Professional Ethos." *New Literary History* 5 (1973/74):565–593.

Peschken, Bernd. *Versuch einer germanistischen Ideologiekritik: Goethe, Lessing, Novalis, Tieck, Hölderlin, Heine in Wilhelm Diltheys und Julian Schmidts Vorstellungen*. Stuttgart: Metzler, 1972.

Reiss, Gunter, ed. *Materialien zur Ideologiegeschichte der deutschen Literaturwissenschaft. I. Von Scherer bis zum ersten Weltkrieg. II. Vom ersten Weltkrieg bis 1945*. Tübingen: Niemeyer, 1973.

Sander, Volkmar. "Wohin treibt die Germanistik?" *Germanic Review* 45 (1970):179–187.

Schiwy, Günther. *Der französische Strukturalismus: Mode, Methode, Ideologie. Mit einem Textanhang*. Rowohlts deutsche Enzyklopädie, Nos. 310/311. Reinbek: Rowohlt, 1969.

Schmoldt, Benno. "Deutschunterricht und politische Bildung." *Der Berliner Germanistentag 1968*, ed. Karl Heinz Borck and Rudolf Henss. Heidelberg: Carl Winter, 1970. Pp.196–206.

Scholes, Robert. "The Illiberal Imagination." *New Literary History* 4 (1972/ 73):521–540.

Schwenke, Olaf, ed. *Kritik der Literaturkritik*. Stuttgart: Kohlhammer, 1973.

Wehrli, Max. "Gibt es eine deutsche Literaturgeschichte?" *Jahrbuch für Internationale Germanistik* 2, No. 1 (1970):13–24.

Weimann, Robert. *Literaturgeschichte und Mythologie: Methodologische und historische Studien*. Berlin: Aufbau-Verlag, 1971.

——. *"New Criticism" und die Entwicklung bürgerlicher Literaturwissenschaft: Geschichte und Kritik neuer Interpretationsmethoden*. Halle: VEB Max Niemeyer Verlag, 1962.

——. "Past Significance and Present Meaning in Literary History." *New Literary History* 1 (1969/70);91–109.

——, et al. *Tradition in der Literaturgeschichte: Beiträge zur Kritik des bürgerlichen Traditionsbegriffs bei Croce, Ortega, Eliot, Leavis, Barthes u. a.* Berlin: Akademie-Verlag, 1972.

Žmegač, Viktor, and Zdenko Škreb, eds. *Zur Kritik literaturwissenschaftlicher Methodologie*. Frankfurt am Main: Athenäum, 1973.

IX. READER RESPONSE AND RECEPTION

Baumgärtner, Alfred Clemens, ed. *Lesen—Ein Handbuch*. Hamburg: Verlag für Buchmarkt-Forschung, 1973.

Beaujean, Marion, Hans Norbert Fügen, Wolfgang R. Langenbucher, and Wolfgang Strauss. *Der Leser als Teil des literarischen Lebens*. Bonn: Bouvier, 1971.

Cohen, Gillian. "The Psychology of Reading." *New Literary History* 4 (1972/ 73):75–90.

Fish, Stanley E. "Literature in the Reader: Affective Stylistics." *New Literary History* 2 (1970/71):123–162.

Girardi, Maria-Rita, Lothar Karl Neffe, and Herbert Steiner, eds. *Buch und Leser in Deutschland: Eine Untersuchung des DIVO-Instituts, Frankfurt am Main* Gütersloh: Verlag für Buchmarkt-Forschung, 1965.

Grey, Lennox. "Literary Audience." *Contemporary Literary Scholarship: A Critical Review*, ed. Lewis Leary. New York: Appleton-Century-Crofts, 1958. Pp.403–461.

Harding, D. W. "Practice at Liking: A Study in Experimental Aesthetics." *Bulletin of the British Psychological Society* 21 (1968):3–10.

Iser, Wolfgang. "The Reading Process: A Phenomenological Approach." *New Literary History* 3 (1971/72):279–299.

Jaeggi, Urs. "Lesen und Schreiben. Thesen zur Literatursoziologie." *Der*

Berliner Germanistentag 1968, ed. Karl Heinz Borck and Rudolf Henss. Heidelberg: Carl Winter, 1970. Pp.157–168.

Jauss, Hans Robert. "Levels of Identification of Heroes and Audience." *New Literary History* 5 (1973/74):283–317.

Link, Hannelore. "'Die Appellstruktur der Texte' und ein 'Paradigmawechsel in der Literaturwissenschaft?'" *Jahrbuch der deutschen Schillergesellschaft* 17 (1973):532–583.

Mandelkow, Karl Robert. "Probleme der Wirkungsgeschichte." *Jahrbuch für Internationale Germanistik* 2, No. 1 (1970):71–84.

Naumann, Manfred, et al. *Gesellschaft, Literatur, Lesen: Literaturrezeption in theoretischer Sicht*. Berlin: Aufbau-Verlag, 1975.

Norman, Liane. "Risk and Redundancy." *PMLA* 90 (1975):285–291.

Poulet, Georges. "Phenomenology of Reading." *New Literary History* 1 (1969/70):53–68.

Rømhild, Lars Peter. *Laesere : Artikler og foredrag*. Copenhagen: Munksgaard, 1971.

Slatoff, Walter J. *With Respect to Readers: Dimensions of Literary Response*. Ithaca: Cornell University Press, 1970.

Turk, Horst. "Wirkungsästhetik: Aristotles, Lessing, Schiller, Brecht. Theorie und Praxis einer politischen Hermeneutik." *Jahrbuch der deutschen Schillergesellschaft* 17 (1973):519–531.

Winter, Lorenz. *Heinrich Mann and His Public: A Socioliterary Study of the Relationship Between an Author and His Public*. Coral Gables: University of Miami Press, 1970.

X. SUBLITERATURE

Appell, J. W. *Die Ritter-, Räuber- und Schauerromantik: Zur Geschichte der deutschen Unterhaltungs-Literatur*. Leipzig: Wilhelm Engelmann, 1859.

Bark, Joachim. "Research in Popular Literature and Praxis-Related Literary Scholarship." Continued as: "Mass Literature, Belles Lettres and Functional Texts: A Discussion of Current Positions and Classroom Praxis." *New German Critique* 1, No. 1 (Winter, 1974):133–141; No. 5 (Spring, 1975):129–148.

Beaujean, Marion. *Der Trivialroman in der zweiten Hälfte des 18. Jahrhunderts*. Bonn: Bouvier, 1964.

Beylin, Pawel. "Der Kitsch als ästhetische und ausserästhetische Erscheinung." *Die nicht mehr schönen Künste: Grenzphänomene des Ästhetischen*, ed. Hans Robert Jauss. Munich: Wilhelm Fink Verlag, 1969. Pp.393–406.

Brown, Roger L. "The Creative Process in the Popular Arts." *International Social Science Journal* 20 (1968):613–624.

Burger, Heinz Otto, ed. *Studien zur Trivialliteratur*. Frankfurt am Main: Vittorio Klostermann, 1968.

Clausse, Roger. "The Mass Public at Grips with Mass Communications." *International Social Science Journal* 20 (1968):625–643.

Dalziel, Margaret. *Popular Fiction 100 Years Ago: An Unexplored Tract of Literary*

History. London: Cohen & West, 1957; Philadelphia: Dufour Edition, 1958.

Denney, Reuel. *The Astonished Muse*. Chicago: University of Chicago Press, 1957.

Giesz, Ludwig. "Das Phänomen des Kitsches." *Deutsche Literatur im 20. Jahrhundert: Strukturen und Gestalten*, ed. Otto Mann and Wolfgang Rothe. 5th ed. Berne: Francke Verlag, 1967. I, 377–390.

Greiner, Martin. *Die Entstehung der modernen Unterhaltungsliteratur*. rororo Enzyklopädie, No. 207. Reinbek: Rowohlt, 1964.

Hartung, Harald. "Das Interesse am Trivialen." *Neue Rundschau* 84 (1973): 345–352.

Killy, Walther. *Deutscher Kitsch: Ein Versuch mit Beispielen*. Göttingen: Vandenhoeck & Ruprecht, 1962.

Klein, Albert. *Die Krise des Unterhaltungsromans im 19. Jahrhundert: Ein Beitrag zur Theorie und Geschichte der ästhetisch geringwertigen Literatur*. Bonn: Bouvier, 1969.

Kreuzer, Helmut. "Trivialliteratur als Forschungsproblem. Zur Kritik des deutschen Trivialromans seit der Aufklärung." *Methodenfragen der deutschen Literaturwissenschaft*, ed. Reinhold Grimm and Jost Hermand. Darmstadt: Wissenschaftliche Buchgesellschaft, 1973. Pp.463–486.

La Motte-Haber, Helga de, ed. *Das Triviale in Literatur, Musik und bildender Kunst*. Frankfurt am Main: Vittorio Klostermann, 1972.

Leavis, Q. D. *Fiction and the Reading Public*. London: Chatto & Windus, 1932.

Lowenthal, Leo. *Literature, Popular Culture and Society*. Englewood Cliffs, New Jersey: Prentice-Hall, 1961.

Munch-Petersen, Erland. "Trivial Literature and Mass Reading." *Orbis Litterarum* 27 (1972):157–178.

Nutz, Walter. *Der Trivialroman, seine Formen und seine Hersteller*. Cologne: Westdeutscher Verlag, 1962.

Rosenberg, Bernard, and David Manning White, eds. *Mass Culture: The Popular Arts in America*. Glencoe, Ill.: The Free Press, 1957.

Schenda, Rudolf. *Volk ohne Buch: Studien zur Sozialgeschichte der populären Lesestoffe 1770–1910*. Frankfurt am Main: Vittorio Klostermann, 1970.

Schulte-Sasse, Jochen. *Die Kritik an der Trivialliteratur seit der Aufklärung*. Munich: Fink, 1971.

Smith, Henry Nash. "The Scribbling Women and the Cosmic Success Story." *Critical Inquiry* 1 (1974/75):47–70.

Thalmann, Marianne. *Der Trivialroman des 18. Jahrhunderts und der romantische Roman*. Berlin: E. Ebering, 1923.

Winterscheidt, Friedrich. *Deutsche Unterhaltungsliteratur der Jahre 1850–1860*. Bonn: Bouvier, 1970.

XI. EVALUATION

Beardsley, Monroe C. "Intrinsic Value." *Philosophy and Phenomenological Research* 26 (1965/66):1–17.

Fokkema, D. W. "The Problem of Generalization and the Procedure of Literary Evaluation." *Neophilologus* 58 (1974):253–272.

Hass, Hans-Egon. *Das Problem der literarischen Wertung*. Darmstadt: Wissenschaftliche Buchgesellschaft, 1970.

Hirsch, Eric Donald, Jr. "Privileged Criteria in Literary Evaluation." *Yearbook of Comparative Criticism* 2 (1969):22–34.

Ingarden, Roman. *Erlebnis, Kunstwerk und Wert*. Tübingen: Niemeyer, 1969.

Morawski, Stefan. *Inquiries into the Fundamentals of Aesthetics*. Cambridge, Mass.: MIT Press, 1974.

Müller-Seidel, Walter. *Probleme der literarischen Wertung: Über die Wissenschaftlichkeit eines unwissenschaftlichen Themas*. 2nd ed. Stuttgart: Metzler, 1969.

Olson, Elder. "On Value Judgments in the Arts." *Critical Inquiry* 1 (1974/75):71–90.

Peacock, R. *Criticism and Personal Taste*. Oxford: Clarendon Press, 1972.

Rescher, Nicholas. *Introduction to Value Theory*. Englewood Cliffs, New Jersey: Prentice-Hall, 1969.

Strelka, Joseph, ed. *Problems of Literary Evaluation. Yearbook of Comparative Criticism*, Vol. II. University Park: Pennsylvania State University Press, 1969.

XII. ELITISM

Bell, Quentin. "Art and the Elite." *Critical Inquiry* 1 (1974/75):33–46.

Block, Haskell M. "Some Concepts of the Literary Elite at the Turn of the Century." *Mosaic* 5, No. 2 (Winter, 1971/72):57–64.

Bottomore, T. B. *Elites and Society*. New York: Basic Books, 1964.

Gans, Herbert J. *Popular Culture and High Culture: An Analysis and Evaluation of Taste*. New York: Basic Books, 1974.

Kreuzer, Helmut. "Zum Literaturbegriff der sechziger Jahre in der Bundesrepublik Deutschland." *Literatur und Dichtung: Versuch einer Begriffsbestimmung*, ed. Horst Rüdiger (Stuttgart: Kohlhammer, 1973). Pp.144–159.

Pareto, Vilfredo. *The Rise and Fall of Elites: An Application of Theoretical Sociology*. Introduction by Hans L. Zetterberg. Totowa, New Jersey: Bedminster Press, 1968.

XIII. CRITIQUES OF LITERARY SOCIOLOGY AND IDEOLOGICAL CRITICISM

Bisztray, George. "Literary Sociology and Marxist Theory: The Literary Work as a Social Document." *Mosaic* 5, No. 2 (Winter, 1971/72):47–56.

Crane, R. S. *Critical and Historical Principles of Literary History*. Chicago: University of Chicago Press, 1971.

Crews, Frederick. "Offing Culture: Literary Study and the Movement." *TriQuarterly*, Nos. 23/24 (Winter/Spring, 1972):34–56.

Frye, Northrop. *The Critical Path: An Essay on the Social Context of Literary Criticism*. Bloomington: Indiana University Press, 1971.

Gombrich, E. H. *In Search of Cultural History*. Oxford: Clarendon Press, 1969.

Hamburger, Käte. "Zwei Formen literatursoziologischer Betrachtung. Zu Erich Auerbachs 'Mimesis' und Georg Lukács' 'Goethe und seine Zeit.'" *Orbis Litterarum* 7 (1949):142–160.

Harth, Dietrich. "Begriffsbildung in der Literaturwissenschaft. Beobachtungen zum Wandel der 'semantischen Orientierung.'" *Deutsche Vierteljahrsschrift für Literaturwissenschaft und Geistesgeschichte* 45 (1971):397–433.

Mühlmann, Wilhelm Emil. "Tradition and Revolution in Literature: Socioliterary Sketches in the Light of German Writing." *Yearbook of Comparative Criticism* 5 (1973):124–173.

Muir, Edwin. *Essays on Literature and Society*. Enlarged and revised ed. Cambridge, Mass.: Harvard University Press, 1967.

Philippi, Klaus-Peter. "Methodologische Probleme der Literatursoziologie. Kritische Bemerkungen zu einer fragwürdigen Situation." *Wirkendes Wort* 20 (1970):217–230.

Reck, Rima Drell. "The Politics of Literature." *PMLA* 85 (1970):429–432.

Schultz, H. Stefan. "Literatursoziologie, leicht gemacht." With reply by Volkmar Sander, "Notgedrungener Beitrag." *Die Unterrichtspraxis* 5, No. 1 (Spring 1972):82–91.

Silbermann, Alphons. "Literaturphilosophie, soziologische Literaturästhetik oder Literatursoziologie." *Kölner Zeitschrift für Soziologie und Sozialpsychologie* 18 (1966):139–148.

Spearman, Diana. *The Novel and Society*. London: Routledge & Kegan Paul, 1966.

Stöcklein, Paul. "Literatursoziologie. Gesichtspunkte zur augenblicklichen Diskussion." *Literatur und Geistesgeschichte: Festgabe für Heinz Otto Bürger*, ed. Reinhold Grimm and Conrad Wiedemann. Berlin: Erich Schmidt Verlag, 1968. Pp.406–421.

Strelka, Joseph. *Die gelenkten Musen: Dichtung und Gesellschaft*. Vienna: Europa Verlag, 1971.

Tober, Karl. "Poetry, History, and Society? Reflections on Method." *Yearbook of Comparative Criticism* 5 (1973):41–55.

XIV. OTHER USEFUL WORKS

Abrams, M. H., ed. *Literature and Belief: English Institute Essays 1957*. New York: Columbia University Press, 1958.

———. *The Mirror and the Lamp: Romantic Theory and the Critical Tradition*. New York: Oxford University Press, 1953.

———. *Natural Supernaturalism: Tradition and Revolution in Romantic Literature*. New York: W. W. Norton, 1971.

Barthes, Roland. *Essais critiques*. Paris: Editions du Seuil, 1964.

———. *Mythologies*. Tr. Annette Lavers. New York: Hill and Wang, 1972.

———. *Writing Degree Zero* and *Elements of Semiology*. Tr. Annette Lavers and

Colin Smith. Preface by Susan Sontag. Boston: Beacon Press, 1970.

Beardsley, Monroe C. *Aesthetics: Problems in the Philosophy of Criticism*. New York: Harcourt, Brace, 1958.

——. *The Possibility of Criticism*. Detroit: Wayne State University Press, 1970.

Berlin, Isaiah. *Historical Inevitability*. London: Oxford University Press, 1955.

Bersani, Leo. "Is There a Science of Literature?" *Partisan Review* 39 (1972):535–553.

Binder, Wolfgang. *Literatur als Denkschule: Eine Vorlesung mit zwei Kapiteln von Klaus Weimar*. Zurich: Artemis Verlag, 1972.

Booth, Wayne C. *Modern Dogma and the Rhetoric of Assent*. Chicago: University of Chicago Press, 1974.

——. *The Rhetoric of Fiction*. Chicago: University of Chicago Press, 1961.

Brombert, Victor. *The Intellectual Hero: Studies in the French Novel 1880–1955*. Chicago: University of Chicago Press, 1964.

Brooks, Cleanth. *The Well-Wrought Urn: Studies in the Structure of Poetry*. New York: Reynal & Hitchcock, 1947.

Burke, Kenneth. *A Grammar of Motives*. Berkeley: University of California Press, 1969.

——. *The Philosophy of Literary Form: Studies in Symbolic Action*. 3rd ed. Berkeley: University of California Press, 1973.

——. *A Rhetoric of Motives*. Berkeley: University of California Press, 1969.

——. *Terms for Order*, ed. Stanley Edgar Hyman with the assistance of Barbara Karmiller. Bloomington: Indiana University Press, 1964.

Daiches, David. *Critical Approaches to Literature*. Englewood Cliffs, New Jersey: Prentice-Hall, 1956.

Damon, Philipp, ed. *Literary Criticism and the Historical Understanding: Selected Papers from the English Institute*. New York: Columbia University Press, 1967.

Derrida, Jacques. "White Mythology: Metaphor in the Text of Philosophy." *New Literary History* 6 (1974/75):5–74.

Ellis, John M. *The Theory of Literary Criticism: A Logical Analysis*. Berkeley: University of California Press, 1974.

Empson, William. *Some Versions of Pastoral*. Norfolk, Conn.: New Directions, [1950].

Emrich, Wilhelm. *Geist und Widergeist: Wahrheit und Lüge der Literatur. Studien*. Frankfurt am Main: Athenäum, 1965.

——. *Polemik: Streitschriften, Pressefehden und kritische Essays um Prinzipien, Methoden und Maßstäbe der Literaturkritik*. Frankfurt am Main: Athenäum, 1968.

Fellows in American Letters of the Library of Congress. *The Case Against the Saturday Review of Literature*. Chicago: Modern Poetry Association, 1949.

Ferrara, Fernando. "Theory and Model for the Structural Analysis of Fiction." *New Literary History* 5 (1973/74):245–268.

Fieguth, Rolf. "Rezeption contra falsches und richtiges Lesen? oder Missverständnisse mit Ingarden." *Sprache im technischen Zeitalter* No. 38 (April–June, 1971):142–159.

Fizer, John. "The Concept of Strata and Phases in Roman Ingarden's Theory of Literary Structure." *Yearbook of Comparative Criticism* 6 (1973):10–39.

Freud, Sigmund. *Bildende Kunst und Literatur*. Studienausgabe, Vol. X. Frankfurt am Main: Fischer, 1969.

Frye, Northrop. "The Knowledge of Good and Evil." *The Morality of Scholarship*, ed. Max Black. Ithaca: Cornell University Press, 1967. Pp.1–28.

Goodheart, Eugene. *Culture and the Radical Conscience*. Cambridge, Mass.: Harvard University Press, 1973.

Habermas, Jürgen. *Strukturwandel der Öffentlichkeit: Untersuchungen zu einer Kategorie der bürgerlichen Gesellschaft*. 2nd ed. Neuwied: Luchterhand, 1965.

Hartman, Geoffrey H. *Beyond Formalism: Literary Essays 1958–1970*. New Haven: Yale University Press, 1970.

Hawkes, Terence. *Metaphor*. London: Methuen, 1972.

Hermand, Jost. *Synthetisches Interpretieren: Zur Methodik der Literaturwissenschaft*. Munich: Nymphenburger, 1968.

Hernadi, Paul. *Beyond Genre: New Directions in Literary Classification*. Ithaca: Cornell University Press, 1972.

Hirsch, E. D., Jr. "The Paradoxes of Perspectivism." *Lebendige Form: Interpretationen zur deutschen Literatur. Festschrift für Heinrich E. K. Henel*, ed. Jeffrey L. Sammons and Ernst Schürer. Munich: Fink, 1970. Pp.15–20.

——. "Three Dimensions of Hermeneutics." *New Literary History* 3 (1971/72):245–261.

——. *Validity in Interpretation*. New Haven: Yale University Press, 1967.

Holland, Norman N. *The Dynamics of Literary Response*. New York: Oxford University Press, 1968.

Hughes, H. Stuart. *Consciousness and Society: The Reorientation of European Social Thought 1890–1930*. New York: Knopf, 1958.

——. *The Obstructed Path: French Social Thought in the Years of Desperation 1930–1960*. New York: Harper & Row, 1968.

——. *The Sea Change: The Migration of Social Thought, 1930–1965*. New York: Harper & Row, 1975.

Hultberg, Helge. *Semantisk litteraturbetragtning*. 2nd ed. Copenhagen: Munksgaard, 1969.

Ingarden, Roman. *Vom Erkennen des literarischen Kunstwerks*. Darmstadt: Wissenschaftliche Buchgesellschaft, 1968.

Jauss, Hans Robert. "Das Ende der Kunstperiode—Aspekte der literarischen Revolution bei Heine, Hugo und Stendahl." *Beiträge zur französischen Aufklärung und zur spanischen Literatur: Festgabe für Werner Krauss zum 70. Geburtstag*, ed. Werner Bahner. Berlin: Akademie-Verlag, 1971. Pp.141–167.

Kermode, Frank. *The Sense of an Ending: Studies in the Theory of Fiction*. New York: Oxford University Press, 1967.

Konstantinović, Zoran. *Phänomenologie und Literaturwissenschaft: Skizzen zu einer wissenschaftstheoretischen Begründung*. Munich: List Verlag, 1973.

Krieger, Murray. "The Critic as Person and Persona." *Yearbook of Comparative Criticism* 6 (1973):70–92.

——. "Fiction, History, and Empirical Reality." *Critical Inquiry* 1 (1974/75):335–360.

——. *The Play and Place of Criticism*. Baltimore: Johns Hopkins University Press, 1967.

Lane, Michael, ed. *Introduction to Structuralism* New York: Basic Books, 1970.

Leavis, F. R. *The Common Pursuit*. London: Chatto & Windus, 1952.

Leibfried, Erwin. *Kritische Wissenschaft vom Text: Manipulation, Reflexion, transparente Poeţologie*. Stuttgart: Metzler, 1970.

Lepenies, Wolf. *Melancholie und Gesellschaft*. Frankfurt am Main: Suhrkamp, 1969.

Levin, Harry. *The Gates of Horn: A Study of Five French Realists*. New York: Oxford University Press, 1963.

——. *Grounds for Comparison*. Cambridge, Mass.: Harvard University Press, 1972.

Man, Paul de. *Blindness & Insight: Essays in the Rhetoric of Contemporary Criticism*. New York: Oxford University Press, 1971.

Maren-Grisebach, Manon. *Methoden der Literaturwissenschaft*. Berne: Francke Verlag, 1970.

Mecklenburg, Norbert. *Kritisches Interpretieren : Untersuchungen zur Theorie der Literaturkritik*. Munich: Nymphenburger, 1972.

Morris, Wesley. *Toward a New Historicism*. Princeton: Princeton University Press, 1972.

Munro, Thomas. *The Arts and Their Interrelations*. Revised ed. Cleveland: Press of Case Western Reserve University, 1969.

Nierlich, Edmund. "Pragmatik in die Literaturwissenschaft?" *LiLi. Zeitschrift für Literaturwissenschaft und Linguistik* 3, No. 9/10 (1973):9–32.

Ortega y Gasset, José. *The Dehumanization of Art and Other Essays on Art, Culture, and Literature*. Princeton: Princeton University Press, 1968.

Palmer, Richard E. *Hermeneutics: Interpretation Theory in Schleiermacher, Dilthey, Heidegger, and Gadamer*. Evanston: Northwestern University Press, 1969.

Paulsen, Wolfgang, ed. *Psychologie in der Literaturwissenschaft: Viertes Amherster Kolloquium zur modernen deutschen Literatur 1970*. Heidelberg: Lothar Stiehm Verlag, 1971.

Peckham, Morse. *Man's Rage for Chaos: Biology, Behavior, and the Arts*. Philadelphia: Chilton Books, 1965.

Pepper, Stephen C. *The Basis of Criticism in the Arts*. Cambridge, Mass.: Harvard University Press, 1946.

Perrin, Noel. *Dr. Bowdler's Legacy: A History of Expurgated Books*. New York: Atheneum, 1969.

Peyre, Henri. *The Failures of Criticism*. Ithaca: Cornell University Press, 1967.

Popper, K. R. *The Open Society and its Enemies*. 2 Vols. London: George Routledge & Sons, 1945.

Rader, Ralph W. "Fact, Theory, and Literary Explanation." *Critical Inquiry* 1 (1974/75):245–272.

Reiss, Hans. "Problems of Demarcation in the Study of Literature: Some

Reflections." *Deutsche Vierteljahrsschrift für Literaturwissenschaft und Geistesgeschichte* 46 (1972):189–212.

Richards, I. A. *Practical Criticism: A Study of Literary Judgment.* London: K. Paul, Trench, Trubner & Co., 1929.

———. *Principles of Literary Criticism.* London: K. Paul, Trench, Trubner & Co., 1925.

Starobinski, Jean. "On the Fundamental Gestures of Criticism." *New Literary History* 5 (1973/74):491–514.

Trilling, Lionel. *Beyond Culture*: *Essays on Literature and Society.* New York: Viking Press, 1965.

———. *The Liberal Imagination : Essays on Literature and Society.* New York: Viking Press, 1951.

———. *Sincerity and Authenticity.* Cambridge, Mass.:Harvard University Press, 1972.

Walsh, Dorothy. *Literature and Knowledge.* Middletown: Wesleyan University Press, 1969.

Wasiolek, Edward. "Wanted: A New Contextualism." *Critical Inquiry* 1 (1974/75):623–639.

Wellek, René. "The Fall of Literary History." *Geschichte—Ereignis und Erzählung,* ed. Reinhart Koselleck and Wolf-Dieter Stempel. Munich: Wilhelm Fink Verlag, 1973. Pp.427–440.

———. *A History of Criticism 1750–1950.* New Haven: Yale University Press, 1955- .

———, and Austin Warren. *Theory of Literature.* New York: Harcourt Brace, 1949.

Wienold, Götz. *Semiotik der Literatur.* Frankfurt am Main: Athenäum, 1972.

Wilson, Edmund. *Axel's Castle*: *A Study in the Imaginative Literature of 1870–1930.* New York: Scribner's, 1931.

———. *The Triple Thinkers: Twelve Essays on Literary Subjects.* Revised and enlarged ed. New York: Oxford University Press, 1948.

Wimsatt, W. K., Jr. *Hateful Contraries*: *Studies in Literature and Criticism.* Lexington: University of Kentucky Press, 1966.

———. *The Verbal Icon: Studies in the Meaning of Poetry.* Lexington: University of Kentucky Press, 1954.

INDEX

Heidegger, Martin 6, 71
Heine, Heinrich 22, 24–26, 44, 69, 96, 130, 163
Hemingway, Ernest 96, 173
Henel, Heinrich 139
Henry VI, Holy Roman Emperor 21n.
Hermand, Jost 88, 174, 186, 191
Hernadi, Paul 198
Hesiod 43
Hesse, Hermann 24, 87, 92
Hinderer, Walter 133, 180
Hirsch, E. D., Jr. 40, 103, 145, 160, 163–64
Hitler, Adolf 30
Hochhuth, Rolf 53–54
Hodges, H. A. 116
Hoggart, Richard 120–21, 122, 151n., 186
Hölderlin, Friedrich 22, 51
Homer 80, 167, 168
Horace 4, 100
Huaco, George A. 37
Hugo, Victor 101
Hyman, Stanley Edgar 5

Ibsen, Henrik 100
Illich, Ivan 115
Ingarden, Roman 41–42, 139, 153, 155, 195, 198
Isaiah 40
Iser, Wolfgang 105n.

Jaeggi, Urs 200
James, Henry 152
Jameson, Fredric x–xi, 12, 13, 23, 31, 32, 37, 50, 63, 144, 155, 157–58
Jauss, Hans Robert 100, 103, 112, 203
Javits, Jacob 90
Jay, Martin x–xi, 11, 23, 24n., 59n., 75n.
Jefferson, Thomas 171–72
Jeremiah 89
Johnson, Lyndon 18n.
Johnson, Samuel 96

Kafka, Franz 22, 28, 83, 138
Kamenka, Eugene 33n.
Kampf, Louis 76, 97, 127, 129
Kant, Immanuel 29, 60, 80, 83, 107
Karbusicky, Vladimir 23n.
Kautsky, Karl 93n.
Kavolis, Vytautas 97, 116n.
Keats, John 42
Keller, Gottfried 160
Kennedy, John F. 18n.
Kermode, Frank 188
Kernan, Alvin 4
Kinder, Hermann 187
Kipling, Rudyard 175
Királyfalvi, Béla 185
Klein, Albert 117n.
Kleist, Heinrich von 51
Knights, L. C. 166
Köhler, Erich 21n.
Kollwitz, Käthe 63–64
Konstantinović, Zoran 198
Kraus, Wolfgang 97n.
Kreuzer, Helmut 48n., 111–12
Krieger, Murray 103, 199
Kuhn, Hugo 110n.

Lacy, Dan 201
La Fontaine, Jean de 50, 101
Laforgue, Jules 167
Lamartine, Alphonse de 101
Lang, Kurt 193
Laurenson, Diana T. 51, 102, 144
Leavis, F. R. 115, 174
Leavis, Q. D. 31, 119–21, 124, 151n., 196
Leibfried, Erwin 13, 40, 72, 159
Leibniz, Gottfried Wilhelm 60
Lenin, V. I. 8, 29, 33, 44
Lenz, Jakob Michael Reinhold 51
Lessing, Gotthold Ephraim 160, 173–74
Levin, Harry 36, 131, 140, 169
Lévi-Strauss, Claude 35, 59
Lichtheim, George 13